Triumph Revisited

"*Triumph Revisited* provides a fascinating and lively exchange between Moyar and a number of his critics. It makes for great reading and is highly recommended for all those interested in the continuing battle about the war and its meaning and historical interpretation."
—James H. Willbanks, author of *Abandoning Vietnam* and *The Tet Offensive: A Concise History*

"Wiest and Doidge have brought together a marvelous collection of essays that provide context, explanation, and response to recent new ideas about a time and conflict that continue to define the post-World War II American experience. This is a must read for any student of the Vietnam War, and is yet another reminder to us all that 'history' is never static."
—William Thomas Allison, author of *Military Justice in Vietnam* and *The Tet Offensive: A Brief History with Documents* (Routledge)

More than thirty years later, the Vietnam War still stands as one of the most controversial events in the history of the United States, and historians have so far failed to come up with a definitive narrative of the wartime experience. With competing viewpoints already in play, Mark Moyar's recent revisionist approach in *Triumph Forsaken* has created heated debate over who "owns" the history of America's war in Vietnam.

Triumph Revisited: Historians Battle for the Vietnam War collects critiques of *Triumph Forsaken* from both sides of this debate, written by an array of Vietnam scholars, cataloging arguments about how the war should be remembered, how history may be reconstructed, and by whom. A lively introduction and conclusion by editors Andrew Wiest and Michael Doidge provide context and balance to the essays, as well as Moyar's responses, giving students and scholars of the Vietnam era a glimpse into how history is constructed and reconstructed.

Contributors: David L. Anderson, Andrew J. Birtle, Philip E. Catton, Jessica Chapman, James Dingeman, Charles Hill, Scott Laderman, Mark Atwood Lawrence, Michael Lind, James McAllister, Edward Miller, Mark Moyar, Dennis Showalter, William Stueck, Keith W. Taylor, Robert F. Turner, and Qiang Zhai.

Andrew Wiest is Professor of History and Co-Director of the Center for the Study of War and Society at the University of Southern Mississippi. He is the author of *Vietnam's Forgotten Army: Heroism and Betrayal in the ARVN* and co-editor of *America and the Vietnam War: Re-examining the Culture and History of a Generation* (Routledge).

Michael J. Doidge is a doctoral candidate in History at the University of Southern Mississippi. He is currently writing his dissertation, *An Army Worth Fighting For: Doctrinal, Strategic, and Bureaucratic Transformation in the U.S. Army from 1946–1964*.

Triumph Revisited
Historians Battle for the Vietnam War

Edited by Andrew Wiest
and Michael J. Doidge

NEW YORK AND LONDON

First published 2010
by Routledge
711 Third Avenue, New York, NY 10017

Simultaneously published in the UK
by Routledge
2 Park Square, Milton Park, Abingdon, Oxon OX14 4RN

Routledge is an imprint of the Taylor & Francis Group, an informa business

© 2010 Taylor & Francis

Typeset in Minion by RefineCatch Limited, Bungay, Suffolk

All rights reserved. No part of this book may be reprinted or reproduced or utilized in any form or by any electronic, mechanical, or other means, now known or hereafter invented, including photocopying and recording, or in any information storage or retrieval system, without permission in writing from the publishers.

Trademark Notice: Product or corporate names may be trademarks or registered trademarks, and are used only for identification and explanation without intent to infringe.

Library of Congress Cataloging in Publication Data
Triumph revisited : historians battle for the Vietnam War / edited by Andrew Wiest and Michael Doidge.
    p. cm.
  Includes index
1. Vietnam War, 1961–1975 – Historiography. 2. Moyar, Mark, 1971-Triumph forsaken, I. Wiest, Andrew A.   II. Doidge, Michael.
   DS557.74.T757 2010
   959.704′3072 – dc22

                                                2009046037

ISBN10: 0–415–80020-X (hbk)
ISBN10: 0–415–80021–8 (pbk)
ISBN10: 0–203–85211–7 (ebk)

ISBN13: 978–0–415–80020–4 (hbk)
ISBN13: 978–0–415–80021–1 (pbk)
ISBN13: 978–0–203–85211–8 (ebk)

Contents

Foreword
Dennis Showalter ... ix

Acknowledgments ... xiii

Introduction: Historians and the Vietnam War
Andrew Wiest ... 1

Section I   The Vietnam War in an Asian Perspective ... 15

1   The Vietnamese Civil War of 1955–1975 in
    Historical Perspective ... 17
    Keith W. Taylor

2   Ngo Dinh Diem and South Vietnam Reconsidered ... 29
    Philip E. Catton

3   What We Still Do Not Know: Moyar's Treatment of
    Global Communism ... 39
    William Stueck

4   A One-sided Picture of Chinese–Vietnamese Ties
    during the Vietnam War ... 48
    Qiang Zhai

5   Section I Response ... 54
    Mark Moyar

vi • Contents

Section II Debating *Triumph Forsaken* as History   73

6   Triumph Impossible   75
    James Dingeman

7   Fighting Stories   79
    Charles Hill

8   Imperial Revanchism: Attempting to Recover a
    Post-war "Noble Cause"   90
    Scott Laderman

9   *Triumph Forsaken* as a Path to Setting the
    Record Straight   102
    Robert F. Turner

10 Governing the Vietnamese "Masses": The United States,
    Ngo Dinh Diem, and the Notion of *Triumph Forsaken*   113
    Jessica Chapman

11 *Triumph Forsaken* as Military History   124
    Andrew J. Birtle

12 Section II Response   140
    Mark Moyar

Section III Orthodoxy and Revisionism   169

13 Orthodoxy and Revisionism: The Domino Theory as a
    Case Study   171
    David L. Anderson

14 Caricature for Caricature? The Vietnamese Context in
    Triumph Forsaken   175
    Mark Atwood Lawrence

15 Familiar Territory: Mark Moyar's Call to Revisionism
    and the Counterfactual   186
    Michael Lind

16 Throwing Down the Gauntlet: *Triumph Forsaken* and
    the Revisionist Challenge   191
    James McAllister

17 Ngo Dinh Diem and Vietnam War Revisionism in Mark
    Moyar's *Triumph Forsaken*   199
    Edward Miller

18 Section III Response Mark Moyar	208
Conclusion Michael J. Doidge	224
Contributors	233
Index	239

Foreword

DENNIS SHOWALTER

It is beyond a cliché to say that the Vietnam War is unique in the American experience. The country's earlier major conflicts, the Revolutionary and Mexican Wars, the Spanish–American War, and World Wars I and II, have tended to generate consensus history, dominated by a network of recognized mainstream works reflecting a fairly broad agreement on the purpose, course, and nature of the conflict. Even the Civil War, the ultimate divisive experience, eventually found its niche as a tragic "brothers' war" waged in a haze of gunpowder and an aroma of magnolias. Only later did more comprehensive evidence, increased hindsight, and intellectual disagreements combine to generate alternative perspectives. These in any case have been generally confined to specialist military, diplomatic, and academic niches.

Vietnam was different—utterly different. From the early stages of U.S. involvement, Vietnam was presented in the context of value systems. The nonexistence, for practical purposes, of any matrices for understanding Vietnam left a virtual blank screen for the projection of preconceptions and conventions. In consequence, no central body of argument had a chance to form in the context of a war that rapidly became a subject of domestic politics and domestic morality.

Even to its participants the Vietnam War was a chameleon. Its geography varied from jungles to rice paddies to littorals to cities. Each tour of duty, limited to a year, was a unique event: mediate only to itself in the context of individual as opposed to unit rotation. Even professionals who returned for successive tours faced discrete experiences. An officer might begin in 1965 as a lieutenant in a rifle company, return two years later as a captain assigned to headquarters in Saigon, and find himself as a major assigned to a South Vietnamese division as a senior advisor.

The intellectual result was an approach to writing about Vietnam that I have described as tribal. Soldiers, scholars, and popular writers alike have been able to present their research and conclusions in the context of limited, largely self-referencing, enclaves, each staring into its own fires, each acknowledging its own shamans. And like all tribes, with time they evolved into clans and sects. The Tribe of the Soldiers gave birth to the Clans of the Counterinsurgents, the Warriors, and the Airmen. The Tribe of the Diplomats includes the Internationalists and the Domestics. The Tribe of the Moralists, perhaps the most entropic of all, has a faction depicting a government and a people denying and camouflaging its wrongdoing: unmatched power and uncontrolled bureaucratization led to slippery slopes of random killing with ordinary men, front-line grunts, seeking a rite of passage to a spurious manhood by routinely taking ears, scalps, and fingers as trophies from dehumanized "gooks" and "dinks." It has another faction interpreting the Vietnam debacle as appropriate punishment for America's Cold War sins, and yet another calling that defeat merely a beginning of retribution for the fundamental flaws of racism, patriarchy, and capitalism.

And at the opposite end of the Moralist camp is the sect, very much alive, that depicts Vietnam as moral and idealistic: an appropriate application of Western and American values in an imperfect world, conducted without abandoning or denying those values—and above all, justified by the consequences of defeat.

The notion of an orthodox, or even a mainstream, perspective on Vietnam, in other words, should not be confused with the presence of such a perspective in the academic/intellectual community. Here, if anything, the interpretation of Vietnam as an enterprise not merely mistaken, not merely bungled, but evil in a cosmic sense, has metastasized. This has been achieved by the simple process of excluding alternatives by every means from public denunciation to selective hiring to departmental reviews magical in their ability to make a body of inappropriate scholarship disappear.

There is some hyperbole in this description of self-referencing solipsism—but not much. And to extend the tribal metaphor, the Comanche Empire may have dominated the southwest in the eighteenth century—but its Indian, Hispanic, and Anglo neighbors did not disappear in consequence. Tribalism endured, nurtured by the tangible and intangible consequences of an incontrovertible defeat. Vietnam became an all-purpose explanation for anything subsequently perceived as going wrong, anywhere on the American spectrum. And instead of being addressed and resolved, the Vietnam experience became a poisoned weapon in an increasingly polarized public and political consciousness.

Like any poisoned weapon, Vietnam's wounds festered. From Carter through Bush II, successive presidents have proclaimed this or that event, domestic or international, as "putting Vietnam behind us." In defiance of hope and spin, we remain with country singer Charlie Daniels: "Still in Saigon/ in our minds."

The aftermath of 9/11 offers almost too many examples to mention. From the ladies of Code Pink, to college faculty members recalling glory days on the picket line, to journalists identifying with Seymour Hersh and Walter Cronkite, opposition was structured by memories of Vietnam. On the policy side, the U.S. made the mistake of interpreting Iraq from a Vietnam perspective. The Vietnam insurgency was home-grown, homogeneous, integrated top to bottom—and pre-electronic. It was fundamentally different from Iraq's fragmented, horizontally networked, structure of disparate groups.

Confusing one non-Western culture with another, conflating 2005 and 1968, reflect not so much unwillingness to learn from history, as learning too much from the wrong kind of history—history written and sustained by tribes. That was what made Mark Moyar's *Triumph Forsaken*, published in 2006, the right book at the right time.

Considered in the abstract, neither its thesis nor its contents are especially polemical. Moyar demonstrates that the Vietnam War was an ongoing, longstanding, deeply embedded conflict. The U.S. became involved in its middle stages, allied to a country fighting for its very existence against an enemy no less determined on total victory. Brutality was the order of the day long before the Americans arrived—and long after they left as well; the Vietnamese had nothing to learn from the West in that regard. In a wider context, successive administrations accurately processed Vietnam in the context of a global Soviet threat. A general policy of response based on containment and credibility led the U.S. first to seek a middle road of limited aid to the South, then to sanction Diem's removal. The resulting putsch left South Vietnam in such confusion that, within months, America's goal became not to achieve victory by proxy, but to avoid disaster through direct involvement.

Modest enough on the face of it, this set of theses impacted academic orthodoxies on Vietnam with the same force as an earlier set of theses shook the Roman Catholic Church. Moyar indeed has faced Martin Luther's punishments: anathematization and excommunication. Some reviewers and commentators seemed willing at least to consider burning at the stake—professionally if not literally.

This work, by contrast, shows the beginnings of a move away from tribalism and its accompanying orthodoxies. Its introduction and its contributions reflect the readiness of a new generation of scholars not so much to seek new interpretations, but to re-examine evidence and follow its tracks with neither fear nor favor. Traditionalists and revisionists, establishment and outsiders, develop information and exchange ideas with a mixture of intellectual sophistication and personal good will, kindling optimism that the tribes of Vietnam will finally bury the hatchet elsewhere than in each other's backs.

Acknowledgments

The editors would like to thank their colleagues in the History Department and the Center for the Study of War and Society at the University of Southern Mississippi for their support during the formulation and writing of this project. The intellectual atmosphere of and debates fostered by the Department and the Center were critical to the maturation of the ideas expressed in this work. The editors also thank Kimberly Guinta, Matthew Kopel and the staff at Routledge Press for their unflagging support and diligent effort. The editors would also like to thank all the contributors for their hard work, as well as their insightful commentary into what is clearly a lively and significant debate.

Andrew Wiest would like to acknowledge the pivotal role played in this project by his wife Jill and their children Abigail, Luke and Wyatt. Without their support, and willingness cheerfully to allow daddy time away to work, this project would have never reached fruition.

Michael Doidge would like to thank his parents Tom and Sue for their continued patience and support of his work. He would like to extend his special thanks to dad for donating his free time toward the completion of the index. Thanks go as well to his brother Chad, his sister Lori, and their spouses for their continued support. In addition, Michael would like to extend his sincerest appreciation for Adam Chelstowski, Matt Oelfke, Ethan Fox, Andrew Davis, Tristan Nowicki and Angie Manfredi's unwavering support, loyalty and friendship. It has made all the difference. Last, but certainly not least, heartfelt gratitude goes to Jenny Bermudez for all the love and affection she selflessly gives, and the confidence it inspires.

Michael would just like to take this space to tell Jenny that, if in history he has found one of the great loves of his life, it is in her that he has found the other.

Introduction
Historians and the Vietnam War

ANDREW WIEST

On the night of January 29, 1928, Sir Douglas Haig died of an apparent heart attack after attending a Boy Scout rally in London. The unexpected passing of the general who had commanded the British Expeditionary Force (B.E.F.) on the Western Front for most of the Great War—the man who had led the forces of the Empire to their greatest ever military victory—came as a national shock. More than 20,000 mourners braved the London cold every day to file past Haig's body as it lay in state at St. Columba's Church. The national wave of mourning equaled that accorded to Winston Churchill some twenty-five years later.[1]

By the close of the twentieth century, though, the British public's perception of Haig had changed dramatically. On the occasion of the eightieth anniversary of the armistice that ended the First World War, a national British newspaper, the *Express*, ran a story on Haig under the headline, "He Led a Million Men to Their Deaths," and launched a campaign to remove Haig's statue from Whitehall because its close proximity to the monument to Britain's war dead, the Cenotaph, sullied the memory of the glorious fallen.[2] Perhaps, though, the best indicator of the changed popular opinion of Haig is his portrayal in the satirical British television series *Blackadder Goes Forth*, which pillories British officers of the Great War as inept at best and insane at worst—sacrificing the lives of their men for inches of tortured ground. Haig only appears in a short clip in the series, in which he sweeps toy soldiers from a model of the Western Front into a dustpan and tosses them away without a second thought, depicting the commander as an uncaring caricature of military disdain for human life.

The shift in British public opinion regarding Haig, from mourning the loss of a national hero in 1928 to clamoring for the removal of a the statue of a despised butcher in 1998, both mirrored and interacted with trends in the professional scholarly debate over Haig's career and legacy. By the 1970s, most scholars had come to see Haig as misguided at best and a war criminal at worst. Some works, such as John Laffin's *British Butchers and Bunglers of World War One*, do not even require the reader to open the book to discern their contents. Nevertheless, there remained a hardcore group of scholars who viewed Haig with sympathy and even a measure of grudging respect. Whenever representatives of the opposing historical camps met in conferences, even though the more pro-Haig forces were usually badly outnumbered, the results often led to acrimonious debate.

No, you have not picked up the wrong book. But, if that is the case, why should a work that examines the debate surrounding the publication of Mark Moyar's *Triumph Forsaken: The Vietnam War 1954–1965* begin with ruminations on the historical fate of Sir Douglas Haig? Rather than a study of a historical moment, *Triumph Revisited* investigates the processes of historical inquiry itself. These processes are a living, breathing thing: an intellectual organism that is the sum of many parts composed of biases, periodic trends, methodological shifts, and even foregone conclusions. The history of an event is born, stumbles through its gawky adolescent phase, comes of age, and grows old. The scholarly coming of age of the Vietnam War closely resembles the lifespan of its historiographical older sibling the Great War. An understanding of the march of Great War history, a biography of the history of the First World War if you will, can shed valuable light on both the nature of historical processes in general, and the state of the present debate concerning the Vietnam War in particular.

Battling for the Great War

Although the wars were different in almost every way, the British social and cultural experience in and historical treatment of the Great War closely resemble the American experience of Vietnam. Both wars transformed the landscape of their respective home fronts and spawned controversies that reverberated for generations. Neither country would ever be the same after its experience of war. As the aftereffects of the conflicts became clear, historians, journalists, and wartime participants rushed to stake their claim to intellectual ownership of the wars' legacy and meaning, in both cases constructing a historical orthodoxy that was both one-sided and remarkably nationally self-absorbed.

From the time the guns fell silent on the Western Front on November 11, 1918, writers and historians, including Arthur Conan Doyle of Sherlock Holmes fame, ventured into a historical no-man's-land to do battle over the legacy of the Great War. Some of the initial histories were, of course, simply celebratory pieces paying homage to Britain's greatest ever victory, including a spate of memoirs published by military and civilian wartime players anxious to cement their historical legacy. However, as it became clear in the 1920s and 1930s that Britain's enormous sacrifice in the First World War had solved little, and that the world remained a dangerous place, a serious disillusionment began to take hold. Historians, including J.F.C. Fuller and Basil Liddell Hart, began both to question the British military effort in the First World War and to set the stage for the Second. Memoirists, most notably wartime Prime Minister David Lloyd George, savaged the British military's handling of the conflict in general and Haig's command in particular.

While historians darkened their collective perception of Britain's victory as repercussions of the war's imperfect peace swept Europe, public opinion regarding the conflict also shifted dramatically, especially after the appearance of Erich Maria Remarque's *All Quiet on the Western Front* in 1929 opened the floodgates to the publication of works that portrayed the Great War as little more than a futile waste. In Britain, the release of Siegfried Sassoon's *Memoirs of a Fox Hunting Man* (1928) and Robert Graves' *Goodbye to All That* (1929), and the production of R.C. Sherriff's play *Journey's End*, popularized the view, as stated by one war veteran, that the war "had passed the heroic to the blackguardly ... obscene in its ruthlessness and sub human in its mechanisation."[3]

The hagiographers of the Great War had lost the initial historical skirmish, as the new, darker wave of history interacted both with powerful cultural expressions and the sweep of economic and political events to win the day. As Europe first sunk into depression and then lurched toward a more deadly conflict, and while Britain turned toward pacifism and appeasement, the historical orthodoxy of the Great War was set in academic stone. It became accepted wisdom that Britain's efforts in the Great War, although heroic on the level of the ordinary soldier, had been badly planned and poorly led. Instead of being a great victory, British involvement in the First World War had been wrongheaded and doomed to eventual failure (even in victory) from the outset. The Great War had been Britain's Vietnam.

Perhaps understandably, public and academic interest in the Great War dwindled during and immediately after the Second World War. However, the 1960s, a decade that included the fiftieth anniversaries of the important events of the Great War and the opening of most of the archival sources regarding Britain's role in the conflict, witnessed a new surge of interest in and publication on the First World War. Most of the historical publications, best represented by Alan Clark's *The Donkeys* (1961), were reminiscent of Liddell Hart's earlier attacks on the British military's conduct of the war. Of greatest importance to the construction of the public mindset regarding the conflict, though, was the 1963 production of Joan Littlewood's play *Oh! What a Lovely War*, which portrayed the conflict as a pointless waste of young lives.[4]

Especially as the archives opened, though, a new wave of historians began to question what they considered to be the overly simplistic conclusion that the B.E.F. had been led by "Butchers and Bunglers." What is often termed the revisionist field of Great War history began with John Terraine's 1963 publication of *Douglas Haig: The Educated Soldier*. While paying close attention to Haig, Terraine devoted much of his work to the nature of the war itself. What emerged was not a caricature of an overmatched yet over-confident butcher,[5] but a portrait of a thoughtful man who struggled against the insoluble problems posed by trench warfare in the early twentieth century.[6]

Terraine's attack on the herd of historical sacred cows of Britain's Great War experience touched off a heated academic and public debate. Although the historiographical clash centered on the lightning rod of Haig's career, it was in truth a struggle over the historical legacy of Britain's role in the First World War. Had the war been a futile effort commanded by a wrongheaded butcher (Britain's own William Westmoreland), or was it more complex? Was Haig possibly even a good commander given the realities of his time? While Terraine and a growing group of younger scholars defended Haig, attacks poured in from all sides, with historian Denis Winter even contending that Haig had falsified his own diary in an effort to set a trap for unwary historians and to skew history in his favor.[7] Unfortunately, while Terraine's work had jolted the field of First World War studies, it had also mired historians in an increasingly unproductive and insoluble struggle for the soul of the Great War, a period often termed "the Great Haig Debate." The situation became so bad that the historical team of Robin Prior and Trevor Wilson even called for a moratorium on books devoted to Haig, for attention fixated on him had, in their view, helped "to preserve historical writing about the Great War in its ridiculously protracted adolescence."[8]

While the debate concerning the command of Douglas Haig continues, sparked by Terraine's original questioning, the study of the B.E.F. in the Great War has now progressed well beyond simple traditionalism vs. revisionism. Once questioning the doctrine of Great War understanding became acceptable, academics have gotten well beyond the "was it good or bad" stage and have moved on to add critical depth to questions left unasked for decades. Once the lid was off, there was an explosion of new questions, new answers, new angles, and new methodologies. Although a chronicle of the flowering of the field is beyond the scope of this study, a tiny sample of the scholarship is in order. Tim Travers investigated the intellectual framework of the military practitioners of the war in his *The Killing Ground*; Peter Simkins identified who served in the B.E.F. and why in *Kitchener's Army*; Shelford Bidwell and Dominick Graham studied the reality of Great War weaponry in *Fire Power*; Robin Prior and Trevor Wilson explored the maturation of the British command system in *Command on the Western Front*; and G.D. Sheffield explained the functioning of officer–man relations in *Leadership in the Trenches*.

The flowering of Great War studies has also seen important advances in related fields, including a belated interest in what other nations did in the Great War, cultural studies, studies of memorialization, psychology, and literary criticism to name but a few. Given the vibrancy of the field, students today can be forgiven if they have trouble believing that the study of the First World War was once monotonously gray—a field in which history was complete and all was answered and had been for generations. The publication of Terraine's *Douglas Haig: The Educated Soldier* had changed all that and knocked the traditional understanding of the war onto its ear. It was something of a historiographical singularity—a moment in which everything changed. Arguably, the publication of Mark Moyar's *Triumph Forsaken* marks a similar moment in the historiography of the Vietnam War—a moment in which (rightly or wrongly) everything comes into question.

The Vietnam War in Tradition and Memory

The historical debate over American involvement in Vietnam began even before the U.S. Marines splashed ashore outside Da Nang in March 1965. In many ways, Graham Greene's *The Quiet American* (1955) launched the intellectual discussion concerning the naiveté and questionable nature of American goals in Vietnam. Adding more fuel to the historical fire was the fact that American involvement in the conflict followed fast on the heels of the failed French effort to reestablish colonialism in Vietnam. Bernard Fall's *Street Without Joy* (1961) chronicled the bungled French military experience in Vietnam and served as a warning concerning potential American military action in Southeast Asia. Finally, presaging Vietnam's place in history as the "living room war," *New York Times* reporter David Halberstam (who was destined to become one of the most controversial figures of the war) published *The Making of a Quagmire: America and*

Vietnam during the Kennedy Era (1965). Harsh in its criticism of American policy in Vietnam, and especially critical of the regime of President Ngo Dinh Diem in South Vietnam, *The Making of a Quagmire* powerfully interacted with roiling events on the American home front and helped lead to a questioning of the conflict among many of the nation's academics and intelligentsia. What would become the conventional view of the Vietnam War was, then, in some ways well entrenched even before American soldiers entered combat in earnest.

The Great War had been, by and large, a newspaper conflict. Reporters scoured the front lines and military headquarters searching for stories, a task made easier due to the static nature of the war. While there were exceptions, including reporting of the "Shell Scandal" of 1915 and the controversial release of the film *The Battle of the Somme*, which included scenes considered to be graphic at the time, much of the reporting on the war in the United Kingdom followed a rather celebratory pattern, with the brave British "Tommy" persevering against all odds. With changes in technology and in journalistic convention, the American media's coverage of Vietnam was quite different. By 1965, there were over 400 accredited correspondents in South Vietnam, and they enjoyed an unprecedented access to the battlefields of the war-torn nation. Famously, several young journalists, including David Halberstam and Neil Sheehan, began to publish stories that were quite critical of American military tactics and of the South Vietnamese state.

Perhaps of even greater importance to the formation of a traditional viewpoint regarding the Vietnam War was the interaction between reporting and the powerful imagery provided by modern camera and broadcasting technology. A pivotal moment in the media war was Morley Safer's August 1965 report on the burning of the village of Cam Ne, which showed U.S. Marines setting fire to several hooches with Zippo lighters. As the village burned to the ground, and the local peasants wept in horror, Safer remarked, "Today's operation shows the frustration of Vietnam in miniature. There is little doubt that American firepower can win a military victory here. But to a Vietnamese peasant whose home means a lifetime of backbreaking labor, it will take more than presidential promises to convince him that we are on his side." When combined with the iconic still images of the war, including South Vietnamese General Nguyen Ngoc Loan's summary execution of a Viet Cong prisoner during the Tet Offensive and 10-year-old Thim Kim Phuc fleeing, burned and naked, from a napalm attack on her village in 1972, television did much to formulate America's reaction to its war in Vietnam.[9]

Although the role of the media in Vietnam is complex and remains controversial, reporting on the conflict certainly played a role, especially when combined with the general societal turmoil that permeated the 1960s and 1970s, in shaping American perceptions of the Vietnam War and its era. While there had been a brief time between 1918 and 1929 in Britain when there was a debate over the conduct and nature of the Great War, Americans needed no such period of rumination before judging their national adventure in Vietnam. Like Siegfried Sassoon and Robert Graves before them, post-Vietnam War fiction writers and memoirists played a major role in completing the edifice of the public's understanding of the traditional view of the Vietnam War, which had begun with Greene's *The Quiet American.* Ron Kovic's *Born on the Fourth of July* (1976), Michael Herr's *Dispatches* (1977), and Tim O'Brien's *Going After Cacciato* (1978) achieved wide success and acclaim, while dramatically portraying the physical and mental cost, sacrifice, futility, and disjointed randomness that was the American experience in Vietnam.[10]

Perhaps of even greater importance to the formation of American public opinion regarding the Vietnam War, though, was its portrayal, and the portrayal of its aftermath, in film. The first depiction of the war on the big screen, John Wayne's *The Green Berets* (1968), failed to seize the moment with its flattering portrayal of the American war effort, losing out to Robert Altman's *M*A*S*H* (1969), which, although nominally about the Korean War, lampooned American involvement in Vietnam. After the fall of Saigon, film portrayals of the Vietnam experience darkened considerably. In Martin Scorcese's *Taxi Driver* (1976), physically scarred and mentally unbalanced Travis Bickle embodied the Vietnam veteran as a ticking time bomb, a topic reprised and given greater depth in Michael Cimino's *The Deer Hunter* (1978). Francis Ford Coppola's *Apocalypse Now* (1978) took allegorical filmmaking even further with Marlon Brando's Colonel Kurtz representing the ultimate portrayal of American wartime intentions having gone horribly wrong.[11]

As had been the case in Britain after the Great War, academics and writers quickly began to enter the fray in the battle for the history of America's role in the Vietnam War. Building on a surge of anti-war sentiment, and aided by the dimming popular portrayals of the war, Vietnam's academic detractors had a relatively easy task. After only a few efforts, including William Westmoreland's *A Soldier Reports* (1976), the major players in the war and their defenders ceded the historigraphical battlefield to the intellectual steamroller that was to become the orthodox view of America's failed war. The written works, as often by journalists as by historians, that form the bedrock of the orthodox view are many and have continued to appear in great numbers over the years. Some stand clear as formative pieces to the field: Frances FitzGerald's Pulitzer Prize-winning *Fire in the Lake: The Vietnamese and the Americans in Vietnam* (1973) provides a popular and eminently readable account of stalwart Vietnamese communists, an inefficient and misguided South Vietnamese leadership, and a befuddled U.S. policy that was not wedded to the reality of Vietnam. Stanley Karnow's massive *Vietnam: A History* (1983) is a riveting and detail-filled account of bumbling American policy and military efforts in a part of the world that Americans have almost always failed to understand. Gabriel Kolko, in *Anatomy of a War: Vietnam, the United States and the Modern Historical Experience* (1985), went even further and portrayed the war as part of an effort to impose an American order in the world.

Whether bumbling and misinformed, or imperialistically aggressive, this traditional view of the Vietnam War painted a public and academic portrait of an America that was predestined to fail in Vietnam. It became accepted wisdom that America's war in Vietnam had been a mistake and a tragedy. The first fundamental mistake was that, blinded by the Cold War concept of containment, the United States chose not to side with the stalwart Vietnamese nationalists of Ho Chi Minh, but instead to defend ramshackle and morally bankrupt South Vietnam at any cost. Once in the war, the Americans committed their second major mistake by relying on brutal and ham-fisted military tactics better suited to conventional war in Europe than to a people's war in Vietnam. In short, the United States fought the wrong war, in the wrong place, backing the wrong ally in the wrong way. The American war was doomed to failure.[12]

Although the orthodoxy had been set, revisionist historians and writers kept up something of an academic rearguard action that, while it made little headway in the public sphere, conceived of the American war in Vietnam quite differently. Some of the most influential revisionist works include Guenter Lewy's *America in Vietnam* (1978), which took issue with most of the conclusions of the traditional school, and the "ideological fervor" of the school's adherents. Lewy was sympathetic to the American reasoning for the conflict, and condemned the media and American society for much of the blame for America's failed war.[13] Harry Summers' *On Strategy: A Critical Analysis of the Vietnam War* (1981) looked at the conflict in a military light, depicting an American war effort that erred by not being traditional enough and by being too closely linked to the political whimsy of the time. Michael Lind's *Vietnam: The Necessary War* (1999) built on the idea that there were valid and compelling reasons for American military action in Vietnam while questioning the tactical nature of those actions.

Although distinctly outnumbered and on the defensive, revisionist scholars and writers stood starkly at odds with the traditional view of the Vietnam War. They characterized the conflict as necessary, the enemy as committed communists as much as Vietnamese nationalists, and the war itself as winnable. Although the military certainly made mistakes in its prosecution of the war, the revisionist view saved its greatest criticism for the media, politicians, and crumbling American morale on the home front.

Far from being divided only into two separate camps, Vietnam War historiography also included a great many works that did not fit easily into either school, but instead provided depth to both. Although again the list of works is vast, two formative pieces stand as representative. Andrew Krepinevich's *The Army and Vietnam* (1986) investigated military tactical culture and the inability to move beyond the American techniques of attrition in a war that cried out for the use of counterinsurgency. H.R. McMaster, in *Dereliction of Duty: Lyndon Johnson, Robert McNamara, the Joint Chiefs of Staff, and the Lies that Led to Vietnam* (1997), depicted a broken national security structure as perhaps the chief culprit in leading America into a war that it would lose.

As Vietnam historiography entered the new century, and began to look at the war through the experience of ongoing wars in Iraq and Afghanistan, the traditional view continued to dominate the field even as new methodologies and historical points of view began to move to the forefront. The reasoning behind and deepening of American involvement in Vietnam proved especially fertile ground for study. Fredrik Logevall's *Choosing War: The Lost Chance for Peace and the Escalation of the War in Vietnam* (1999) does not portray the war as inevitable due to Cold War belief structures, but instead contends that Johnson and his advisors brought America into what they knew would be a difficult war for reasons of political expediency. Mark Bradley, in *Imagining Vietnam and America: The Making of Postcolonial Vietnam, 1919–1950* (2000), broadened the field by considering the Vietnamese side of the equation (something few others did amidst an overly American-centered historiography). Focusing mainly on the communists in Vietnam, a trait shared with traditional works, Bradley contends that American and Vietnamese actions were shaped mainly by what they imagined the other to be rather than what they truly were. Seth Jacobs' *America's Miracle Man in Vietnam: Ngo Dinh Diem, Religion, Race, and U.S. Intervention in Southeast Asia* (2004) argues that American policy makers backed the failed Diem regime in South Vietnam mainly for flawed cultural and religious reasons.

Although different in their reasoning, the works of Logevall, Bradley, and Jacobs are still traditionalist in nature. Instead of blaming U.S. entry into Vietnam on simple Cold War dynamics, they see other culprits—grasping politicians, an imperfect imagined understanding of Vietnam, or cultural and religious ties to Ngo Dinh Diem. Whatever the causes, though, the results were the same: getting the United States involved in a quagmire in which it backed the wrong Vietnamese with tragic results. The field of

Vietnam War studies had broadened considerably, but in some ways the arguments remained the same. The traditionalist view of the Vietnam War dominated the field to the point that revisionists, try as they might, were limited only to sniping from the sidelines—sniping that never really moved to the level of a full-fledged academic argument. The debate, such as it was, seemed long since over.

Mark Moyar's *Triumph Forsaken* (2006) represented a very conscious effort to set the field of Vietnam War studies onto its ear and to correct many of the works of the traditionalist interpretation of the war that the author found to be, in his words, "inadequate."[14] The resulting study is the most clear and thorough presentation of the revisionist school's arguments, although it sometimes disagrees with other revisionist works in points of interpretation or detail. In almost every way, Moyar inverts the traditionalist understanding of the Vietnam War. Moyar's points are many, and a discussion of those points will form the remainder of this work. However, outlining a few of Moyar's most important claims will illustrate the role that his work has played in the historiographical development of the field.

In *Triumph Forsaken*, Ho Chi Minh is a convinced communist who needed stopping, while Ngo Dinh Diem was an effective leader—the leader that South Vietnam and Vietnam as a whole required. The United States was correct to enter Vietnam, lest the fall of South Vietnam trigger a domino effect in strategically vital Southeast Asia. The U.S./South Vietnamese joint military effort was not failing, but instead had achieved marked success in thwarting communist revolution. It was flawed media reporting of events such as the Buddhist Crisis and the Battle of Ap Bac in 1963 that had given the public and many politicians the mistaken impression that South Vietnam teetered on the brink of collapse. The truth was, in Moyar's view, that American and South Vietnamese forces were nearing victory until the ill-fated decision to oust Ngo Dinh Diem from power cast South Vietnam into a political turbulence from which it could not recover without the aid of U.S. combat forces.

Although more revisionist scholarship had preceded Moyar's work than that of his Great War historical compatriot, in many ways the publication of *Triumph Forsaken* was for the field of Vietnam War studies the same pivotal moment that John Terraine's *Douglas Haig: The Educated Soldier* was for the study of the First World War. Moyar's assault on nearly all of the assumptions held most dear regarding America's role in Vietnam has resulted in a heated academic debate. There have been both vitriolic attacks on Moyar's work, as well as spirited defenses of the revived revisionist school. Like their Great War colleagues before them, Vietnam War historians now trade barbs at conferences in what often become quite spirited discussions. The reason for this vigorous, sometimes cut-throat, academic debate is simple—the battle for the soul of the Vietnam War has been reopened. Was the United States correct in its actions? Was the war in Vietnam nearly won? Or were the Americans misguided and doomed to failure?

There is little reason to believe that the debate concerning the efficacy of U.S. involvement in Vietnam will center around William Westmoreland, like the Great War debate centered rather too closely on Haig. However, it remains to be seen whether the renewed arguments concerning the Vietnam War will become bogged in academic mudslinging about who was and is right and who was and is wrong—miring the field in a "protracted adolescence" reminiscent of the historiographical life of the Great War. Signs within the field, though (as demonstrated by the reviews and responses contained in this study), are quite hopeful. In agreeing with or questioning Moyar's conclusions or the dependability of his research, many scholars have taken his reopening of old questions as a chance to add historical depth to once-dark corners of the history of the Vietnam War.

Of course, *Triumph Forsaken* is but one book among an explosion of scholarship concerning the Vietnam War. A wide range of scholars, who are often not associated with either the traditionalist or revisionist schools, have recently produced works (some even pre-dating the release of *Triumph Forsaken*) based on new points of view or methodologies that invigorate the once again dynamic field of Vietnam War studies. A single example of the rich nature of the ongoing research concerns the study of the nature of the South Vietnamese state and its military. Even though it was long written off as simply predestined to failure and not worthy of interest, in the last few years an increasing number of scholars have devoted time to trying to understand *why* South Vietnam failed. Recent works include Phillip Catton's *Diem's Final Failure: Prelude to America's War in Vietnam* (2002), which provides a nuanced view of the oft-despised president of South Vietnam, and James Carter's *Inventing Vietnam: The United States and State Building, 1954–1968* (2008). James Willbanks' *The Battle of An Loc* (2005) and Andrew Wiest's *Vietnam's Forgotten Army: Heroism and Betrayal in the ARVN* (2008) are among an important group of recent works that attempt to discern both the strengths and weaknesses of South Vietnam's military at war.

The surge of academic interest in the once-fallow historical ground of South Vietnam will likely continue. At least three recent dissertations on the topic are being revised for publication: Matthew Masur's "Hearts and Minds: Cultural Nation Building in South Vietnam"; Jessica Chapman's "Debating the Will of Heaven: South Vietnamese Politics and Nationalism in International Perspective, 1953–1956"; and Martin Loicano's "Negotiating Strategy: Republic of Vietnam and United States Military Relations, 1968–1973."

While *Triumph Forsaken* is, in truth, only one book amid a welter of important new scholarship on the Vietnam War, its publication has touched a singular historical nerve, and, like John Terraine before him, Mark Moyar has helped to touch off a vigorous and multifaceted debate. On one hand, *Triumph Forsaken* has led to an open, and often intense, confrontation between the larger traditionalist and revisionist schools regarding the very nature of the American war in Vietnam. On another, Moyar's work fits into an already established general trend of re-asking old questions and utilizing new sources and methodologies to provide new answers. For both reasons, the field of Vietnam War studies finds itself in an exciting period of flux—a historiographical singularity. Authors and academics on both sides of the historical divide have taken note of the moment, and have responded to Moyar's work and assertions. The future of the field is being formed in the historiographical present. *Triumph Revisited* is a collection of responses to *Triumph Forsaken* by the leading traditionalist and revisionist figures in the field, as well as by the up-and-coming historians of the future. The goal of this collection is neither to judge Moyar nor his defenders and detractors. Instead, this study allows each to have their say. The field of Vietnam War studies is changing rapidly, changing in large part due to the work of the contributors to this volume. Readers will be able to put their fingers on the pulse of history as it is changing; to see the arguments, evidence, biases, and epiphanies that make up a critical historiographic moment in time. *Triumph Revisited* is history come alive.

The reviews and critiques of *Triumph Forsaken* contained in this volume have been arranged into three thematic sections. The first focuses on the connections between Moyar's work and Asian history, especially the history of Vietnam. The second section includes pieces that center more on Moyar's work as history, and especially his use of source materials. The third section details Moyar's place in the ongoing conflict between the "orthodox" and "revisionist" schools of the study of the Vietnam War. Each section concludes with a response from Moyar himself.

Notes

1. Daniel Todman, " 'Sans peur et sans reproche': The Retirement, Death and Mourning of Sir Douglas Haig, 1918–1928," *Journal of Military History* (October 2003, Vol. 67. No. 4), 1,088.
2. J.M. Bourne, "Haig and the Historians," in Brian Bond and Nigel Cave, eds., *Haig: A Reappraisal 70 Years On* (London: Leo Cooper, 1999), 1.
3. Max Plowman, *The Right to Live* (London: Dakers, 1942), quoted in Gary Sheffield, *Forgotten Victory: The First World War: Myths and Realities* (London: Headline, 2001), 7–8.
4. Sheffield, *Forgotten Victory*, 20; Brian Bond, "The Somme in British History," in

Geoffrey Jensen and Andrew Wiest, eds., *War in the Age of Technology* (New York: New York University Press, 2001), 204.
5. Sheffield, *Forgotten Victory*, 135.
6. Wiest, *Haig*, xiii.
7. Denis Winter, *Haig's Command* (London: Viking, 1991). For treatments of Haig and his place in history, see J.M. Bourne, "Haig and the Historians," in Brian Bond and Nigel Cave, eds., *Haig: A Reappraisal 70 Years On* (London: Leo Cooper, 1999), and Keith Simpson, "The Reputation of Sir Douglas Haig," in Brian Bond, ed., *The First World War and British Military History* (London: Clarendon, 1991).
8. Robin Prior and Trevor Wilson, "Review of Denis Winter, *Haig's Command: A Reassessment*," *Australian War Memorial Journal* (23, October 1993), 57.
9. Daniel Hallin, "The 'Living Room War': Media and Public Opinion in Limited War," in Andrew Wiest, ed., *Rolling Thunder in a Gentle Land: The Vietnam War Revisited* (Oxford, UK: Osprey, 2006), 281–285.
10. See Maureen Ryan, *The Other Side of Grief: The Home Front and the Aftermath in American Narratives of the Vietnam War* (Amherst: University of Massachusetts Press, 2008).
11. See Thomas Doherty, "Vietnam: The Movies," in Andrew Wiest, Glenn Robins, and Mary Kathryn Barbier, *America and the Vietnam War: Re-examining the Culture and History of a Generation* (New York: Routledge, 2010).
12. See Matthew Masur, "Historians and the Vietnam War," in Andrew Wiest, Glenn Robins, and Mary Kathryn Barbier, *America and the Vietnam War: Re-examining the Culture and History of a Generation* (New York: Routledge, 2010).
13. See "Vietnam and National Security Revisionism" in *The Encyclopedia of American Foreign Relations*, http://www.americanforeignrelations.com/O-W/Revisionism-Vietnam-and-national-security-revisionism.html
14. Mark Moyar, *Triumph Forsaken: The Vietnam War 1954–1965* (Cambridge: Cambridge University Press, 2006), xi.

Section I

The Vietnam War in an Asian Perspective

CHAPTER 1
The Vietnamese Civil War of 1955–1975 in Historical Perspective

KEITH W. TAYLOR

Mark Moyar's *Triumph Forsaken* offers new perspectives not only on the events of the 1950s and 1960s, but also on the historical context of those events. Most books about the mid-twentieth-century Vietnamese wars provide a prefatory myth about the Vietnamese being a unified people who for millennia have been enemies of the Chinese, and consequently have become experts at resisting foreign aggression. Mark Moyar sees this myth for what it is, an exuberant nationalist flourish, and instead offers a more sober and accurate evaluation of Vietnamese history as displaying a long, complicated, and overwhelmingly peaceful relationship with China, on the one hand, and centuries of division and internecine war among the Vietnamese, on the other hand.

Fashionable interpretations of modern Vietnam have used nationalist propaganda to portray the Vietnamese as incomparable underdogs of history whose devotion to national unity and independence have made them the bane of any would-be foreign aggressors. Mark Moyar's book points to historical evidence beyond the clichés, particularly the cliché of the Vietnamese having suffered unremitting Chinese aggression for the past thousand years and the cliché that the Vietnamese always were, have been, and always will be a united people, and that divisions among them have resulted only from the policies of predatory foreign powers.

This essay takes a look at these ideas and finds that they cannot be sustained by historical evidence. The argument here makes the following points. Pre-modern Chinese and Vietnamese were closely related as members of a common civilization and shared centuries of political and cultural history. Times of Sino-Vietnamese warfare were rare, and untypical of a relationship that was fundamentally peaceful. As for the unity of the Vietnamese people, from the time that Vietnamese in the south were numerous enough to establish their own political system in the late sixteenth century, they asserted their separation from the northern Vietnamese and defended their northern border through fifty years of war during the seventeenth century. It was not until the beginning of the nineteenth century that the Vietnamese were united under one regime and the country of Vietnam as we know it today, from the Chinese border in the north to the Gulf of Siam in the south, came into existence.

The war of 1955–1975 was a war between two Vietnamese visions of the future of the country. These visions primarily came from contrasting northern and southern perspectives on ideology, economics, society, and politics that have existed for over four centuries, ever since southern Vietnamese began to form their own structure of authority. The major world powers entered this conflict in pursuit of their global interests, and the outcome was a result of their policies.

Sino-Vietnamese Relations

It is widely believed that a Vietnamese "identity" can be traced back more than two thousand years, before the time when the Han Empire of China extended its supremacy over the inhabitants of the Red River plain in northern Vietnam. Modern Vietnamese are taught to hail the Trung Sisters, who led an uprising against Han, as Vietnamese heroines, and Vietnamese scholars claim the archaeological sites named Dong Son, which date prior to the Han conquest, as early manifestations of Vietnamese culture.[1]

However, it is implausible to associate either the Trung Sisters or the Dong Son sites with anything resembling Vietnamese culture. The distinctive features of Vietnamese culture appeared during the centuries when dynasties in China directly governed northern Vietnam, during the first millennium C.E.[2] Language, literature, philosophy, religion, government, society, cuisine, art, architecture, music, technology—in all of these aspects, distinctive features of Vietnamese culture were derived from, inspired by, or modeled upon ideas and practices common to the larger world of East Asian civilization, not upon Dong Son.

In the tenth century, the status of jurisdictions in northern Vietnam changed from being provinces of the northern empire to being part of a local kingdom. This resulted from a fundamental reorientation of imperial government. A martial aristocracy had ruled before and during the Tang dynasty (618–907), but a class of bureaucratic administrators educated in history, philosophy, and literature governed the Song dynasty (960–1279). Song leaders distrusted military men, kept them on a short leash, and the imperial borders accordingly shrank. This enabled the rise of a tributary kingdom in northern Vietnam.

At this time, the dominant language among people in the Red River plain shifted toward what today is recognizably Vietnamese. During the preceding millennium, the prestige language spoken by officials and a significant portion of the population in the Red River plain was Chinese. From this time, these people began to speak the vernacular while transforming it with vocabulary and syntactic features of Chinese, thus giving rise to an early form of the Vietnamese language, as we know it today. Around three-quarters of the vocabulary in Vietnamese derives from Chinese, and this includes particles and function words, which indicate something more than the mere borrowing of words.[3]

Vietnamese speakers emerged from centuries of acculturation, intermarriage, and bilingualism during which streams of administrators, scholars, monks, priests, soldiers, merchants, farmers, and adventurers from China settled in northern Vietnam. As one modern Vietnamese historian has written, albeit without reference to linguistics and with some hyperbole, ". . . the Vietnamese people were descendants of Chinese colons . . . To insist that the Vietnamese were the descendants of the [Dong Son people], for example, is similar to insist that the American people are descendants of, say, the Sioux."[4] American English does not display features of indigenous North American languages to the extent that Vietnamese displays features of the Mon-Khmer (Viet-Muong) spoken by people in northern Vietnam. But the point remains that pre-Han inhabitants of northern Vietnam resembled the Sioux in having a culture that was as utterly different from what in later centuries would be called Vietnamese as the Sioux were from what today we call American.

Rather than being a "thousand years of Chinese domination," the millennium during which the inhabitants of northern Vietnam lived within the borders of Chinese empires was a time of relative prosperity when they benefited from the imperial peace that enabled opportunities for trade and education. Rebellions occurred when northern dynasties were weak and unable to protect the frontiers or when there was turmoil in dynastic administration. Rebels were typically ambitious imperial commanders, not "indigenous" leaders.[5]

When the Tang dynasty became too weak to govern the region in the late ninth century, local leaders continued to pose as loyal imperial officials until, in the 930s, the disorders of the imperial breakdown in the north finally spread into northern Vietnam. The famous victory of Ngo Quyen at

Bach Dang River in 939, generally taken as the beginning of Vietnamese "independence," was against a local dynasty in the southern Chinese provinces of Guangdong and Guangxi, and Ngo Quyen did no more than emulate the many small kingdoms that, at that time, had partitioned the empire in the north.

In 980, after restoring the empire, the Song dynasty sent an expedition to pacify the northern Vietnamese region. The expedition was not successful and demonstrated that the reach of imperial armies was not what it had been during the previous millennium. The Vietnamese king quickly sent envoys to establish a stable tributary relationship with the empire, and the Song court understood that maintaining the Han and Tang frontiers was beyond its capability. During the following decades, efforts to demarcate a border between Song administrators and the new kingdom failed, and resulted in an inconclusive war in the 1070s in which a Song expedition responded to a Vietnamese attack into the modern Chinese province of Guangxi. In the wake of this war, a border was negotiated that has remained essentially unchanged to the present time. Thereafter, relations between Vietnamese rulers and the Song dynasty were peaceful.

When the Mongols conquered Song China in the thirteenth century, thousands of Song refugees fled to northern Vietnam. And when the Mongols attacked the Vietnamese kingdom, the Vietnamese kings understood their role as picking up the fallen sword of Song civilization, and an army composed of Song refugee soldiers fought with them, playing important roles in some critical battles. Far from being resistance to Chinese aggression, the wars of the thirteenth century found the Vietnamese allied with the Song Chinese against the Mongol "barbarians."

In the early fifteenth century, partisans of a recently fallen Vietnamese dynasty appealed for Chinese assistance against a new dynasty. Emperor Zhu Di (r. 1402–1424) of the ascendant Ming dynasty, ambitious to reclaim the supposed glories of the Han and Tang empires, took the opportunity to conquer and re-establish imperial rule in northern Vietnam. Thousands of educated Vietnamese welcomed this and assisted the Ming in setting up a provincial government. After Zhu Di's death, however, Ming emperors turned away from his ambitious policies, which had included sending huge fleets through Southeast Asia to India and Africa. The idea of directly governing northern Vietnam was abandoned by Zhu Di's successors. Sensing the shift in imperial policy, armies from the less Sinicized southern provinces of northern Vietnam pressed forward and hastened the withdrawal of Ming garrisons. By the late 1420s, the Vietnamese relationship to the northern empire had returned to the well-worn status of tributary vassal.[6]

During the following three-and-a-half centuries, the Sino-Vietnamese relationship was peaceful. All problems were resolved by negotiation. Then, in the 1780s, the Vietnamese royal family appealed to the Qing emperor for assistance against rebels that had seized their capital at Hanoi. The emperor was not interested in getting involved in the situation, but felt obligated, as the suzerain of the Vietnamese king, to assist him against the rebels. An army was quickly mobilized from border provinces and sent to place the Vietnamese king back on his throne in Hanoi. Considering their task accomplished, Qing officials were preparing to withdraw back to their borders when the rebel leader surprised and defeated them during the New Year celebrations of 1789.[7]

The Qing Empire did not intervene in Vietnam again until the 1880s, when the Vietnamese king called for help against French invaders. Chinese armies fought several battles with the French in the mountains of northern Vietnam before France forced China to surrender its claim of suzerainty over Vietnam.

In the 1950s and 1960s, Chinese leaders assisted their Vietnamese communist allies against anti-communist Vietnamese who, for their part, looked first to the French and then to the U.S. for assistance. By the time this war came to an end in 1975, the Chinese were turning away from their erstwhile Vietnamese allies, who had turned to the Soviet rivals of the Chinese. The Sino-Vietnamese war of 1979–1989 was an aspect of the Sino-Soviet struggle for supremacy in Indochina that followed U.S. withdrawal from the region. Since the collapse of the Soviet Union, Vietnamese leaders have returned to the well-worn policy of vigilant deference toward the Chinese.

Considering the historical evidence, it is incorrect to say that the Vietnamese have been resisting Chinese aggression for the last thousand years. Since the beginning of Vietnamese "independence" in the mid-tenth century, setting aside the Mongol wars of the thirteenth century, which cannot be attributed to "Chinese aggression," it is possible to count seven episodes of Chinese military intervention in Vietnam. These episodes resulted from particular situations that defy the simplistic label of "aggression." In 980, the Song emperor was doing no more than attempting, as previous dynasties had done for centuries before, to restore the imperial boundaries after a time of disorder and dynastic change. When it was clear that this was no longer possible, the imperial court accordingly adjusted its view of its southern frontier and adapted to the new state of affairs. In the 1070s, confronted by accumulating problems along disputed borderlands and stung by a destructive Vietnamese attack into a southern province, the Song court mobilized a punitive expedition. In the resulting stalemate, negotiations eventually settled outstanding issues.

Most Chinese interventions in Vietnamese affairs came in response to appeals for assistance by Vietnamese leaders. In the early fifteenth century, political turmoil in Vietnam elicited the interest of the Ming emperor. A new Vietnamese dynasty had provoked regional animosities and members of the deposed dynasty, still supported by a large part of the Vietnamese population, appealed to the Ming court for help. When the Ming decided to occupy the region and to dispense with any Vietnamese king at all, many Vietnamese were content to be part of the northern empire. The so-called "war of liberation" that accompanied the eventual Ming withdrawal was also a civil war between Vietnamese in the Red River plain who remained loyal to Ming and the less Sinicized population of the southern provinces of Thanh Hoa and Nghe An (commonly called Muong), whose leaders were determined to gain supremacy over the Vietnamese.[8]

The brief Qing interventions in Vietnam of the 1780s and 1880s were in response to requests by Vietnamese kings, were limited in scope, and were motivated by a suzerain's responsibility to protect a vassal rather than by any intent to conquer. The same could also be said for Chinese interventions in Vietnam during the 1950s and 1960s, although the feudal rhetoric was changed to the rhetoric of international socialist solidarity. The Sino-Vietnamese war of 1979–1989 was an aspect of Sino-Soviet competition in Southeast Asia.

The supposed inevitability of the 1975 conquest of the Republic of Vietnam by the Democratic Republic of Vietnam has often been asserted by claiming that "the Vietnamese" had been fighting "the Chinese" for centuries and so were some kind of indomitable experts in resisting "foreign aggression." However, this ignores the fact that this was first of all a war between rival Vietnamese governments, which became an aspect of the global Cold War. It also ignores the fact that, with rare exceptions, Sino-Vietnamese relations were peaceful and, furthermore, that Vietnamese have fought Vietnamese much more than they have ever fought against any foreign aggressor.

Northerners and Southerners

An early major episode of warfare among the inhabitants of northern Vietnam was in the 860s when ancestors of the Vietnamese, supported by Tang Chinese armies, fought ancestors of the Muong, supported by the Yunnan kingdom of Nan Zhao, ruled by Tibeto-Burmans. The Muong are linguistically related to the Vietnamese, but without the same degree of linguistic and cultural influence from China that was absorbed by the Vietnamese. The Muong inhabited the southern provinces of the Tang jurisdiction of An Nam (the "Vietnam" of that time), what today are the provinces of Thanh Hoa, Nghe An, and Ha Tinh. Today, they inhabit the upland hinterlands of these three provinces, having been pushed out of the lowlands through the centuries by the Vietnamese.

In the 860s, as Tang power was receding from the region, Muong leaders called upon Nan Zhao to assist in taking control of the Red River plain. The inhabitants of the Red River plain appealed to Tang for protection from this threat. In one last demonstration of imperial might, a famous Tang general defeated the Nan Zhao and Muong armies and pacified the region. When, a few years later, Tang administrators departed with their garrisons, they left the region in the hands of men who kept the peace and remained loyal to the imperial ideal for another half-century. Although armies recruited among the Muong of the southern provinces played prominent roles in battles among warlords in the mid-tenth century, Vietnamese kings in the late tenth and early eleventh centuries repeatedly mobilized men from the Red River plain to attack and subdue these provinces.

The tension between the Muong and the Vietnamese came to be expressed in a persistent competition for ascendancy between the inhabitants of the southern provinces, where Chinese influence was relatively low, and the inhabitants of the Red River plain, where Chinese influence was relatively high. This rivalry became a dominant theme of Vietnamese politics from the late fourteenth century to the mid-eighteenth century. In the 1370s, royal princes whose maternal families were based in Thanh Hoa took the throne. Within three decades, one of their maternal kinsmen had seized the throne and moved the capital to Thanh Hoa. This provoked resistance among people in the Red River plain, who subsequently welcomed Ming intervention, preferring Ming rule to the rule of leaders from the southern provinces. When Ming armies withdrew, people from Thanh Hoa established the Le dynastic regime. A century later, war broke out between the Le dynasty of Thanh Hoa and the aspiring Mac dynasty, which was based in the Red River plain.

In the 1590s, after decades of war between the two regions, the Mac were driven into the mountains, and the men of Thanh Hoa, under the leadership of the Trinh family, organized a military occupation of the Red River plain. The Trinh never resolved the underlying tension between the two regions. Mac leaders in the mountains retained the loyalty of many people in the Red River plain. In the early seventeenth century, they found several opportunities to return to the lowlands and to mobilize armies against the Trinh, but they were weakened over time and were finally eliminated in the 1670s.

The Trinh never won over the people they had conquered. In the mid-eighteenth century, after generations of misgovernment, the people of the

Red River plain rose up in rebellion against the Trinh. The Trinh mobilized armies from the southern provinces and eventually regained control of the Red River plain after fifteen years of fighting, which left both regions exhausted for decades thereafter.

In the mid-sixteenth century, Vietnamese in the far south, under the leadership of the Nguyen family in the region of the modern city of Hue, began to build a new kind of Vietnamese realm based on international trade, sea power, a monetized economy, a diverse population that included Chams, Chinese, Khmers, and peoples of the Central Highlands, and new patterns of war and diplomacy with the Siamese. From the 1620s to the 1670s, seven wars were fought with the Trinh in the north. Six of these wars were initiated by northern efforts to invade the south. In the 1630s, the southerners built a system of walls between the mountains and the sea in the basin of the Nhat Le River in the vicinity of the modern city of Dong Hoi. Artillery was mounted on the walls and thousands of soldiers were permanently garrisoned there for a century and a half. The northern armies never penetrated these walls. In the 1650s, southern armies invaded the north and occupied the modern province of Ha Tinh for several years.[9]

Southern society was more prosperous, more open to the outside world, and afforded more possibilities for exercising personal freedom than were possible in the north. During the two-and-a-half centuries that southerners were separate from and independent of the north, they created a new version of being Vietnamese, less disciplined by poverty and oppression than were northerners, less awed by authority, less constrained by notions of fate and cyclic passivity, more self-reliant, and more susceptible to opportunity.[10] Unlike the typical gated village in the north that was surrounded by a bamboo hedge, southerners tended to build their homes along the banks of rivers and canals, open to the outside world. Southern seaports welcomed foreign merchants. In the north, the Trinh encouraged foreign merchants to obtain weapons during the decades of war with the south. However, when fighting stopped in the late seventeenth century, Trinh harassment of foreign merchants caused most of them to depart by the beginning of the eighteenth century.

During the seventeenth century, Vietnamese in the south pushed into Cham and Khmer territories on their southern frontier. They gained dominance over the lower Mekong River plain assisted by thousands of Chinese immigrants, Ming refugees from the Manchu conquest of China. By the mid-eighteenth century, the Vietnamese border with Cambodia was established more or less along the line that it follows today, and Saigon had become an important seat of regional administration and a center of international commerce.

Between the Hue/Da Nang region and Saigon, the third most important administrative and economic center of the southern Vietnamese domain was at the modern city of Qui Nhon, in Binh Dinh province. It was a major seaport and a critical link between Hue and Saigon as well as being the terminus of the main route from the sea across the Central Highlands to the Mekong, and beyond to Siam. In the 1770s, when the leadership at Hue fell into corruption and incompetence, a rebel regime appeared at Qui Nhon, the Trinh occupied Hue, and surviving members of the Nguyen family re-established themselves at Saigon. During the "Thirty Years War" (1771–1802) that ensued from these events, the northerners passively watched the powers based at Saigon and Qui Nhon fight for ascendancy. In the 1780s, the Trinh regime collapsed and the north came under the control of an aspiring regime at Hue that was allied with Qui Nhon. In the 1790s, leaders at Qui Nhon and Hue allied with Chinese pirates from the coasts of Guangdong and Guangxi in an effort to counter the rising sea power of Saigon.

The leader at Saigon, Nguyen Phuc Anh, was a gifted administrator and a great shipbuilder. He constructed a set of international friendships and alliances: with the kings of Siam, Cambodia, and Laos; with the Sultan of Johore; with the Portuguese at Macau and the Dutch at Batavia; and with deserters from the French navy. From his friends and allies he obtained supplies, modern weapons, and technology. From Siam, Cambodia, and Laos he also obtained thousands of allied soldiers who joined him in battle. Unlike his enemies at Qui Nhon and Hue, who were limited by their rivalries and their provincial attachments, he had a broad vision that included all Vietnamese speakers, and he understood how to build and maintain a government. When he finally defeated the last stand of his enemies at Qui Nhon in 1802, the north accepted him without battle.

Nguyen Phuc Anh assembled for the first time in one kingdom all of the territories inhabited by Vietnamese speakers to form the country of Vietnam as it appears on the map today. He made his capital at Hue, the city where his ancestors had governed. He was an astute ruler who understood that his kingdom was comprised of diverse peoples who had never before been subject to a single regime. Consequently, he was content to rely upon trusted subordinates to adjust his authority to regional conditions. In Saigon, he relied upon Le Van Duyet, a man who had served him from the beginning of his career in the 1770s and who became his most trusted general during the final years of the war.

A eunuch, Le Van Duyet adopted into his entourage a wide variety of talented men, including Chinese merchants. He continued to govern at Saigon until his death in 1832, during which time he successfully resisted Hue policies that threatened the distinctive multicultural and international environment of Saigon. For example, he refused to enforce royal edicts against Christianity. He protected European missionaries and promoted trade with foreign merchants. When he died, centralizing Hue policies provoked a brief rebellion led by one of his adopted sons. The Hue court established direct control of Saigon in 1835—but only twenty-four years later, in 1859, the French seized Saigon.

For the next twenty years, the French navy governed Saigon, which became the capital of the French colony of Cochinchina, comprised of the lower Mekong plain. When France conquered the rest of Vietnam in the 1880s and 1890s, Cochinchina became the only part of French Indochina that was governed as a direct colony subject to French metropolitan law, unlike the rest of Vietnam, which was governed as a "protectorate" through Vietnamese magistrates of the royal court at Hue. Consequently, Cochinchina experienced the weight of "colonial modernization" to a much greater degree than other parts of Vietnam.

Vernacular newspapers and publishing houses in Saigon were less restricted than in the north, the economy was more integrated into international trade than in the north, and politics were more lively and included limited participation by Vietnamese. Elections were held for Vietnamese representatives on the Saigon Municipal Council and the Cochinchinese Colonial Council. In the 1920s and 1930s, the Vietnamese electorate was expanded, and Vietnamese candidates, including "constitutionalists" who sought democratic reform and communists of both Stalinist and Trotskyist factions, ran campaigns and were elected, although communists were not allowed to take the seats they had won. Vietnamese politics in the 1920s and 1930s were lively and included a wide spectrum of ideological predispositions.[11]

Society and culture in Cochinchina developed its own distinctive features. Direct French rule had swept away the administrative structures of village society as well as all obstacles to a regime of large landholdings, thereby producing a rural population of landless people who turned to new religions such as the Cao Dai and the Hoa Hao for a sense of community and for mutual assistance.[12] Colonial administration in Saigon nurtured a new class of urban, "middle-class," educated Vietnamese. The development of rubber plantations, factories, shipyards, and railroads led to labor movements and strikes. Cochinchina was more integrated into the modern world than other parts of Vietnam. During the August Revolution of 1945 when Vietnamese communists seized power at Hanoi, power in Saigon was negotiated amongst a great variety of organized groups, of which the communists were only one.[13]

While the Vietnamese communists were members of a highly disciplined hierarchy, Vietnamese anti-communists were committed to a political system that afforded a greater measure of economic, religious, educational, and personal freedom. But, in comparison with their communist rivals, who enjoyed the support of communist governments in other countries, Vietnamese who favored constitutional democracy were orphans. During the late 1940s and early 1950s, they were repeatedly frustrated by the unwillingness of France to step aside and allow them to establish an independent national government. After the departure of the French, they found an ally in the United States, but while their communist enemies received the unfailing support of their allies, they were eventually abandoned by the United States.[14]

The Vietnamese war of 1955–1975 was based on two contrasting Vietnamese visions of what it meant to be Vietnamese and of the future direction of the country. Larger powers placed the Cold War confrontation on top of the struggle between these two visions, and when the United States withdrew its support for the southern cause, the northern cause, with the continued support of its allies, prevailed. The outcome of the war is commonly conflated with the merit of the Vietnamese opponents rather than with the persistence of their respective allies, but this is surely an error. The Hanoi government was no less corrupt and was much more authoritarian than the Saigon government. That it prevailed is a judgment upon the steadfastness of its patrons, not upon the unworthiness of the southern cause.

The southern cause has a genealogy going back to the early seventeenth century when southern leaders built miles of walls and trained thousands of soldiers to preserve their southern freedoms from the hands of northern rulers. They saw the north as a poor country with too many tax collectors, where the accumulation of personal property and wealth was impossible, where economic ventures simply attracted the greedy hands of powerful men, where a privileged class of mandarins lost no chance to control all aspects of one's life. The northern view of southerners was that they were disloyal, lazy, ostentatious, undisciplined, and unorthodox.[15] It is not difficult to see how the modern confrontation between communists and non-communists entered this Vietnamese world in the way that it did.

The country of Vietnam appeared on the map at the beginning of the nineteenth century as a result of the entrepreneurial dynamism, the cultural and ethnic diversity, and the commercial wealth of Saigon. At that time, the north was exhausted and rendered utterly passive by centuries of warfare, misgovernment, and isolation. The Vietnam that came into existence in 1975, sustained by lifelines to foreign allies, brought years of warfare, misgovernment, and isolation to the Vietnamese. Change came with the end of the Cold War, but the northern and southern visions for the future of the country continue in a process of negotiation within the framework of northern primacy.

Notes

1. Bui Quang Tung, "Le Soulevement des Soeurs Trung," *Bulletin de la Société des Études Indochinoises* 36 (1961): 78–85; Stephen O'Harrow, "From Co-loa to the Trung Sister's Revolt: Viet-Nam as the Chinese found it," *Asian Perspectives* 22, 2 (1979): 140–164; Jeremy H.C.S. Davidson, "Archaeology in Northern Viet-Nam since 1954," in R.B. Smith and W. Watson, *Early South East Asia: Essays in Archaeology, History and Historical Geography* (Oxford: Oxford University Press, 1979), 98–124.
2. Stephen O'Harrow, "Men of Hu, Men of Han, Men of the Hundred Man," *Bulletin de l'École Française d'Extrême-Orient* 75 (1986): 249–266.
3. I am indebted to the unpublished work of John Duong Phan (doctoral candidate in East Asian Linguistics and Literature, Cornell University) for my understanding of Sino–Vietnamese historical linguistics.
4. Nguyen Phuong, "The Ancient History of Viet Nam: A New Study" (unpublished manuscript, 1976), 187.
5. K.W. Taylor, *The Birth of Vietnam* (Berkeley: University of California Press, 1983).
6. A.B. Woodside, "Early Ming Expansionism (1406–1427): China's Abortive Conquest of Vietnam," *Papers on China* 17 (Harvard University East Asia Research Center, December 1963): 1–37; John K. Whitmore, *Vietnam, Ho Quy Ly, and the Ming (1371–1421)* (New Haven: Yale Council on Southeast Asia Studies, The Lac Viet Series No. 2, 1985).
7. Truong Buu Lam, "Intervention versus Tribute in Sino–Vietnamese Relations, 1788–1790," in John King Fairbank, ed., *The Chinese World Order* (Cambridge, MA: Harvard University Press, 1968), 165–179.
8. K.W. Taylor, "Surface Orientations in Vietnam: Beyond Histories of Nation and Region," *Journal of Asian Studies* 57 (1998): 949–978. On the Muong, see K.W. Taylor, "On Being Muonged," *Asian Ethnicity*, vol. 2, no. 1 (March 2001): 25–34.
9. L. Cadiere, "Le Mur de Dong-Hoi," *Bulletin de l'École Française d'Extreme-Orient*, 6 (1906): 87–254.
10. Li Tana, *Nguyen Cochinchina: Southern Vietnam in the Seventeenth and Eighteenth Centuries* (Ithaca, NY: Cornell Southeast Asia Program, 1998); Alexander Woodside, "Central Vietnam's Trading World in the Eighteenth Century as Seen in Le Quy Don's 'Frontier Chronicles'," in K.W. Taylor and John K. Whitmore, eds., *Essays into Vietnamese Pasts* (Ithaca: Cornell University Southeast Asia Program, 1995), 156–172; Olga Dror and K.W. Taylor, *Views of Seventeenth-Century Vietnam: Christoforo Borri on Cochinchina and Samuel Baron on Tonkin* (Ithaca: Cornell Southeast Asia Program Publications: 2006).
11. Hue-Tam Ho Tai, *Radicalism and the Origins of the Vietnamese Revolution* (Cambridge, MA: Harvard University Press, 1992).
12. Hue-Tam Ho Tai, *Millenarianism and Peasant Politics in Vietnam* (Cambridge, MA: Harvard University Press, 1983).
13. Shawn Frederick McHale, *Print and Power: Confucianism, Communism, and Buddhism in the Making of Modern Vietnam* (Honolulu: University of Hawai'i Press, 2004); David G. Marr, *Vietnamese Tradition on Trial, 1920–1945* (Berkeley: University of California Press, 1981); David G. Marr, *Vietnam 1945: The Quest for Power* (Berkeley: University of California Press, 1995).
14. Edward Miller, "Grand Designs: Vision, Power, and Nation Building in America's Alliance with Ngo Dinh Diem, 1954–60" (PhD Dissertation: Harvard University, 2004); Philip E. Catton, *Diem's Final Failure: Prelude to America's War in Vietnam* (Lawrence, KS: University of Kansas Press, 2002).
15. K.W. Taylor, "Nguyen Hoang and the beginning of Viet Nam's southward expansion," in Anthony Reid, ed., *Southeast Asia in the Early Modern Era* (Ithaca: Cornell University Press, 1993), 42–65.

CHAPTER 2

Ngo Dinh Diem and South Vietnam Reconsidered[1]

PHILIP E. CATTON

The story of the Vietnam conflict is no stranger to controversy and, in spite of the ever-expanding list of works devoted to it, there seems little sign of an emerging consensus about the war's origins, conduct, and meaning. Not surprisingly, there is considerable disagreement in the literature about Ngo Dinh Diem, the leader of South Vietnam from 1954 to 1963 and one of the conflict's key protagonists. Writing shortly after Diem's demise, Bernard Fall, the veteran journalist, observed that the treatment of the former South Vietnamese president consisted "either of totally uncritical eulogy or of equally partisan condemnation."[2] Little has changed in the intervening four decades. Staunch patriot or bumbling stooge, far-sighted statesman or blinkered reactionary—Diem has always elicited sharply defined, and divergent, judgments of his character and leadership. Which—to borrow the opening line of a recent journal article—begs the question, "Who was Ngo Dinh Diem?"[3]

From the moment he assumed office in the summer of 1954, the Vietnamese Communists sought to pigeonhole Diem as a traitor and American puppet, one more in a long line of individuals in Vietnam's history who had sold out their country to a foreign power. Diem, in this view, was merely a U.S. client, in charge of an illegitimate rump state that the Americans had created below the seventeenth parallel. In light of Saigon's strained relationship with Washington, however, this propaganda line was rather difficult to swallow. If Diem was a puppet, he proved remarkably uncooperative in responding to the promptings of his American masters. As one U.S. official put it, Diem was "a puppet who pulled his own strings—and ours as well."[4] Indeed, the Americans eventually found him to be so troublesome that they connived in his overthrow in November 1963. Given the tensions that plagued U.S.–South Vietnamese relations, most historians have portrayed Diem as a man of some independence, even though many of them characterize the state over which he presided as essentially a neo-colonial creation. Instead of an American stooge, the prevailing image that has emerged in the historiography is that of Diem as the backward-looking "Last of the Mandarins" or "Last Confucian."[5] He is invariably viewed as an old-fashioned patriot, intensely nationalistic and steeped in the autocratic culture of the Vietnamese past—a man who rejected U.S. advice because of a prickly sensitivity to foreign pressure and his belief that the Americans simply did not understand his country and its traditions.

Although this image of Diem has come to dominate the literature, its exponents have drawn from it very different conclusions about the former president's role in the history of the Vietnam conflict. On the one hand, the "Orthodox," and majority, opinion in the historiography casts Diem as narrow-minded and out of touch, as a patriot without a program; he was a Confucian/Catholic despot and dyed-in-the-wool reactionary who sought to govern by the outmoded precepts of a long-dead past. "His love for his country in the abstract was profound, but he was an elitist who had little sensitivity to the needs and problems of the Vietnamese people," wrote George Herring. "He had no blueprint for building a modern nation or mobilizing his people."[6] It follows from this analysis that the United States backed a losing horse by supporting Diem and that its nation-building efforts in South Vietnam had little chance of success. This view bolsters the broader "Orthodox" thesis that U.S. intervention in Vietnam was a tragic mistake and the war ultimately unwinnable.

On the other hand, the "Revisionist," and minority, interpretation praises Diem for his traditional style of autocratic government. Rather than a hopeless reactionary, "Revisionists" portray him as a far-sighted leader. Diem recognized that only his one-man rule could hold South Vietnam together, they contend, and understood the mentality of his fellow countrymen far better than the Americans. In this view, he provided the kind of charismatic leadership that Vietnamese traditionally expected of their rulers and that was critical to the establishment of an effective southern state. Consequently, his presence was vital to the outcome of the struggle in Vietnam; indeed, some "Revisionists" argue that the conflict could have been won if he had remained at the helm. The most recent and most forthright expression of this viewpoint is Mark Moyar's *Triumph Forsaken*, in which Diem is described as a "very wise and effective leader" and U.S. involvement in his overthrow as "by far the worst American mistake of the Vietnam War."[7]

While these "Orthodox" and "Revisionist" views offer conflicting opinions of Diem's fitness for office—and thus, by extension, of the whole nation-building enterprise in South Vietnam—they may not be quite as far apart as they at first appear.[8] After all, they both draw on the same essential picture of Diem as the old-fashioned mandarin patriot. They disagree over the consequences of his character and style of government, not so much about the man himself. What if this basic image of Diem is a false or distorted one, however? And, if he were not the "Last of the Mandarins," how would that affect interpretations of his regime and the course of the conflict in the period 1954–1963?

In the literature, the former president's image appears remarkably underdeveloped and fixed in time. It reflects the enduring influence of interpretations put forward in the earliest histories of the conflict, many of them journalistic "first drafts of history," like those of David Halberstam, Joseph Buttinger, Frances FitzGerald, and Stanley Karnow.[9] While eager students of Vietnamese history and perceptive observers of the drama unfolding before them, most of these commentators were not experts on Vietnam or Southeast Asia. Nor did they enjoy the advantages traditionally afforded the historian; they lacked the benefit of access to the documentary record and the perspective that comes from viewing the past from a greater distance in time. Writing close to the events that they recorded, and struggling to make sense of a complex and controversial conflict, they naturally sought a satisfying framework to help explain Diem's South Vietnam. They found it in the portrait of Diem as the backward-looking mandarin, which became the stock image in the first histories of the war.

And the image stuck. Perhaps its persistence can be attributed in large part to the lopsided nature of the literature that followed these early works on the war. Most studies of the Vietnam conflict examine events from an American perspective and generally give short shrift to that of the Vietnamese. The historiography, noted Robert McMahon, is dominated by "American scholars asking American-oriented questions and seeking answers in documents produced by Americans."[10] As a result, the Vietnamese side of the story is all too often relegated to the margins. Or, as historian Huynh Kim Khanh observed, Vietnam is treated merely "as a battlefield or a piece of real estate to be fought over" and its people "as passive bystanders in a historical process engineered elsewhere."[11] In this context, scholars focused on exploring the U.S. experience in Vietnam seem to have taken Diem's character as a given and accepted uncritically the stereotypical image of the traditional mandarin.

When viewed through the prism of Vietnamese and Southeast Asian history, however, this portrait appears one-dimensional. Diem was certainly a conservative in terms of his approach to nation-building, especially compared with his communist rivals. Nevertheless, his thinking reflected the broadly progressive concerns of other Vietnamese nationalists and Southeast Asian leaders at the time. Like Vietnamese from all parts of the political spectrum, he realized that his country's traditional practices had proved a weak reed in the face of Western imperialism and the challenges presented by the modern world; he recognized the need for change and was determined to strengthen Vietnam. While drawing on older ideas and customs, he wanted to build a version of a modern nation rather than recreate a replica of the Vietnamese past. As he once told journalist Marguerite Higgins, "We are not going to go back to a sterile copy of the mandarin past. But we are going to adapt the best of our heritage to the modern situation."[12] In short, Diem was a conservative modernizer rather than a traditional autocrat; he was looking forward, not backward.

There is considerable evidence to support such an interpretation—if historians are prepared to take a fresh look at the information available and examine seriously what his regime had to say about itself. English-language sources on the Saigon government abound. Scholars have also benefited in recent years from improved access to Vietnamese-language materials that help to illuminate the regime's policies. Indeed, a number of historians have already used such materials to challenge the prevailing image of Diem and paint a more well-rounded, less caricatured, portrait of his government.[13] Above all, to better understand Diem, we need to analyze him on his own terms and in the context of Vietnamese history, not just as a bit-part player in the story of America's involvement in Vietnam.

For Diem, as for other Vietnamese nationalists, the great struggle facing mid-twentieth-century Vietnam was not only to throw off the yoke of French colonialism, but also to overcome the societal weaknesses that had facilitated the country's subjugation in the first place. Politically engaged Vietnamese focused in particular on the problem of group cohesion and unity. They argued that the nation had lost its independence because of a lack of national consciousness and the absence of the kind of organized social structures that could connect the individual/family with the rest of society.[14] These problems animated non-communist Vietnamese as much as they did their communist compatriots, but Diem rejected Marxism-Leninism as the solution. Instead, he sought an alternative ideology to guide the country's development. He found it in the philosophy of Personalism, a rather obscure doctrinal import from Europe that was most closely associated with the Frenchman Emmanuel Mounier. Personalism sought to promote a sense of community and an engaged citizenry by avoiding the perceived excesses of existing ideologies; it advocated a third, or middle, way between the anarchic tendencies of capitalism/individualism and the suffocating collectivism of Marxism-Leninism. Diem's brother, Ngo Dinh Nhu, the regime's self-appointed intellectual, led the way in promoting these ideas. Nhu and Diem believed that a Vietnamese version of Personalism, transposing the basic tenets of the European original, could serve as a framework for mobilizing the population and modernizing South Vietnam. The philosophy effectively became the state ideology of Diem's South Vietnam, the Saigon government routinely speaking of its desire to promote a Personalist Revolution.[15]

With few exceptions, studies of the Diem period, most of them focused on the trials and tribulations of American policy, devote little attention to these ideas. Personalism is usually viewed as an intellectual curiosity and casually dismissed as a cover for Diem's authoritarian style of rule.[16] This pattern of analysis is most evident in "Orthodox" works, but also appears in Mark Moyar's "Revisionist" history. Representative of the "Orthodox" view is James Carter's recent study of nation-building in South Vietnam—that is, American efforts at nation-building. Since his focus is on the U.S. side of the story, Carter leaves the thinking of the Diem government largely unexamined. Not surprisingly, Personalism is covered in a single paragraph and described as merely another weapon in the "panoply used by the regime to silence opposition and safeguard the Ngo hold on power."[17] Moyar's treatment of the topic is not much more substantial than Carter's and ultimately quite similar. He argues that Personalism was an unnecessary ideological contrivance because what really mattered was Diem's ability to lead the country by playing the part of the traditional strongman. Thus, Moyar offers a brief summary of Personalism before it disappears from his analysis.[18]

Both Carter and Moyar effectively gloss over the philosophy. They treat it in ways that fail to take seriously the Saigon regime's ideological preoccupations and serve to bolster the stereotype of Diem as an old-fashioned autocrat. Like so much of the scholarly literature, their approach appears to draw upon ideas and images cemented in the historiography by those influential, early journalistic accounts of the period. In 1965, in *The Lost Revolution*, Asia correspondent Robert Shaplen informed readers that they should take Ngo Dinh Nhu's expositions on Personalism with a large dose of salt because, whatever the philosophy was, "it was only a theory, while in practice it was what Nhu wanted it to be."[19] In other words, it served essentially as an intellectual smokescreen for the Ngo family's dictatorship. Unfortunately, historians seem to have taken Shaplen's advice to heart and ignored the philosophy's influence on the thinking of the Diem regime. Whatever its deficiencies as a practical guide to government—David Halberstam once described it as "a confusing counterideology to

Communism, which no one else in Vietnam ever understood"[20]—Personalism requires closer examination because it played an important part in shaping the regime's approach to nation-building.

Perhaps the best illustration of the regime's efforts to put its ideological precepts into practice is the Strategic Hamlet program, the scheme in the early 1960s to fortify most of the settlements in the South Vietnamese countryside.[21] Much of the literature on strategic hamlets routinely ascribes their origins to foreign thinking and advice, notably that of the State Department's Roger Hilsman and British counterinsurgency expert Robert Thompson. In addition, the program is usually portrayed as a straightforward counterinsurgency measure, the Saigon government's broader explanations of its purpose being dismissed as mere propaganda.[22] Hence, for the most part, the literature denies the Diem regime much agency in developing the scheme and characterizes it simply in terms of securing the countryside. Yet the documentary record suggests otherwise. The Strategic Hamlet program represented not only a Vietnamese initiative, but also an elaborate nation-building project—it was, in fact, the last and most ambitious of the regime's plans for developing South Vietnam and implementing its Personalist Revolution.

The Diem government began to promote the strategic hamlet concept in the fall of 1961. Obviously, the burgeoning insurgency, spearheaded by the newly created National Liberation Front (N.L.F.), required some response and served to encourage the program's emergence, but there were several other important stimuli as well. First, the growing threat from the N.L.F. prompted the Americans to increase their pressure on Diem to accept a U.S. plan of action to win the war—a plan that required all kinds of political reform that Diem regarded as unwise and meddlesome. One way of deflecting this unwanted attention from Washington was for Saigon to come up with its own solution to the insurgency. Second, the success of the insurgents had exposed the weak foundations on which the Diem regime was built. In particular, it demonstrated the government's failure to reach into the countryside and successfully mobilize South Vietnam's peasantry. Diem was anxious to overcome the isolation of the rural population and tie the country's villages into a cohesive state. This concern—so redolent of the long-standing interest of Vietnamese nationalists in fostering group cohesion and solidarity—had preoccupied the regime since 1954 and influenced its previous rural schemes, such as the Agroville program. With the N.L.F. stepping up operations in the countryside, the Diem government decided that it had to find a new means of effectively engaging the peasant population. Thus, the Strategic Hamlet program aimed at killing several birds with one stone: it would stamp out the insurgency, sideline the troublesome Americans, and serve to mobilize the country. Not surprisingly, the Diem regime used the term "strategic" to describe its efforts because it saw the program as a multifaceted one.

Even though the United States supported the hamlet scheme, the Vietnamese and Americans held quite different conceptions of its purpose. U.S. officials saw the program as a useful framework for bringing security and the benefits of American largesse to the rural population; the Diem regime viewed it as a way of encouraging peasants to pull themselves up by their own bootstraps. Ngo Dinh Nhu, who became the driving force behind the program, was particularly insistent that rural inhabitants should not be passive recipients of outside support. He argued that lavish U.S. aid would just make the peasantry dependent on the government and ultimately increase South Vietnam's dependence on the United States—something that the hyper-nationalistic Ngo family considered intolerable. Instead, he emphasized the importance of self-reliance and the part that peasants must play in establishing their own strategic hamlets. Indeed, the Diem regime believed that the hamlet program would serve as a handmaiden for its Personalist Revolution: active peasant participation in the program would promote civic engagement and kindle a new sense of group solidarity among the rural population. In this way, the bonds of a cohesive nation might gradually be forged from the bottom up. The regime's expectations explain what lay behind Nhu's proposal only to lend weapons to the inhabitants of strategic hamlets for a period of six months, during which time he wanted them to arm themselves by capturing guns from the insurgents. On the face of it, the idea sounds absurd, but it makes sense—in theory at least—if we put ourselves in the Diem government's shoes and try to understand the benefits that it hoped would follow from encouraging peasants to help themselves.

Examining the nation-building ideas that lay behind the Strategic Hamlet program paints a different picture of Ngo Dinh Diem from the prevailing one of the unimaginative autocrat. Similarly, the broader conclusion that can be drawn from this analysis—that Diem was a forward-thinking nationalist rather than backward-looking mandarin—does not fit neatly into the existing historiography. Although historians from both sides of the "Orthodox/Revisionist" divide have embraced this image of Diem as the "Last of the Mandarins," the argument that he was a modernizer, with his own nation-building agenda, poses a potentially bigger problem for those belonging to the former school of thought rather than the latter. One of the cornerstones of the "Orthodox" thesis is that the United States was attempting essentially to make something out of nothing in South Vietnam. In this view, there was never any solid basis for establishing an anti-communist state to the south of the seventeenth parallel; in fact, the only Vietnamese who offered a coherent nation-building program and vision of the future were the communists. Thus, to suggest that the Diem government—and non-communist nationalism in general—had some real ideological substance to them is to question a fundamental assumption of the "Orthodox" interpretation. Given the fiercely contested nature of the historiography, merely raising such a possibility can attract some barbed responses. Recently, one historian peremptorily dismissed the new scholarship on Diem as "poor history" and suggested that it was part of a politically motivated campaign to legitimize America's intervention in Vietnam (and U.S. foreign policy more generally).[23]

Not only is this accusation an unfair slight on honest and scholarly efforts to understand the past, but it also fails to appreciate that reconsidering Diem's image does not necessarily require subscribing to the tenets of "Revisionism" or, indeed, rejecting the broader "Orthodox" interpretation of the war. One can argue, as I have done elsewhere, that Diem may have been a modern nationalist, but that there still remained enormous obstacles to the creation of a viable South Vietnam, including his style of leadership, the bases of his support, conceptual flaws in his vision of nation-building, and the effectiveness of the Vietnamese communists. Such a conclusion, in fact, is not incompatible with the "Orthodox" view that the war was ultimately unwinnable. In other words, Diem "revisionism," with a small "r," should not be regarded as synonymous with Vietnam War "Revisionism" with a capital "R." Perhaps it is also worth emphasizing in this context that while Mark Moyar's *Triumph Forsaken* is most certainly a "Revisionist" work, it is not really an example of Diem "revisionism." Not only is its argument that Diem was a successful leader one that has been made before, but its portrait of the former president is also closer to the traditional view of him as the mandarin autocrat than it is to the interpretations put forward in the new scholarship on Diem.

Revising the character and role of Ngo Dinh Diem is not about trying to score points for one side or the other in the great "Orthodox/Revisionist" debate over the Vietnam conflict. That is only likely to lead to the kind of simplistic judgments of Diem—"uncritical eulogy" or "partisan condemnation"—that Bernard Fall identified more than forty years ago. Instead, it is about bringing the Vietnamese side of events from out of the historical shadows. The South Vietnamese, or non-communist, perspective is a notably neglected aspect of the historiography. George Herring pointed to this gap in the literature in his presidential address to the Society for Historians of American Foreign Relations in 1989.[24] Twenty years later, coverage of this dimension of the conflict still remains patchy. Hopefully, the recent appearance of new studies of Diem, as well as of other aspects of South Vietnamese society, has begun to remedy this omission.[25] Such work helps to illuminate the Vietnamese experience of the war; it also offers fresh insights into those long-standing disputes that continue to animate debates over the struggle in Vietnam. After all, how can we adequately explain either the roots of the war or its eventual outcome without a better understanding of Vietnamese political and cultural dynamics?

Notes

1. The title is borrowed from a panel that was part of a conference held at Williams College in March 2007 on "The New Vietnam War Revisionism: Implications and Lessons." The author would like to thank Edward Miller, Stephen Taaffe, and Andrew Wiest for their advice and comments on drafts of this essay.
2. Bernard B. Fall, *The Two Viet-Nams: A Political and Military Analysis*, 2nd rev. edn. (New York: Frederick A. Praeger, 1967), 235.
3. Edward Miller, "Vision, Power, and Agency: The Ascent of Ngo Dinh Diem," *Journal of Southeast Asian Studies*, October 2004, 433.
4. Quoted in Stanley Karnow, *Vietnam: A History*, rev., up. edn. (New York: Viking Penguin, 1991), 251.
5. These are the titles of two of the earliest books on Diem: Anthony Trawick Bouscaren, *The Last of the Mandarins: Diem of Vietnam* (Pittsburgh, PA: Duquesne University Press, 1965); and Denis Warner, *The Last Confucian: Vietnam, South-East Asia, and the West* (Harmondsworth, Middlesex: Penguin Books, 1964). Although their authors both view Diem as the embodiment of an older, traditional Vietnam, they hold diametrically opposed opinions of his fitness for office: Bouscaren's work is a hagiography, whereas Warner's is highly critical.
6. George C. Herring, *America's Longest War: The United States and Vietnam, 1950–1975*, 4th edn. (New York: McGraw-Hill, 2002), 59.
7. Mark Moyar, *Triumph Forsaken: The Vietnam War, 1954–1965* (Cambridge: Cambridge University Press, 2006), xiv–xvii. Although Moyar gives a nod to recent scholarship, which argues that the Diem regime was not as backward-looking as it is generally portrayed, his work emphasizes that old-fashioned autocracy was Diem's basic approach to government and the secret of his success. For example, see 35–37.
8. Miller, 433–434.
9. David Halberstam, *The Making of a Quagmire* (New York: Random House, 1965); Joseph Buttinger, *Vietnam: A Dragon Embattled*, vols. 1 and 2 (New York: Frederick A. Praeger, 1967); Frances FitzGerald, *Fire in the Lake: The Vietnamese and the Americans in Vietnam* (New York: Vintage Books, 1973); Karnow, *Vietnam*.
10. Robert J. McMahon, "U.S.–Vietnamese Relations: A Historiographical Survey," in Warren I. Cohen, ed., *Pacific Passage: The Study of American–East Asian Relations on the Eve of the Twenty-First Century* (New York: Columbia University Press, 1996), 314.
11. Huynh Kim Khanh, "The Making and Unmaking of 'Free Vietnam'," *Pacific Affairs*, Fall 1987, 474.
12. Quoted in Marguerite Higgins, *Our Vietnam Nightmare* (New York: Harper & Row, 1965), 166.
13. Philip E. Catton, *Diem's Final Failure: Prelude to America's War in Vietnam* (Lawrence: University Press of Kansas, 2002); Miller, "Vision, Power, and Agency"; Stan B.-H. Tan, " 'Swiddens, Resettlements, Sedentarizations, and Villages': State Formation among the Central Highlanders of Vietnam under the First Republic, 1955–1961," *Journal of Vietnamese Studies*, February/August 2006, 210–251; Jessica M. Chapman, "Staging Democracy: South Vietnam's 1955 Referendum to Depose Bao Dai," *Diplomatic History*, September 2006, 671–703; Matthew Masur, "Exhibiting Signs of Resistance: South Vietnam's Struggle for Legitimacy, 1954–1960," *Diplomatic History*, April 2009, 293–313. For information on Vietnamese-language materials available in Vietnam

that cover the non-communist side of the conflict, see Matthew Masur and Edward Miller, "Saigon Revisited: Researching South Vietnam's Republican Era (1954–1975) at Archives and Libraries in Ho Chi Minh City," Cold War International History Project, September 2006, http://www.wilsoncenter.org/topics/docs/Saigon-Masur_Miller.pdf
14. For example, see David G. Marr, *Vietnamese Tradition on Trial, 1920–1945* (Berkeley: University of California Press, 1984); and Alexander B. Woodside, *Community and Revolution in Modern Vietnam* (Boston: Houghton Mifflin, 1976).
15. Catton, 41–47.
16. A recent, notable exception is Seth Jacobs, *America's Miracle Man in Vietnam: Ngo Dinh Diem, Religion, Race, and U.S. Intervention in Southeast Asia, 1950–1957* (Durham, NC: Duke University Press, 2004), 36–37.
17. James M. Carter, *Inventing Vietnam: The United States and State Building, 1954–1968* (Cambridge: Cambridge University Press, 2008), 109.
18. Moyar, *Triumph Forsaken*, 36–37.
19. Robert Shaplen, *The Lost Revolution: The Story of Twenty Years of Neglected Opportunities in Vietnam and of America's Failure to Foster Democracy There* (New York: Harper & Row, 1965), 131.
20. Halberstam, *The Making of a Quagmire*, 50.
21. The following analysis of the Strategic Hamlet program comes from Catton, especially 73–161.
22. For example, see several popular surveys: Marilyn B. Young, *The Vietnam Wars, 1945–1990* (New York: HarperCollins, 1991), 82–84; James S. Olson and Randy Roberts, *Where the Domino Fell: America and Vietnam, 1945–2006*, 5th edn. (Maplecrest, NY: Brandywine Press, 2006), 89–90. For an example of an in-depth analysis of the hamlet program that emphasizes the role of foreign initiative and downplays Diem's ideological concerns, see Michael E. Latham, *Modernization as Ideology: American Social Science and "Nation Building" in the Kennedy Era* (Chapel Hill: University of North Carolina Press, 2000). In spite of the subsequent publication of my *Diem's Final Failure*, which highlighted the Saigon government's role in the program, Latham repeated his original argument unchanged in a later article ("Redirecting the Revolution? The USA and the failure of nation-building in South Vietnam," *Third World Quarterly*, February 2006, 27–41). His persistence on this point suggests that many commentators—including serious and capable scholars like Latham—simply cannot shake the conviction that the Diem regime lacked ideas and agency.
23. Robert Buzzanco, "Fear and (Self) Loathing in Lubbock, Texas, or How I Learned to Quit Worrying and Love Vietnam and Iraq," *Passport*, December 2005, 5–14.
24. George C. Herring, " 'Peoples Quite Apart': Americans, South Vietnamese, and the War in Vietnam," *Diplomatic History*, Winter 1990, 1–23.
25. In addition to the works cited in footnote 12, see Robert K. Brigham, *ARVN: Life and Death in the South Vietnamese Army* (Lawrence: University Press of Kansas, 2006); Nu-Anh Tran, "South Vietnamese Identity, American Intervention, and the Newspaper *Chinh Luan* [Political Discussion], 1965–1969," *Journal of Vietnamese Studies*, February/August 2006, 169–209; Andrew Wiest, *Vietnam's Forgotten Army: Heroism and Betrayal in the ARVN* (New York: New York University Press, 2008); James McAllister, " 'Only Religions Count in Vietnam': Thich Tri Quang and the Vietnam War," *Modern Asian Studies*, 2008, 751–782.

CHAPTER 3

What We Still Do Not Know
Moyar's Treatment of Global Communism

WILLIAM STUECK[1]

For the sake of full disclosure, I begin with the promotional blurb I provided for Cambridge University Press for the book under review: "Mark Moyar has produced the best 'revisionist' study to date of the U.S. intervention in Vietnam. Engagingly written and broadly researched, this book establishes Moyar as the leading voice of a new generation of historians intent on challenging conventional wisdom." This statement was not an endorsement of the book's central argument, but rather a reflection of the beliefs (1) that Moyar is a serious scholar whose work deserves careful consideration, especially because of his use of sources from the North Vietnamese side, and (2) that re-examining the evidence and arguments for the orthodox view is a healthy development, especially for people such as me who spent a good portion of the late 1960s and early 1970s either protesting the war, dodging the draft, or a combination of the two. The extensive early attention devoted to *Triumph Forsaken* greatly reinforces my sense that the field of diplomatic history is alive and well.

Since the Vietnam War is not my primary area of research, I want to avoid any pretense at making authoritative judgments about the arguments and evidence Moyar puts forth. Rather, as a person who, over the years, has dabbled in U.S. primary sources on Vietnam and more than a little in the English-language secondary literature, I will comment on the arguments that strike me as most persuasive, those that strike me as least so, and where the debate that is just beginning might most fruitfully focus.

In a text of 416 pages, Moyar devotes a mere thirty-one to getting through the Geneva Accords of the summer of 1954. In that brief space, however, he makes assertions about Vietnamese history, the legitimacy of U.S. concerns for Vietnam after World War II, the military balance in Indochina in early 1954, and the negotiations at Geneva during June and July of that year that represent important foundations for what comes later. He emphasizes factionalism, disunity, authoritarianism, and violence in Vietnam's political history and China's relatively benign approach to Vietnam over the centuries. When China did intervene militarily in Vietnam, Moyar asserts, it was generally because it was dragged in at the behest of one of the smaller land's warring factions. Furthermore, according to Moyar, by 1945, Ngo Dinh Diem possessed nationalist credentials with his countrymen comparable to those of Ho Chi Minh, who in fact was a staunch internationalist holding "to the Leninist principle that Communist nations should subordinate their interests" to those of the broader revolutionary movement.[2] American concern from 1949 onward that the fall of Vietnam to communism would produce a "domino" effect in the region was sound, but its unwillingness to provide France with air support in the spring of 1954 was a serious mistake, because such aid probably would have averted the debacle at Dienbienphu and reinforced the essentially favorable military position that the French enjoyed at the time. Even after Dienbienphu, Ho recognized the weaknesses of his own forces and readily accepted partition of Vietnam rather than a continued armed struggle. That partition along the seventeenth parallel was not far from the division of the country from the late sixteenth century through most of the eighteenth.

Moyar is on strongest ground in his assertions regarding Vietnamese political history. The secondary literature makes it hard to dispute that unity was the exception rather than the rule or that Vietnam lacked a liberal tradition. Those facts, in turn, suggest that partition somewhere in the area of the seventeenth parallel was far from a historical aberration and that Vietnamese leaders need to be evaluated by some standard other than a predisposition toward liberal democracy. In addition, recent scholarship suggests that Ngo Dinh Diem possessed personal qualities and nationalist credentials that made him a potentially viable alternative to Ho. Finally, although the nature of China's traditional relationship with Vietnam may be debated endlessly, there can be no doubt that, from early 1950 onward, the People's Republic of China gave important support to the communist-led Viet Minh, support that was essential to the French defeat at Dienbienphu.

Moyar is far less persuasive in other areas, however. For example, he asserts that "the French and their Vietnamese cohorts were on the verge of crushing the Viet Minh in early 1954," a claim based largely on *Khrushchev*

Remembers and Hungarian diplomat Janos Radvanyi's recollection of statements in 1959 by Viet Minh General Vo Nguyen Giap. Former Soviet premier and party leader Nikita Khrushchev's memoirs provide immensely useful insights and have been proven accurate on numerous issues, but they must be read with a wary eye. Khrushchev's account of events regarding Indochina from April through July 1954 is particularly problematic. He is clearly wrong in stating that "at the first session of the [Geneva] conference, the French head of state, Mendes-France, proposed to restrict the northern reach of French forces to the seventeenth parallel," a proposal that he claimed to be a "surprise" to the Soviets, who regarded the line as "the absolute maximum" of what could be attained by the communist side. In fact, although Mendes-France did not become French premier until June 18, over six weeks into the conference, he initially insisted on the eighteenth parallel as the demarcation line, and the Soviets consistently hoped that the demarcation line would be no further north than the sixteenth parallel.[3] Moyar quotes Khrushchev as having been told by Zhou Enlai in early April that Ho characterized the Viet Minh military position as " 'hopeless,' " a statement that does not appear in the leading secondary sources on the Chinese side, books by Qiang Zhai and Chen Jian.[4]

To be sure, it is clear that the Viet Minh suffered serious losses at Dienbienphu during the early months of 1954, that Viet Minh troops suffered from morale problems in early April, at which time victory was by no means assured, and that Ho lobbied at the time for more aid from Beijing, including Chinese troops. Yet Moyar's use of *Khrushchev Remembers* to put the Viet Minh in a position of extreme distress is highly dubious. Even if Ho did say to Zhou what Khrushchev claims, the Viet Minh leader had every reason to exaggerate conditions in order to get more Chinese aid. Even if Radvanyi's account of Giap's lecture to a group of Hungarian officials five years after the event is precise, the lecture could easily have been an exaggeration to dramatize the heroism of the Vietnamese communists.[5] Giap's 1964 published account, as well as later oral accounts to journalist Stanley Karnow, are, after all, quite different.[6]

Placing the Khrushchev and Radyanji stories against some undisputed facts does not strengthen Moyar's interpretation. The Viet Minh outnumbered the surrounded French by five to one in manpower at Dienbienphu, they controlled the high ground on which their ample Chinese-supplied artillery and antiaircraft weapons were protected through camouflage and deployment partially underground, and they hid and shielded their troops through carefully constructed tunnels and trenches. During the first stage of their offensive in mid-March, Viet Minh units captured three key outer French defense posts and, through artillery and antiaircraft fire, closed the enemy airstrip, thus greatly restricting France's capacity to resupply and reinforce its troops. The French suffered over a thousand casualties, hundreds of defections by T'ai (a Vietnamese ethnic minority loyal to the French) soldiers, and a crisis of command both at the tactical and strategic levels. Paris's desperate appeal to Washington was not without cause.

It is entirely possible that U.S. bombing of the high ground around Dienbienphu could have brought some relief to the French. However, Giap had constructed in-ground shelters for his manpower and heavy weaponry with great care, and monsoon rains hit the area harder and earlier than usual in mid-April, flooding the French-held low ground and reducing the potential for precision bombing. The bottom line is that, with any outcome short of the annihilation of communist forces at Dienbienphu, the Viet Minh was far better positioned than the French to continue the military struggle over a prolonged period. The Viet Minh already occupied substantial portions of Vietnam, Laos, and Cambodia, and Mao was actively planning large-scale aid to his ally over a protracted period, all at a time when public support in France for the war was in decline.[7] New evidence from the Vietnamese side may eventually alter prevailing wisdom. At this point, however, the most plausible reading of Ho Chi Minh's perspective in the early spring of 1954 is that, after fighting the French for nearly eight years, he was anxious to win a decisive victory that would lead to the early independence and unification of Vietnam under his control, but that he was far from desperate or unprepared to fight on indefinitely.

This interpretation also fits Ho's course following the French surrender at Dienbienphu, and it does not jibe with Moyar's account. Again the direct documentation on Ho's thinking is far from conclusive, but Shai, Chen, and Ilya V. Gaiduk (on the Soviet side) all present substantial evidence of discontent within the Viet Minh leadership over Chinese and Soviet pressure for partition, especially at the seventeenth parallel, and for withdrawal of forces from Laos and Cambodia. True, Ho was well aware of his ongoing dependence on Chinese material support, which surely dictated caution in resisting Beijing's views; yet as a Vietnamese leader he could hardly have helped but possess local priorities divergent from Mao, who had recently experienced a costly military struggle with the Americans in Korea and faced the unfinished business of securing Taiwan to complete his own country's unification. Although Moyar cites Zhai, Chen, and Gaiduk on some specifics, he ignores other details, as well as these authors' conclusions.

The above excursion into Moyar's use of sources in a specific case falls well short of dismantling the overall argument of the book. It does suggest, however, that such key areas as his portrayal of the state of the war in South Vietnam during 1962 and 1963 and Mao's willingness to intervene with

Chinese ground forces during 1964 and 1965—or lack thereof—require the same kind of scrutiny. In the first case, Moyar argues that the war was going fairly well for the Diem government and would have gone even better had the United States been more supportive of its leader. Moyar bases his claims largely on pro-Diem elements among U.S. observers and previously untapped North Vietnamese sources that he did not read but had translated for him. I am persuaded that at least part of Diem's growing problems in the countryside during 1963 were a result of increased aid to the Viet Cong from North Vietnam and China, that the United States erred in pressing Diem to accommodate Buddhist dissidents and in giving a South Vietnamese military faction the green light for a coup in the fall of 1963, and that anti-Diem journalists such as Neil Sheehan and David Halberstam carried more weight in the United States than their knowledge or wisdom warranted. Nonetheless, I find suspect Moyar's glowing description of Diem's leadership and his downplaying of the issue of land distribution. Moyar is certainly correct to rebut orthodox portrayals of Diem as an unthinking reactionary and to emphasize security as a primary concern of the peasants, but the extent to which he goes in these directions strikes me as excessive. That Moyar sometimes uses block citations in the middle or at the end of declaratory paragraphs, thus making it virtually impossible to identify which point is supported by which source, does not inspire confidence. Over the next decade, a new generation of scholars, armed with appropriate language skills and a determination to uncover new materials in archives in Vietnam and France, are sure to have much to say on these matters.

There also remains much to uncover on Chinese intentions regarding Vietnam in 1964 and 1965. It is well known, of course, that Chinese troops began moving into North Vietnam in May 1965 to assist with logistics and man antiaircraft weapons. Rather than see this fact as an indication that China would have sent troops into North Vietnam at any point before that had the United States crossed the seventeenth parallel, Moyar argues that it was U.S. timidity during the summer and fall of 1964 that emboldened Mao to commit forces to his ally to the south. Moyar views China's response to U.S. bombing of the North after the Gulf of Tonkin incident as weak. "After the Gulf of Tonkin reprisals," Moyar claims, "in violation of previous promises, the Chinese made clear to Hanoi that if American forces invaded North Vietnam, China would not send its troops to fight the Americans."[8] To support the assertion, he cites an account of an October 5, 1964, meeting between Mao and two North Vietnamese leaders in Beijing that is translated and published through the Cold War International History Project.[9] Yet the document is ambiguous. Neither Chen Jian nor Qiang Zhai, the leading authorities on Chinese policy at this time, interpret it as

Moyar does.[10] Nor do they regard China's response to the U.S. bombing of North Vietnam in August as weak. Moyar is correct in stating that the available evidence suggests that China's position at this time was less committal than it had been earlier in the year or during the spring and summer of 1965, but it is a stretch to suggest that Mao would not have intervened on a major scale in late 1964 had the United States invaded the North. As on the Diem issue, while new evidence may prove Moyar correct, the weight of the current documentation is against him.

A better chance existed that Mao would not have sent troops had the United States invaded Laos, especially if it had restricted itself to southern areas being used by the North Vietnamese for infiltration routes into South Vietnam. Yet Moyar fails to analyze the potential logistical problems for American forces in launching such a campaign during the second half of 1964. Overall, if we accept Moyar's argument that the fall of South Vietnam in the mid-1960s would have led to a major erosion of the U.S. position in Asia and perhaps worldwide, rapid American escalation of the war in August 1964 might make sense, but the prudence and/or feasibility of carrying the *ground* war to North Vietnam and Laos remains doubtful. Given the internal problems faced by the South Vietnamese government during 1964, it is also doubtful that a giant infusion of U.S. armed forces a year earlier than it actually occurred would have brought victory over a relatively brief period and at less than an enormous cost in life and treasure.

This leaves us with Moyar's analysis of the domino theory, which is the most extensive to date.[11] Moyar asserts, rightly I believe, that the failure of dominoes to fall beyond Indochina after South Vietnam went communist in 1975 does not necessarily mean that the same outcome would have resulted if South Vietnam had gone communist a decade earlier. Indonesia, after all, was far more firmly anti-communist in 1975 than it had been in 1965, Thailand was much stronger, and Chinese influence was far less threatening. Moyar briefly examines the positions of governments in and the internal conditions of anti-communist nations on the Pacific rim and concludes that, in all likelihood, an American withdrawal from Vietnam during 1965 would have had a devastating effect on U.S. alliances and the anti-communist cause in the region and that the United States would have wound up fighting somewhere else, most probably in Indonesia, under even less favorable conditions than in South Vietnam.

Moyar makes a strong case, but I still have reservations. Most important, with the countries I know best, South Korea, Japan, and Taiwan, it is unlikely that a U.S. withdrawal from South Vietnam would have seriously compromised American alliances. Moyar is correct in claiming that leaders in South Korea and Taiwan and, to a lesser extent, Japan, favored U.S.

escalation in Vietnam; yet the option of abandoning the U.S. security system lacked strong appeal, even if the American government proved unreliable in defending its South Vietnamese ally. For one thing, where else could the three countries find protection? Japan had the most viable option of the three, a turn toward neutrality, because its boundaries were less threatened than the other two. Even so, Japan was in the midst of a U.S.-brokered settlement with South Korea that could not help but provide economic benefits over the long term; it possessed a strong, not to mention privileged, trade relationship with the United States and a profitable one with western Europe as well; and it even carried on significant trade with China, despite American reticence. The spread of communism through Southeast Asia would not necessarily have precluded trade with the area. Economically, breaking the alliance with the United States was potentially much more disruptive to Japan than sticking to it. What is more, the United States had never concluded security treaties with South Vietnam as it had with Japan, South Korea, and Taiwan. So long as it countered a withdrawal from South Vietnam with a reinforcement of commitments to the others, the loss of confidence on the part of the others arguably would have been minimal. Moyar essentially concedes that the same would have been the case with Australia and New Zealand, and I would add the Philippines to the list.

Moyar is on stronger ground with regard to Thailand and Indonesia. In the first case, though, the United States would have retained the option of offering a military alliance, which it had never done with South Vietnam, and the stationing of troops. Despite turmoil at the top, Thailand had a much more functional government and social system than did South Vietnam, and it had historically feared expansion by China and Vietnam. Furthermore, the United States could have made military commitments to Malaya and Singapore, which, given their size, location, and relatively stable internal situations, were readily defensible. Control of one side of the Strait of Malacca, a major strategic prize, should have been sufficient to keep it open to shipping. Indonesia was the biggest problem, but even here, it is far from clear that the conservative military, if given support by the United States, would have done anything other than what it actually did in the fall of 1965—namely, purge the communists and overthrow the increasingly leftist regime of Sukarno. What, after all, would they have preferred to rely upon: the good will of the communists if they seized power, or the immediate assistance of the United States? In other words, much of the impact of a U.S. withdrawal from Vietnam would have been determined by what Washington did as a follow-up.

Moyar does an excellent job of documenting the very real fears of President Johnson and his top advisors during 1965, but in becoming their advocate, he overstates the most likely consequences of a retreat in Vietnam rather than escalation. This overstatement includes not only his estimates of the reactions of anti-communist governments and groups but also of the capacity of China, about to become embroiled in the Cultural Revolution, to consolidate its position in Southeast Asia and possibly beyond. Given the history of Vietnam, both before 1965 and after 1975, it is by no means certain that the Vietnamese communists would have easily consolidated their position in the South, even after a U.S. withdrawal, or found China cooperative in expanding their power into Laos and Cambodia (or in pushing westward beyond that). Under any circumstances, Southeast Asia was destined to be in turmoil for some time and was just as likely to cause indigestion to a communist China and a communist Vietnam as a readily absorbed treat to be exploited for further gain. It was also likely to be a source of further acrimony between the Soviet Union and China. Moyar assists us in understanding why American leaders calculated differently at the time and he provides much grist for a healthy "argument without end." For this aging diplomatic historian, however, while sparking some embarrassing memories of the self-righteousness and naiveté of youth and generating a salutary mental workout, he has failed to persuade on the key point that the United States did the right thing in escalating the war in Vietnam during 1965.

Notes

1. The author wishes to thank Richard Immerman, Chen Jian, and Qiang Zhai for helpful comments on an earlier draft of this review.
2. Mark Moyar, *Triumph Forsaken: The Vietnam War, 1954–1965* (Cambridge: Cambridge University Press, 2006), 9.
3. Nikita Khrushchev, *Khrushchev Remembers*, trans. Strobe Talbott (Boston: Little, Brown, 1970), 482–483. For a recent account based largely on Soviet documents, see Ilya V. Gaiduk, *Confronting Vietnam: Soviet Policy toward the Indochina Conflict, 1954–1963* (Washington, DC: Woodrow Wilson Center Press, 2003), 21–25.
4. Moyar, *Triumph Forsaken*, 27; Qiang Zhai, *China and the Vietnam Wars, 1950–1975* (Chapel Hill, NC: University of North Carolina Press, 2000), 46–49; Chen Jian, *Mao's China and the Cold War* (Chapel Hill, NC: University of North Carolina Press, 2001), 134–138.
5. Janos Radvanyi, *Delusion and Reality: Gambits, Hoaxes, and Diplomatic One-Upmanship in Vietnam* (South Bend, Indiana: Gateway Editions, 1978), 8–9. Radvanyi's prudence in accepting the accounts of others is called into question by his unquestioning acceptance of Khrushchev's account.
6. Vo Nguyen Giap, *Dien Bien Phu* (Hanoi: Foreign Languages Press, 1964); Stanley Karnow, *Vietnam: A History*, rev. & updated edn. (New York: Viking, 1991), 204–214.
7. On Mao's plans, see Zhai, *China and the Vietnam Wars*, 47–48.
8. Moyar, *Triumph Forsaken*, 321.
9. Odd Arne Westad, Chen Jian, Stein Tonnesson, Nguyen Vu Tung, and James G. Hershberg (eds.), "77 Conversations Between Chinese and Foreign Leaders on the Wars in Indochina, 1964–1977," Working Paper No. 22, Cold War International

History Project (Washington, DC: Woodrow Wilson International Center for Scholars, May 1998), 74–77.
10. James G. Hershberg and Chen Jian, "Reading and Warning the Likely Enemy: China's Signals to the United States about Vietnam in 1965," *International History Review* 27 (March 2005): 62. Hershberg and Chen state simply that Mao "did not offer Chinese direct military intervention in response to the invasion." See also Zhai, *China and Vietnam Wars*, 133.
11. Moyar, *Triumph Forsaken*, 376–391.

CHAPTER 4

A One-sided Picture of the Chinese–Vietnamese Ties during the Vietnam War

QIANG ZHAI

Moyar's book provides a detailed treatment of the American involvement in Vietnam from the French defeat at Dien Bien Phu in 1954 to President Lyndon Johnson's escalation of U.S. intervention in 1965. Unlike most other general accounts of the Vietnam conflict, which tend to focus only on the American perspective, Moyar's study also offers an extensive coverage of both the communist (Hanoi and Beijing) and South Vietnamese policymaking. He has conducted research in American and British archives, and is familiar with most of the recent scholarship on the subject. He has incorporated Vietnamese-language sources, as well as communist documents translated and published by the Cold War International History Project.

Although I commend Moyar's efforts to pay attention to both the American and communist sides of the story, I find his treatment of Chinese and Vietnamese history and culture simplistic, and his accounts of Beijing's foreign policy and the Chinese–Vietnamese communist relationship misleading. The image of Ho Chi Minh that emerges from Moyar's narrative is a devoted communist internationalist, a familiar characterization that many of Ho's detractors in the past have proposed. Moyar emphasizes Ho's dedication to communism, portraying Ho as a true believer in the Leninist doctrine that communist nations should subordinate their interest to those of the international communist movement. Is this an accurate characterization of Ho? While it is true that Ho was motivated by Marxist–Leninist communism, it is also true that he drew his inspirations from traditional Confucian humanism. Ho was well versed in the perennial Chinese–Vietnamese philosophy that combined Confucianism with Buddhism and Daoism. Ho retained his classical Confucian education and then closely blended it with Leninist principles, which essentially shaped the strategy and tactics of revolution and the taking of political power. In his childhood, Ho was steeped in Confucian moral and political indoctrination. The Confucian teaching on communal responsibility and the perfectibility of man led Ho, in the disillusioned and desperate years after the First World War, to the appeal of Marxism–Leninism. From Ho's perspective, communism constituted the realization of Confucian ideals in a modern historical setting. In comparison with other Asian communist leaders—like Mao Zedong and Kim Il Sung—who operated in a region once under strong Confucian influence, Ho retained the most traces of Confucian humanism and was the least constricted by communist ideology. William Duiker has judiciously characterized Ho as "half Gandhi and half Lenin," but in Moyar's view, Ho was 100 percent Leninist. Moyar totally misses the influence of Confucian humanism in Ho's mental universe. For a long time, Ho Chi Minh has remained a controversial and shadowy figure in the West. Instead of demystifying Ho, Moyar continues to hold the stereotype of the Vietnamese leader as a ruthless communist operator, who displayed "single-minded and unswerving dedication to one objective: the imposition of communist government in Vietnam and the rest of the World."[1] There is no doubt that Ho believed in communism, but there is also no doubt that he believed in it as an instrument to realize his real purpose: the independence and unification of his country. In emphasizing that Ho was a communist internationalist, Moyar refuses to allow that Ho could also be a Vietnamese nationalist.

While Moyar is correct to emphasize that the Chinese and Vietnamese communists shared many common values and international solidarity, and that Ho Chi Minh admired his Chinese comrades, he tends to overlook the differences and disagreements that constantly emerged as a result of their divergent assessments of their respective national interests. The Sino-Vietnamese negotiations over the settlement of the Indochina conflict during the Geneva Conference of 1954 provide a clear example of the policy gap between the two communist parties. Moyar tends to highlight agreement and unity among the Soviet, Chinese, and Vietnamese communist delegations at Geneva. In fact, the Chinese and Vietnamese communists disagreed over a number of issues at the conference. The Chinese were eager to restore peace in Indochina because they wanted to concentrate on domestic rebuilding, a process that had been disrupted by the Korean War.

They did not want to become involved in another Korea-type conflict with the United States. They feared that if the fighting in Indochina continued, it might trigger an American intervention. As a result, Premier Zhou Enlai, head of the Chinese delegation, showed great flexibility and did his utmost to facilitate a settlement at the Geneva Conference.

At Geneva, the Chinese and Vietnamese communists disagreed over three issues: (1) the representation of Laos and Cambodia at the conference; (2) the withdrawal of foreign troops from Laos and Cambodia; (3) the location of the demarcation line. On all three issues, Zhou Enlai exerted pressure on Pham Van Dong, head of the Vietnamese communist delegation, to modify his position and to accommodate Western views. On the first issue, Western countries preferred to accept the delegates sent by the Royal Governments of Laos and Cambodia to represent their respective countries at the conference while Pham Van Dong promoted the delegates of the "resistance movements" in Laos and Cambodia. These people had been trained and nurtured by the Vietnamese communists. Under Zhou Enlai's pressure, Pham Van Dong gave up and accepted the Western choices. On the second issue, the French insisted that if they were to withdraw their troops from Indochina, the Vietnamese communists should also pull their soldiers out of Laos and Cambodia. Pham Van Dong at first refused to admit the presence of Vietnamese troops in Laos and Cambodia, but because of Zhou Enlai's arm-twisting, he relented in the end, agreeing to withdraw Vietnamese "volunteers" (a euphemism for soldiers) from Laos and Cambodia. The third issue was the thorniest. Zhou Enlai was willing to accept the French proposal of dividing Vietnam at the seventeenth parallel, but Pham Van Dong at first rejected the French suggestion. He wanted the demarcation line to be located as far south as possible, at either fifteenth or fourteenth parallel. Because of Pham Van Dong's rejection of the seventeenth parallel as the demarcation line, the negotiations at Geneva stalled. An anxious Zhou Enlai had to turn to Ho Chi Minh to pressure Pham Van Dong. During a break of the Geneva Conference, Zhou met with Ho Chi Minh in Liuzhou, a city in southern China, from July 3 to July 5. At the meeting, Zhou pointed out the importance of achieving peace in Indochina while French Prime Minister Pierre Mendes-France was still in office. The Chinese premier believed that Washington was putting pressure on the French leader and that if the Vietnamese communists were to insist on Paris accepting "unacceptable" demands, the Americans would take advantage of this, the pro-war faction in France would gain the upper hand, and the Mendes-France Cabinet would fall. The Soviets agreed with Zhou's analysis. Taking the Chinese advice, Ho Chi Minh instructed Pham Van Dong not to drag his feet at Geneva and to accept the seventeenth parallel as the demarcation line.

During the Geneva Conference, the Chinese communists resisted the Vietnamese tendency of promoting what they called the "Indochina federation" idea. They worried about the Vietnamese intention to create a military bloc of the three Indochinese states after ousting the French from the region. They resented the Vietnamese effort to subordinate the interests of Laos and Cambodia to those of the Democratic Republic of Vietnam (D.R.V.). Zhou Enlai declared that the "Indochina federation" notion violated the sovereignty and independence of Laos and Cambodia, and that since conditions for revolution in those countries were not ripe, "revolution cannot be exported." The outcome of the Geneva Conference clearly indicates that Chinese national self-interests outweigh any ideological obligation to assist the struggle of a fraternal communist party. The Chinese and Vietnamese fracture and fissures at the Geneva Conference represented a clash of two visions about what Indochina should look like in the post-French era. Moyar, however, says nothing about the Chinese suspicion of their Vietnamese comrades' intention and effort to dominate Laos and Cambodia.

In discussing developments in North and South Vietnam after the Geneva Conference, Moyar makes frequent references to Beijing's economic and military assistance to Hanoi, but not a single mention of Taiwan's role in Ngo Dinh Diem's efforts to consolidate his power in Saigon. In the early 1960s, General Wang Sheng, a psychological warfare specialist in Chiang Kai-shek's army, made nine visits to South Vietnam and established a close personal relationship with Diem. At the request of Diem and General William Westmoreland, Wang helped the South Vietnam government create a Political Warfare School to train officers on how to conduct campaigns to win the "hearts and minds" of the Vietnamese population.

Moyar's interpretation of Beijing's response to the American intervention in Vietnam after the Gulf of Tonkin Incident is off the mark. He describes China's reaction as "feeble" and Mao as "frightened" of the American power. Citing a conversation between Mao and Pham Van Dong on October 5, 1964, Moyar asserts that Mao broke his promise to send troops to fight the Americans if the United States launched a ground invasion of North Vietnam. Moyar contends that Beijing did not change its timid policy until late February and March 1965, when it became clear that the Johnson administration was showing restraint in fighting North Vietnam and that "the risks associated with greater involvement were decreasing while the risks associated with less involvement were increasing."[2] Revelations from new Chinese sources do not support Moyar's explanations. China's policy toward the Vietnam conflict from the second half of 1964 to the first half of 1965 was generally consistent and firm. Shortly after the Gulf of Tonkin Incident, the leaders in Beijing instructed the Kunming and

Guangzhou Military Regions and the air force and naval units stationed in south and southwest China to begin a state of combat-readiness. Four air divisions and one antiaircraft division were dispatched into areas adjoining Vietnam and put on a heightened alert status. In August, China sent approximately fifteen MIG-15 and MIG-17 jets to Hanoi, agreed to train North Vietnamese pilots, and began to build new airfields in areas adjacent to the Vietnamese border that would serve as sanctuary and repair and maintenance facilities for Hanoi's jet fighters. By moving new air force units to the border area and constructing new airfields there, Beijing intended to deter further U.S. expansion of war in South Vietnam and bombardment against the D.R.V. Between August and September 1964, the People's Liberation Army (P.L.A.) also sent an inspection team to North Vietnam to investigate the situation in case China later needed to dispatch support troops. The only adjustment in Chinese policy was the decision in mid-1965 to cancel the plan to send Chinese pilots to the D.R.V. I checked the record of the October 5, 1964, conversation between Mao and Pham Van Dong as published in the Cold War International History Project (C.W.I.H.P.) working paper and found no indication that Mao had retreated from his position of sending troops to resist the Americans if Washington conducted a ground invasion of the D.R.V. Moyar misuses the document in this instance.

Moyar develops this interpretation of "China's feeble reaction" to the American punishment of the D.R.V. after the Gulf of Tonkin Incident in order to prove his thesis that President Johnson missed an opportunity to invade North Vietnam in late 1964, which, according to Moyar, was "a better strategic scenario than the one the Americans ultimately accepted by not invading."[3] Would Mao not react strongly to an American invasion of North Vietnam in late 1964? Beijing had substantial security and ideological interests in Vietnam. From the security perspective, Mao and his associates were genuinely concerned about the American threat from Vietnam and adopted significant measures in war preparations at home. From the viewpoint of ideology, China's support for Vietnam served Mao's purposes of demonstrating to the Third World that Beijing was a spokesman for national liberation struggles and of competing with Moscow for leadership in the international communist movement. If the solutions recommended by Moyar had been adopted by the Johnson administration in Vietnam, there would have been a real danger of a Sino-American war, with dire consequences for the world. In retrospect, it appears that Johnson had drawn the correct lesson from the Korean War and had been prudent in his approach to the Vietnam conflict.

Moyar's book is marred by many questionable statements and a superficial understanding of Chinese policymaking. He asserts that the Chinese communists killed over one million people during their land reform campaign in China, but produces no evidence to support this assertion.[4] He declares that, in late 1964, the North Vietnamese and Chinese were considering an invasion of Thailand, but he fails to present evidence to substantiate such a claim.[5] He describes Chen Geng, a Chinese advisor to Ho Chi Minh, as being "so fat that he had to be lifted onto his horse."[6] I wonder from what sources Moyar obtained that description of Chen Geng as an obese man. Neither Chen's photos nor contemporary accounts of him corroborate such a description. It is possible that Moyar's penchant for vivid descriptions carries him too far. Moyar tends to attach positions to Chinese leaders that they never held. For instance, he identifies Mao as "Chinese premier."[7] In fact, that was a position that Zhou Enlai occupied. Mao was the chairman of the Chinese Communist Party Central Committee. Moyar refers to Chiang Kai-shek as "Premier."[8] Chiang actually served as the president of the Republic of China. The high-level Chinese military delegation that visited Hanoi in December 1961 was led by Marshal Ye Jianying, not by Defense Minister Lin Biao, as Moyar claims.[9]

The Sino-Vietnamese relationship during the two Indochina wars was more complicated than Moyar has allowed. There were two strands in China's policy toward Vietnam: cooperation and containment. Mao cooperated with the Vietnamese Communist Party in its struggle against France and the United States by investing enormous amounts of energy and resources. This cooperation served China's geopolitical and ideological interests of eliminating hostile imperialist presence from its southern border and spreading revolution in Indochina. While supporting the effort of Ho Chi Minh's party to preserve independence and achieve reunification, Chinese leaders also sought to contain its tendency to establish hegemony over Laos and Cambodia. These conflicting strands in China's policy made the People's Republic of China (P.R.C.) and the D.R.V. both friends and foes.

Notes

1. Mark Moyar, *Triumph Forsaken: The Vietnam War, 1954–1965* (Cambridge: Cambridge University Press, 2006), 10.
2. Ibid., 361.
3. Ibid., 321–322.
4. Ibid., 23.
5. Ibid., 323.
6. Ibid., 22.
7. Ibid., 61.
8. Ibid., 384.
9. Ibid., 146.

CHAPTER 5

Section I Response

MARK MOYAR

The controversy that erupted with the publication of *Triumph Forsaken* three years ago did not come as a great surprise to me, since my previous book, *Phoenix and the Birds of Prey*, had also elicited sharp attacks from some academic scholars, although in much smaller numbers. In fact, the proliferation of attacks on *Triumph Forsaken* had its benefits, for it helped bring the book to the attention of others. Many historians had deliberately ignored the *Phoenix* book, and thereby constrained public and scholarly awareness. Many, no doubt, had wished the same fate for *Triumph Forsaken*, and several took action aimed at that outcome. One of the peer reviewers who advised a publisher to reject the manuscript predicted that the book "will be ignored by the scholarly community, because it will be far too long and expensive," and that it "will briefly get on the radar due to the author's last book, but will be thereafter dismissed." *Triumph Forsaken*, however, was able to develop enough momentum that academic historians decided they could not ignore it.

The hostile responses to the book did hold much surprise for outside observers unfamiliar with the workings of American history departments. Considering that the most prominent academic historians had been in confident agreement on the war's big issues, one might not expect that a single challenge to the orthodoxy, from a junior scholar at a university that few people knew existed, would cause legions of academics to unsheathe their swords. If the historical profession maintained the atmosphere of free inquiry it purported to maintain, indeed, a challenge to popular ideas would have been welcomed as a guardian against complacency, and a stimulus of debate in place of mutual back-patting.

The book aroused the wrath of other historians because it challenged ideas about which they spent many years writing and which, for the Baby Boomers among them, had been central to the formative period of their lives. Few people are especially receptive to new information and ideas that undermine principles they have held for decades. Exacerbating their anger was the existence of many footnotes in *Triumph Forsaken* specifying the historians who had espoused interpretations that I was contesting. I had not originally intended to include such a naming of names, but was forced into it by scholars who, prior to the book's publication, accused me of producing "straw men" or charged that "no one really believes that" after I had laid out in general terms what I viewed as common interpretations. The inclusion of these footnotes has prevented the repetition of those charges since the book's publication.

The opposition to the book was further intensified by the politicization of American history departments, which has encouraged ostracism of research that challenges the politically popular points of view, as mine does. In recent decades, out of the sight of the American public, moderate and conservative viewpoints have all but disappeared from those departments as professors of the Left have hired only like-minded individuals to replace retiring professors. There are a few moderates and conservatives left—individuals who entered the department decades ago before things got really bad, or who kept their political views secret until they received tenure, or who gained greater exposure to the real world after getting tenure and changed their minds—but too few to halt the alarming trends. The absence of dissent has promoted intellectual laziness and made it ever easier to rationalize the exclusion of other voices from the history department, in addition to channeling professorial argumentativeness into trivial departmental politics and denunciations of George W. Bush. The use of history for political purposes has become so accepted that the American Historical Association, in 2007, followed the lead of the group Historians Against the War in calling on Association members to "do whatever they can to bring the Iraq war to a speedy conclusion."

I have found encouraging exceptions to the rule of closed-mindedness among left-of-center academic historians, especially diplomatic and military historians, since their fields are inherently more resistant to the academic fads that have helped justify faculty politicization. Quite a few have spoken favorably of *Triumph Forsaken* in private, to me and to others. Few, however, have been willing to say the same things in public, and some who did initially make positive comments publicly were attacked by other historians and subsequently went quiet or came out against the book. Several of the individuals who contributed to this book belong to that category. Senior scholars have warned more than a few younger scholars that they should avoid embracing the interpretations of *Triumph Forsaken* if they wish to "get ahead" in the profession.

Because of this intellectual climate, nearly all revisionist historians of Vietnam operate outside the academic mainstream. Some of them, including me, are fortunate that the alternative galaxy of higher education within the U.S. military allows the continuation of scholarly work without the pressures and pettiness of ideological conformity. Another result of the ideological intolerance is that scholarly forums on Vietnam regularly exclude revisionist views. Take, for instance, a 2008 edited volume from Oxford University Press that billed itself as "the most up-to-date collection of scholarship on the controversial historiography of the Vietnam Wars." It contained plenty of contributions from the most left-wing of historians—like Gareth Porter, Marilyn Young, and David Hunt—as well as less radical scholars of orthodox persuasion—like Mark Bradley, Mark Lawrence, and David Elliott—but no contributions from revisionists.[1] A 2007 volume that purported to "bring together the country's leading historians of the Vietnam experience" included some of the aforementioned characters as well as Howard Zinn, Walter Lafeber, John Prados, and Alfred McCoy, but not a single revisionist.[2] A volume from the same period stated in its self-description, "The eminent scholars featured in *The War That Never Ends* present the newest perspectives on the war in Vietnam, from the homefront to Ho Chi Minh City, from the government halls to the hotbeds of activist opposition." The editors feature many of the orthodox scholars in the other volumes plus George Herring and Robert Buzzanco, and chose not to fill any of its sixteen slots with a revisionist.[3]

Very few institutions of higher education are sufficiently committed to free inquiry to invite people of contrary viewpoints on Vietnam. One such place is Williams College, which hosted a conference on March 2–3, 2007, that focused on *Triumph Forsaken* and yielded presentations that were incorporated into some of this volume's essays. I readily agreed with the conference's organizers that the event should include people who differed sharply with me on Vietnam. I was confident that my research would withstand their barbs, and I thought that some of them might actually be prepared to change their minds. The list of participants therefore included the likes of David Kaiser, Mark Lawrence, Richard Immerman, Seth Jacobs, Edward Miller, and Jessica Chapman, as well as some who were more favorably inclined toward the book. Yet when Williams held another conference in April 2009 that discussed a book highly critical of American involvement in Vietnam, the organizers (not the same set as for the first event) invited neither me nor anyone else on my side of the debate.[4]

The aversion of academic historians to recognition—not to mention praise—of *Triumph Forsaken* can also be viewed in the books and articles that have appeared since its publication. Although most of these works put forth some of the new information presented in *Triumph Forsaken*, many do not mention whence it came, and their use of that information does not stop them from denouncing the book and/or me in strong terms. Historians cannot be expected to cite other historians for every single new fact that they have discovered, and it is much more important that the truth gets out than that I or anyone else receives credit for it. If historians are honest enough to accept new information that contradicts their views but too afraid of faculty ideologues to acknowledge the validity of the source, so be it. Historians, nevertheless, should be expected to refrain from blanket attacks on, or conspicuous omission of, books from which they obtain valuable information.

John Prados, for example, makes a few unfounded attacks on me in his book *Vietnam: The History of an Unwinnable War*, while invoking some of the book's discoveries, such as the North Vietnamese decision in 1964 to send an entire division to South Vietnam, without footnoting them and without even mentioning the book in a nineteen-page bibliographic essay.[5] Rufus Phillips, in *Why Vietnam Matters*, borrows considerably more from *Triumph Forsaken* and accepts more of its interpretations, such as my characterization of the outbreak of the Buddhist crisis in May 1963 and the White House's last-minute reservations about the coup against Diem, while also neglecting to cite the book in his footnotes or his section on sources.[6] Mark Lawrence cites several findings from *Triumph Forsaken* and uses others, like the impact of the Tonkin Gulf incidents on North Vietnamese strategy, without citation, but does not list the book in his section on further reading.[7] Less egregious is William S. Turley. Although he criticizes some of my positions by name and does not mention my name in connection with those he accepts, such as the rapid decline of the South Vietnamese war effort after Diem's assassination, Turley at least describes my book in the bibliographic note as "a richly documented account of the war."[8]

A better display of scholarly disagreement comes from James McAllister, who disagrees with some of my conclusions, but comments, "Despite my obvious differences with Moyar concerning Tri Quang, all students of the war will have to seriously grapple with his extensive research and revisionist assessment of many elements of the Vietnam War."[9] Gary Hess's *Explaining the Vietnam War* also takes the book seriously and avoids snide comments aimed at belittling it, even while he disputes a variety of its conclusions.[10] I hope that others will learn from their example.

A minority of historians, like Andrew Wiest, Peter Dale Scott, Arthur Herman, and several of the contributors to this book, have stated openly that *Triumph Forsaken* contains valuable new revelations and adjusted prior conclusions accordingly.[11] In addition, quite a few graduate students and recent PhDs have embraced ideas contained in *Triumph Forsaken* (I won't mention their names in order to avoid damaging their careers). I have also been privileged to receive a flood of letters from American and Vietnamese veterans of the war thanking me for setting the record straight on the events in which they participated.

Given human nature, historians are more likely to desist from convenient falsehoods that have been disproven than they are to acknowledge inconvenient truths that have been proven. Consequently, some of the most significant changes, in this case and many others concerning the modification of history, involve what disappears rather than what appears. In most of the aforementioned works, one will find conspicuously absent certain long-standing interpretations that were debunked in *Triumph Forsaken*. For instance, the portrayal of Paul Harkins as a fool has largely disappeared. David Halberstam and Neil Sheehan are no longer depicted as impartial truth-tellers. The Ho Chi Minh Trail is not dismissed as a factor of minor importance in the early years of the war.

Many of this volume's contributors devoted their essays to attacks on a few sections of *Triumph Forsaken*, ignoring numerous sections of great historical import and saying little about what the book's new findings mean for future historical research. As a consequence, the refutation of their allegations comprises the bulk of my responses. When working on *Triumph Forsaken*, I had anticipated most of the objections raised by the commentators and had written the book in such a way as to counter them, but, owing to space considerations, I did not specifically address all of them directly. This volume therefore provides a good vehicle for defending the book more explicitly on certain counts.

I was pleased to contribute to *Battling for the Vietnam War* for several additional reasons. This volume makes the debate available to a larger audience. My responses to the criticisms will, I believe, convince the open-minded that the attacks have distorted the book and have lacked supporting evidence. The responses should also help graduate students and other aspiring scholars understand academia's aversion to alternative viewpoints, and hence the need to keep quiet on controversial subjects prior to receiving tenure. In certain sections, moreover, the volume shows how historians agree and disagree productively and respectfully.

My responses will generally follow the order of the essays, so I will begin with Keith Taylor's essay. Taylor's piece belongs to the category that I had hoped would be the largest, that of essays exploring both the implications of *Triumph Forsaken* for further historical inquiry and other historical discoveries that are pertinent to its themes. The world's preeminent historian of pre-modern Vietnamese history, Taylor draws upon his vast knowledge to bolster the linkages I drew between the Vietnam of 1954–1965 and the Vietnam of prior decades and centuries. Many of these linkages could have been identified long ago by specialists in Vietnamese history, had that field possessed many scholars who, like Taylor, examine the large political issues and do so dispassionately. Some Vietnam specialists have lost sight of those issues by drifting into microhistories and race–class–gender studies, or by focusing narrowly on a single time period. Most have been disinclined to question the incorrect linkages drawn by earlier commentators who argued that the United States should have stayed out of Vietnam, since they concurred with that assessment of U.S. policy. Furthermore, historians of Vietnam shy away from the authoritarian and violent aspects of the political culture for the same reason as historians of other non-Western areas—because they undermine the notion that white males are the principal source of trouble in the world.

In his essay, Taylor provides an exploration of Vietnam's origins that not only discredits the widely believed myth of historical Sino-Vietnamese enmity, but also illuminates Vietnam's political heritage in ways that should help change the minds of other historians. In the past few years, specialists in Vietnamese history have begun accepting my contention in *Triumph Forsaken* that historical Sino-Vietnamese animosity has been vastly overstated, but, given that my book was focused on the war and that I did not know the literature of the pre-modern period nearly as well as Keith Taylor, I did not provide the same level of detail or citation that he includes in his essay. Taylor also elaborates sagely on the point that the rare instances of Chinese involvement in Vietnam were usually the result of one Vietnamese faction enlisting Chinese help in putting down another.

I have admired Philip Catton's work on Ngo Dinh Diem since I first read his doctoral dissertation "Parallel Agendas," which formed the basis for his book *Diem's Final Failure: Prelude to America's War in Vietnam*. Catton was among the first academic historians to approach Diem without hostility and to question the popular portraits of Diem propagated by people like David Halberstam, Frances FitzGerald, and Stanley Karnow. By giving serious study to Diem's words and deeds, Catton found that Diem was a serious thinker who tried to adapt Vietnamese traditions to the modern world. As Catton notes in his essay, this view of Diem contradicted the orthodox version of Diem as an old-fashioned autocrat seeking an idealized version of the Vietnamese past, and it has aroused angry condemnations from certain orthodox historians. I differ with Catton on other points of significance, especially the viability of the Diem regime, allowing me to break Catton's record for the number of attacks sustained, but our agreement on the seriousness of Diem as a historical figure separates both of us from the large majority of historians.

I was therefore surprised to find that his essay depicts his interpretations of Diem as wholly different from mine. Catton contends that both I and the orthodox school "draw on the same essential picture of Diem as the old-fashioned mandarin patriot," whereas the "new scholarship" on Diem takes a different view. Catton describes the view of the "new scholarship" on Diem as follows: "[Diem's] thinking reflected the broadly progressive concerns of other Vietnamese nationalists and Southeast Asian leaders at the time . . . Diem was a conservative modernizer rather than a traditional autocrat; he was looking forward, not backward."

Compare that description with what I actually state in *Triumph Forsaken*:

> Diem and Nhu both favored revolutionary changes but at the same time wanted to preserve central elements of Vietnamese culture . . . Personalism, as professed by the Ngo brothers, was not a mere rehashing of ancient Confucian precepts or other traditional ideas. Diem and Nhu recognized that a return to pre-colonial ways was not feasible. "The nationalism that would surrender to reaction is doomed," Diem declared, "just as nationalism which allies itself with communism is bound to end up in treason." Vietnamese Personalism, rather, was a synthesis of old and new ideas that would allow Vietnam and its traditions to prosper in the modern environment brought on by French colonialism and other outside influences. (35–36)[12]

Only the most imaginative postmodernist could explain how the foregoing passages characterize Diem as an "old-fashioned mandarin patriot."

Those passages also contradict Catton's allegation that, in *Triumph Forsaken*, Personalism "is usually viewed as an intellectual curiosity and casually dismissed as a cover for Diem's authoritarian style of rule." Many other sections of *Triumph Forsaken* likewise demonstrate that I share Catton's view that Personalism helped guide Diem and Nhu in their efforts to build a South Vietnamese polity. For instance: "As a cornerstone of their Personalist movement, Diem and Nhu were intent on redistributing land, which they believed would promote the well-being and dignity of every individual, build support for the government, and deny the Viet Minh the opportunity to institute their own land reform" (36). I describe other development initiatives that reflected Personalist influences, such as Diem's efforts to modernize the economy through government investment and his extension of credit to farmers of modest means (74–75). With respect to the Strategic Hamlet program, I noted that Nhu sought leaders who would become part of a Personalist revolution (158), and I mentioned the importance of family and community in defending the hamlets (156). It is true that I did not refer to Personalism in every instance in which it influenced the Diem government's policies. In a work focused narrowly on Diem or his government, that would have been the right thing to do, but in the broad history I was writing, it was not necessary to provide such constant reminders. In histories of the American Civil War, scholars do not make reference to Abraham Lincoln's philosophical views every time that he makes a policy decision. In the case of the Strategic Hamlet program, moreover, space precluded a lengthy exposition on the origins of the program, so in a footnote I referred readers to Catton's own book for more information on its origins (445, note 27).

Like many historians who focus on ideas, Catton tends to accord too much influence to those ideas and too little to pragmatism and external necessity. Consequently, I view Personalism's impact as more limited than he does. I differ from both the "new scholarship" and the older scholarship by arguing that while Diem and Nhu believed in Personalism and based their actions upon it, few other Vietnamese understood it, and yet the lack of widespread ideological fervor made little difference because most Vietnamese cared more about the personal qualities of leaders and effective governance than about ideology (36–37). Other leading figures in the Diem regime rarely espoused the Personalist philosophy, and a variety of observers have noted that the discourses of Diem and Nhu on Personalism usually went over the heads of listeners. Some of the Personalist aspects of the Strategic Hamlet program, particularly the development of a new elite class among the peasants, fell well short of expectations. I do think that core principles of Personalism filtered down—such as benevolent authoritarianism, communal solidarity, and family life—because they were readily comprehensible and consistent with Vietnamese traditions, and because Diem and Nhu emphasized them. Provincial chiefs could and did govern their provinces effectively and destroy the insurgents by adhering to those principles, without comprehending the Personalist philosophy of Emmanuel Mounier.

Catton contends that the Americans viewed the Strategic Hamlet program as "a useful framework for bringing security and the benefits of American largesse to the rural population," while the Diem government viewed it in a different way, as a means of promoting self-reliance and civic engagement and group solidarity. Catton's phrasing suggests that these views were mutually exclusive, but they were not. Diem clearly was very concerned about security as well as social improvements, out of practical necessity. Throughout his time in office, Diem devoted a great deal of his time and energy to security matters, such as militias, roads for military use, and the infiltration of North Vietnamese personnel through Laos. When the Strategic Hamlet program began, the Diem government were losing many battles and losing control of the population, both of which generated widespread discontent in and out of the government, so restoring security was essential.

Catton does not dispute my contention that the Strategic Hamlet program and the rest of the war effort were going well during 1962 and 1963, a contention that runs contrary to what he had written in his book. It appears to be an example of a disproven falsehood disappearing quietly. In light of Catton's characterization of my writings of Diem as old wine in a new bottle, it should be noted that my conclusions on this score, like others mentioned above, were new. Not even strong Diem supporters like Ellen Hammer and Francis Winters had argued that the war effort was robust.

Catton's essay goes too far in disavowing mandarin influences on Diem, for modernizing tendencies did not cause Diem to abandon the mandarin tradition wholesale. Diem's reluctance to delegate authority, his suppression of organized political dissent, and his rigging of elections are consistent with mandarin tradition, as are his erudition, his asceticism, and his paternalistic affection for the governed. Ho Chi Minh and the Vietnamese communists also emulated aspects of the mandarin tradition in their manner of governance, especially when they tried to woo the Southern peasants. Like most Vietnamese, both Diem and Ho liked the good mandarins, while they had contempt for arrogant mandarins who served themselves instead of the people.

Catton characterizes my depiction of Diem as an "uncritical eulogy." I do believe that Diem was one of the finest national leaders of the Cold War, and that many of his alleged faults were not faults at all. But I do note that Diem and his government had their flaws. For example, I criticize Diem's land reform program for setting the landholding limit too high (73). I contend that political oppositionists were sometimes tortured (75–76). Diem's government, I show, did a poor job of combating the insurgents during the first two years of the insurgency, because government leaders in the provinces were less virtuous than their communist opponents (87–147).

Catton argues at the end that a more nuanced interpretation of Diem does not necessarily support the revisionist view over the orthodox view of the Vietnam War. He reasons that South Vietnamese chances of winning would not have been any higher with a somewhat flawed Diem than a thoroughly flawed Diem, because a plethora of other factors ensured that South Vietnam stood no chance of prevailing. This argument might have been plausible if Diem had died of a heart attack in 1961, but its plausibility disappears in the light of the dramatic improvements in the security situation in 1962 and 1963 and the catastrophic collapse of the war effort after Diem's assassination. South Vietnam was holding its own during that period even in the face of massive infiltration of men and materiel from North Vietnam. As is argued in *Triumph Forsaken*, Hanoi might never have launched a conventional invasion as it did in late 1964 had it not been for the post-coup crumbling of South Vietnam. And if it had launched such an invasion, South Vietnam would have been much better prepared to cope with it in 1965 and later (286).

South Vietnam eventually rebounded and was able, in 1972, to repulse a fourteen-division North Vietnamese Army offensive without American ground troops, another indication that North Vietnamese victory was not predestined. South Vietnam likely could have done the same in 1975 had the United States not slashed aid and withheld its air power.

William Stueck calls into question my assertion that the Viet Minh were in serious trouble at the time of Dien Bien Phu, and argues that unless the communist forces at Dien Bien Phu had been completely annihilated, the communists would have occupied a favorable military position across Indochina after the battle. He asserts that my argument is based primarily on Khrushchev's memoirs and Janos Radvanyi's book. But the two endnotes supporting my interpretation (426, notes 63 and 64) cite six different sources. One of the sources is a book by Ilya Gaiduk, for whom Stueck expresses respect elsewhere. Two of the other sources, written by North Vietnamese leader Le Duan and North Vietnamese witness Bui Tin, show that the Viet Minh had sent most of their mobile armed forces to Dien Bien Phu, refuting the view that the Viet Minh had great numbers of troops elsewhere that would have pressed on to victory had the Dien Bien Phu attack failed. Just after the completion of *Triumph Forsaken*, additional communist sources emerged that showed deep trouble on the communist side in early 1954.

The early stages of Dien Bien Phu, contends Stueck, were very favorable for the Viet Minh, which he says casts doubt on Khrushchev's claim that the Viet Minh were in dire straits during the battle. Owing to space constraints, I did not get into the details of this battle in my book, but communist sources, as well as some Western accounts, show that the Viet Minh did suffer major reverses in March 1954. A decade ago, Pierre Asselin revealed that the Viet Minh suffered a whopping 9,000 casualties in the first four days at Dien Bien Phu. Asselin reported that the staggering losses compelled the Viet Minh to turn away from the use of human wave tactics.[13]

Stueck also criticizes me for using multiple sources in a single endnote at the middle or end of a paragraph. Many other scholars of the Vietnam

War, and many other historians, have done the same, which was why I cited sources in this manner. Examples of books on Vietnam include: Fredrik Logevall's *Choosing War* (University of California Press, 1999); Mark Bradley, *Imagining Vietnam & America* (University of North Carolina Press, 2000); Howard Jones, *Death of a Generation* (Oxford University Press, 2003); Seth Jacobs, *America's Miracle Man in Vietnam* (Duke University Press, 2004). I do not recall seeing any reviewers assert that these or other historians undermined their credibility by citing sources in this way.

Stueck maintains that I overlooked the logistical challenges involved in putting U.S. forces into North Vietnam or Laos and that these challenges would have been very difficult to overcome, if not insurmountable. In *Triumph Forsaken*, I did not discuss the logistics of an invasion of North Vietnam because it did not seem necessary. In the 1960s, the United States was the world's greatest air and naval power, and possessed the ability to land huge numbers of troops amphibiously and by air. As the North Vietnamese and Chinese had agreed explicitly on October 5, 1964, the North Vietnamese did not intend to try keeping the Americans out of North Vietnam, but instead planned to retreat from the coast and engage primarily in guerrilla warfare. It was a wise plan on their part, for American naval and air power would have pulverized North Vietnamese ground forces had they tried to stand firm on the coasts. Once in control of the North Vietnamese coast, the United States would not have had much trouble bringing supplies in by sea. The French had been able to sustain a war against the Viet Minh with far fewer naval resources. With respect to Laos, I do discuss the logistical feasibility of severing the Ho Chi Minh Trail (322–324 and 481, notes 64 and 65).

In Stueck's view, the spread of communism across Asia would not necessarily have cut off American trade with Asia. It is an interesting point, and one upon which I perhaps should have elaborated in *Triumph Forsaken*. Asian countries taken over by communists in the mid-1960s might well have chosen to stop trading with the United States because of hatred of capitalists and capitalism, as North Vietnam did in 1954. Or they might have caused the United States to stop trading with them by nationalizing American businesses, as Cuba did in 1960. Indonesia and Cambodia may offer insights into what would have happened in countries like Thailand, where non-communist governments probably would have bent to the will of China rather than being overthrown right away, since Indonesia and Cambodia were drawing close to China in 1964 and 1965. During those two years, the Indonesian and Cambodian governments became openly hostile to the United States, renounced American aid, confiscated American and other foreign businesses, and increased trade with China. Asian countries like Japan that might have moved to neutralism in

1965, rather than complete subservience to China, probably would have been more inclined to maintain some trade with the United States, but in the long term, Chinese pressure could have compelled them to cut back on this commerce. One could argue that the ultimate futility of communism eventually would have led the countries of Asia to abandon socialist economic practices. But even if they did move toward capitalism as China eventually did, the United States might not have benefited economically because those countries could have erected trade barriers against the West, with Chinese encouragement or pressure. Capitalist dictatorships could have posed an even greater security threat because of their greater economic power—World War II illustrated that danger.

Stueck argues that had Johnson withdrawn from Vietnam in 1965, the United States could have prevented other countries of Asia—including Japan, South Korea, Taiwan, the Philippines, Thailand, Malaya, and Singapore—from falling to communism through increases in American commitments, by means of military alliances or the stationing of troops. He also says that these countries would have been loath to abandon the protection afforded by friendship with the United States. As I state in the book, we cannot be certain about what would have happened had South Vietnam fallen, but we can talk about probabilities, and the evidence indicates that, for many dominoes, the probability of falling was high no matter what remedial measures the United States attempted. In the case of Japan, American Ambassador Edwin Reischauer—far from a Cold War hawk—predicted that the Japanese would turn toward neutralism and abandon U.S. protection if the Americans were to suffer defeat in Vietnam (388). Neutralism was a serious threat in the Philippines and Thailand both in 1961, when Kennedy was pondering his options, and in 1965 (139–141, 382–383, 385). Those two countries and Malaya and Singapore seemed very unlikely to have confidence in any U.S. offers of commitment if the Americans let South Vietnam go after committing to its defense through S.E.A.T.O., lavishing it with money and advisors, and expressing support for its defense on repeated occasions. Why antagonize Beijing and Hanoi and invite war by strengthening relations with Washington, when the Americans might very well decide to bail out on short notice and expose their erstwhile allies to communist retribution? Furthermore, making a stand in one of those countries would have been more difficult militarily than making a stand in Vietnam (389–390). South Korea and Taiwan would have been less likely to turn away from the United States in the short term, but from a strategic point of view, South Korea and Taiwan were not worth nearly as much as other Southeast Asian countries.

Stueck contends that the U.S. stand in Vietnam may have had little impact on the Indonesian military's overthrow of Sukarno and the destruction of the Indonesian Communist Party in late 1965 because:

> ... it is far from clear that the conservative military, if given support by the United States, would have done anything other than what it actually did in the fall of 1965, namely purge the Communists and overthrow the increasingly leftist regime of Sukarno. What, after all, would they have preferred to rely upon, the good will of the Communists if they seized power or the immediate assistance of the United States?

But much evidence, including statements from leading anti-communists, shows that the Indonesian military would have acted differently had the United States abandoned Vietnam in 1965 (380–382). Had the United States abandoned South Vietnam in 1965, a large number of fence-sitters in the Indonesian military likely would have joined forces with the rebels or Sukarno after the putsch began. Even if the rebels had been suppressed by the military, the generals might have avoided easing Sukarno out of power in the months afterward, in the belief that Sukarno would fare better in dealing with the Chinese than would the generals. With Sukarno still in power, Indonesia would have remained a friend of China and an enemy of the United States.

Had South Vietnam fallen in 1965, Stueck argues, the Chinese and North Vietnamese might not have collaborated harmoniously in spreading communism across Southeast Asia, and they might have had trouble consolidating South Vietnam and other Southeast Asian countries. I do not see reason to believe that relations between China and North Vietnam would have soured in 1965 as they did in later years. America's intervention in Vietnam did much to drive the two countries apart. The war forced the North Vietnamese to become reliant on the Soviet Union, which fostered Chinese suspicions of North Vietnamese motives (361–362). The Cultural Revolution and China's accompanying turn away from foreign affairs were influenced by Chinese setbacks in Vietnam and Indonesia; the precise nature of this influence is something I will explore in volume two of *Triumph Forsaken*. North Vietnam and China had different leaders in 1965 than they did when they turned against each other; I very much doubt that relations between them would have deteriorated at all prior to Ho Chi Minh's death in 1969. Frictions might have occurred later as new leaders took power, but by then most of the dominoes would probably have fallen. Ultimately, I believe, Vietnam would have remained a partner of China in terms of foreign policy as has historically been the case and as is the case today. The 1979 war between North Vietnam and China was an aberration that arose from problems created by American intervention in Vietnam.

Qiang Zhai takes issue with my portrayal of Ho Chi Minh as a committed Leninist, contending that he was instead "half Gandhi and half Lenin." But he offers no evidence to suggest Gandhi-like characteristics, while there is much evidence that Ho was far closer to Lenin than Gandhi on key issues like pluralism, religion, and the use of violence. Nor does Zhai provide any support for his assertion that Ho was less constricted by communist ideology than other Asian communist leaders. Confucianism did indeed have some influence on Ho Chi Minh, as it did on every Vietnamese politician of his generation, and, as noted above, Ho did teach the leaders of the Viet Cong to behave with the good graces of the mandarins. But I have not seen evidence that Confucianism lay at the center of his thinking as Zhai maintains, whereas communism clearly did. Confucianism was definitely not at the center of his actions; Ho's deeds of Marxist–Leninist character, like the brutal land reform, the persecution of religious groups, and the confiscation of private property, were not accompanied by large initiatives of a more Confucian type.

Zhai contends, "In emphasizing that Ho was a Communist internationalist, Moyar refuses to allow that Ho could also be a Vietnamese nationalist." To resolve this dispute, one need only look at page 9 of *Triumph Forsaken*, which states,

> Ho Chi Minh was a nationalist in the sense that he had a special affection for Vietnam's people and favored Vietnamese unification and independence, but, from his reading of Lenin's Theses onward, he firmly adhered to the Leninist principle that Communist nations should subordinate their interests to those of the international Communist movement.

Zhai also contends that Ho's "real purpose" was "the independence and unification of his country." As I indicate in many chapters of *Triumph Forsaken*, Ho wanted not only unification, but unification under communist rule, and he spent a great deal of his time on activities designed to spread communist rule beyond Vietnam, as for instance in founding communist parties in other Asian countries, serving in the Chinese Army during World War II, striving to mend relations between China and the Soviet Union, and underwriting communist insurgents in Thailand and Laos.

Many Westerners have claimed that Ho Chi Minh's nationalism was such that it would have caused him to turn against China had the United States been smarter, as Tito's nationalism had caused Tito to turn against the Soviet Union. But Lenin, Ho Chi Minh, and many other communists and non-communists recognized a fundamental contradiction between communism and a nationalism that put national interests before all else, for the communism of Lenin demanded that the national interests of communist countries had to be subordinated to the interests of the world communist movement. Had Ho Chi Minh turned against China for nationalist reasons, he would have violated this central tenet of Marxism–Leninism. The evidence overwhelmingly indicates that Ho was averse to violating that tenet (1–10).

Qiang Zhai contends that *Triumph Forsaken* overlooked disagreements between China and North Vietnam. In actuality, the book covers disagreements on such subjects as radical agrarian policies (62), the timing of armed insurrection (79), the scale of the insurgency (101–102, 146), Chinese protection of North Vietnam (320–321, 361) and Soviet military aid (362).

Concerning the 1954 Geneva conference, Zhai elaborates on Stueck's objection to my claim that the Soviets and Chinese did not pressure the Vietnamese communists into accepting a non-communist South Vietnam. As proof, Zhai asserts that the Chinese and Vietnamese communists differed over the location of the demarcation line between northern and southern Vietnam, but in fact this assertion supports my position, for it shows that the Vietnamese were ready to accept some type of partition of Vietnam into communist and non-communist sections. In his own book, Zhai states that the Vietnamese Communist Party's Politburo decided in March 1954 that "it would be beneficial to divide Vietnam into the northern and southern parts."[14] In May, after the fall of Dien Bien Phu, a Vietnamese negotiator at Geneva told communist compatriots that the Vietnamese communists sought an end to the fighting, rather than a military conquest of all Vietnam, because the exhausted armed forces required "a breathing-space."[15]

In addition, the fact that Vietnamese negotiators sometimes asked for a partition line south of the seventeenth parallel, the line eventually chosen, does not necessarily mean that they had their hearts set on that line, for any decent negotiator asks for more than what is really desired. Considerable evidence shows that the Vietnamese communists were indeed satisfied with the seventeenth parallel. According to Nikita Khrushchev's memoirs, the communist parties at Geneva were ecstatic to get the dividing line so far south as the seventeenth parallel.[16] A French diplomat reported that the Viet Minh proposed a partition north of the seventeenth parallel on June 10, well before communist negotiator Pham Van Dong was asking for a line further to the south.[17] Zhai himself notes that when Mao urged Ho Chi Minh to accept the seventeenth parallel, Ho readily agreed.[18] Pham Van Dong took longer to accept the seventeenth parallel explicitly, but he seems to have agreed to go along with the seventeenth parallel without pressure.[19] One must also keep in mind that the Vietnamese were not dealing with the Soviets and Chinese as equal partners at Geneva, but as junior partners dependent upon their great power allies for assistance in combating France and the United States. The Vietnamese communists were smart enough to know that they could not impose their negotiating views on the Chinese and the Soviets, any more than a 20-year-old mobster can tell his boss how to negotiate with a rival boss over the young man's businesses.

In his book, Zhai contends that Chinese pressure at Geneva probably alienated Pham Van Dong and other Vietnamese negotiators.[20] But his only evidence is a Vietnamese White Paper from 1979, which is highly suspect because Vietnam and China fought a war that year and in the process exchanged all sorts of nasty accusations. Hoang Van Hoan, North Vietnam's first ambassador to China, produced a devastating refutation of Hanoi's White Paper in which he asserted that the Vietnamese, Soviet, and Chinese negotiators at Geneva worked harmoniously together and that the Chinese did not pressure the Vietnamese to accept the final settlement.[21] While researching the North Vietnamese during the period from 1954 to 1965, I came across no evidence of North Vietnamese discontent with China's behavior at Geneva.

Zhai and Stueck question my interpretation of Chinese intentions from the second half of 1964 to the first half of 1965, arguing that China maintained a consistent and firm policy during that period. Shortly before the Tonkin Gulf incidents of August 1964, the Chinese promised the North Vietnamese that they would retaliate against an American attack on North Vietnam, whether by air, land, or sea. Yet when the United States bombed North Vietnam on August 5, the Chinese did nothing in retaliation. Chinese public rhetoric after August 5 was very subdued, emphasizing that China would be restrained and that America would receive its punishment from North Vietnam rather than China (320). In short, China was neither consistent nor firm.

Zhai mentions that, after August 5, the Chinese went on a heightened state of military alert and moved air and antiaircraft forces close to the Vietnamese border, which he says resulted from Chinese desires to deter a further expansion of American activities within Vietnam, as well as to provide sanctuary and maintenance for North Vietnamese jet fighters. But the more likely explanation is that the purpose of these preparations was to defend China, not to discourage American action inside Vietnamese borders or to attack into North Vietnam (480, note 57). Zhai's commentary omits the most significant Chinese decision at this time: the decision to develop industry in western and southwestern China, which was designed to enable the Chinese communists to retreat westward in the event of an American invasion, an eventuality they now greatly feared (321). Attempting to fight with Chinese forces in Vietnam was incompatible, logically and logistically, with a Chinese communist retreat from eastern China.

Both Zhai and Stueck dispute my assertion that the October 5, 1964, conversation between Chinese and North Vietnamese leaders shows that China would not have sent its troops into North Vietnam to counter an American invasion, but they provide nothing to support their conclusion. According to the meeting notes, Mao told the North Vietnamese that if the Americans tried to invade North Vietnam's interior,

> ... you may allow them to do so. You should pay attention to your strategy. You must not engage your main forces in a head-to-head confrontation with them, and must well maintain your main forces. My opinion is that so long as the green mountain is there, how can you ever lack firewood?[22]

Had the Chinese intended to send combat troops to help the North Vietnamese fight the Americans, they surely would have referred to joint strategy and joint operations and talked about "we" instead of "you."

Zhai and Stueck neglect to mention Mao's stunning remark to Edgar Snow in January 1965 that China would not fight outside its borders (360–361). I cannot believe that Mao would have made this statement insincerely, for he could not have gained anything and could have lost much by lying on this score—luring American ground forces into North Vietnam by promising to stay out would have frustrated his ambitions in Southeast Asia, endangered the survival of his North Vietnamese allies, and produced a military situation in which he could not make good use of his relatively modest military resources.

Zhai asserts that I did not cite a source when asserting that the Chinese communist land reform campaign killed more than one million people. I am not sure why he raised this issue, since today's most prominent scholars all put the death toll at between one and three or more million.[23] Zhai contends that I provided no source for my contention that the North Vietnamese and Chinese were considering an invasion of Thailand. But elsewhere in the book I do cite sources stating that they discussed the matter, on August 13, 1964, and again on May 16, 1965 (482, note 78; 489, note 61). My source on the corpulence of General Chen Geng is Bui Tin, a North Vietnamese colonel who defected to the West.[24]

Zhai complains that I refer to Mao as "the Chinese premier." Had I capitalized the word premier, Zhai would have been correct; in lower case, the term is a synonym for "head of state," which is how I was using it. In the case of Chiang Kai-shek, I used a capital P and thus was incorrect. After Zhai brought this typo to my attention, I asked Cambridge University Press to change it to lower case for the paperback edition, and they did so. According to Zhai, I claimed that the Chinese defense minister led the Chinese military delegation to Hanoi in December 1961. In truth, I did not state who led the delegation, but instead merely recounted what the defense minister had said, based upon a source that lists Marshal Yeh Chien-ying as the head of the Chinese delegation.[25]

Notes

1. Mark Philip Bradley and Marilyn B. Young, eds., *Making Sense of the Vietnam Wars: Local, National, and Transnational Perspectives* (New York: Oxford University Press, 2008). Quote is from http://www.amazon.com/Making-Sense-Vietnam-Wars-Reinterpreting/dp/0195315146/ref=sr_1_1?ie=UTF8&s=books&qid=1250950442&sr=1-1#
2. Lloyd C. Gardner and Marilyn B. Young, eds., *Iraq and the Lessons of Vietnam, Or, How not to Learn from the Past* (New York: New Press, 2007). Quote is from http://www.thenewpress.com/index.php?option=com_title&task=view_title&metaproductid=1645. For my review of this book, see http://www.nysun.com/arts/wrong-analogy/68019/
3. David L. Anderson and John Ernst, *The War that Never Ends: New Perspectives on the Vietnam War* (Lexington: University Press of Kentucky, 2007). Quote is from http://www.kentuckypress.com/viewbook.cfm?Category_ID=1&Group=170&ID=1407
4. http://www.h-net.org/~diplo/williams2009/
5. John Prados, *Vietnam: The History of an Unwinnable War, 1945–1975* (Lawrence: University Press of Kansas, 2009), 114–115, 613–631.
6. Rufus Phillips, *Why Vietnam Matters: An Eyewitness Account of Lessons not Learned* (Annapolis: Naval Institute Press, 2008), 154–155, 202, 385–388.
7. Mark Atwood Lawrence, *The Vietnam War: A Concise International History* (Oxford, New York: Oxford University Press, 2008), 87, 201–204.
8. William S. Turley, *The Second Indochina War: A Concise Political and Military History*, 2nd edn. (Lanham, MD: Rowman & Littlefield, 2009), 80, 272.
9. James McAllister, "'Only Religions Count in Vietnam': Thich Tri Quang and the Vietnam War," *Modern Asian Studies*, vol. 42, no. 4 (July 2008), 753.
10. Gary R. Hess, *Vietnam: Explaining America's Lost War* (Malden, MA; Oxford: Blackwell Publishing, 2009).
11. Andrew Wiest, *Vietnam's Forgotten Army: Heroism and Betrayal in the ARVN* (New York: New York University Press, 2007); Peter Dale Scott, *The War Conspiracy: JFK, 9/11, and the Deep Politics of War* (Ipswich, MA: Mary Ferrell Foundation Press, 2008); Arthur Herman, "Who Owns the Vietnam War?" *Commentary*, vol. 124, no. 5 (December 2007), 42–52.
12. Numbers in parentheses refer to pages of *Triumph Forsaken*.
13. Pierre Asselin, "New Perspectives on Dien Bien Phu," *Explorations in Southeast Asian Studies*, vol. 1, no. 2, Fall 1997.
14. Qiang Zhai, *China and the Vietnam Wars, 1950–1975* (Chapel Hill: University of North Carolina Press, 2000), 51.
15. Ilya V. Gaiduk, *Confronting Vietnam: Soviet Policy Toward the Indochina Conflict, 1954–1963* (Stanford: Stanford University Press, 2003), 33.
16. Nikita S. Khrushchev, *Khrushchev Remembers*, trans. Strobe Talbott (Boston: Little, Brown, 1970), 482–483.
17. Saigon to State, 27 October 1954, FRUS, 1952–1954, vol. 13, 2, 2191.
18. Zhai, *China and the Vietnam Wars*, 59–60.
19. Chen Jian, *Mao's China and the Cold War* (Chapel Hill: University of North Carolina Press, 2001), 143.
20. Zhai, *China and the Vietnam Wars*, 63.

21. *Beijing Review*, December 7, 1979.
22. Memcon, Mao Zedong and Pham Van Dong, Hoang Van Hoan, October 5, 1964, CWIHP.
23. Benjamin Valentino, *Final Solutions: Mass Killing and Genocide in the Twentieth Century* (Ithaca: Cornell University Press, 2004), 121; Jean-Louis Margolin, "China: A Long March Into Night," in Stephane Courtois et al., eds., *The Black Book of Communism: Crimes, Terror, Repression* (Cambridge, MA: Harvard University Press, 1999), 479; Philip Short, *Mao: A Life* (New York: Henry Holt, 2000), 436; Jung Chang and Jon Halliday, *Mao: The Unknown Story* (New York: Knopf, 2005), 324.
24. Bui Tin, *From Enemy to Friend: A North Vietnamese Perspective on the War*, trans. Nguyen Ngoc Bich (Annapolis: Naval Institute Press, 2002), 98.
25. Bui Tin, *Following Ho Chi Minh: The Memoirs of a North Vietnamese Colonel*, trans. Judy Stowe and Do Van (Honolulu: University of Hawaii Press, 1995), 45.

Section II

Debating *Triumph Forsaken* as History

CHAPTER **6**
Triumph Impossible

JAMES DINGEMAN

Who has ownership of the meaning of the Vietnam War? This is an especially compelling question in view of our involvement in a new series of difficult conflicts around the world as a result of 9/11—virtually a global counterinsurgency campaign. The U.S. armed forces have had to relearn the sobering lessons of fighting a counterinsurgency war after decades of deliberately turning away from this kind of warfare after Vietnam. A fierce debate rages about the mindset of our senior policymakers concerning what lessons they did or did not take from the Vietnam War as they crafted our intervention into Iraq. Comparisons between the wars in Iraq and Vietnam dominate the U.S. political landscape, and many Americans feel that Iraq is a new Vietnam. Into this imbroglio a new comprehensive interpretation of the Vietnam War has arrived that renders the war as just, necessary, and winnable, a sharp contrast to the view of the majority of Americans who feel, in poll after poll, that the Vietnam War was unjust, unnecessary, and unwinnable.

The ideas of Mark Moyar are part of the complicated, diverse body of thought on the issue of why the U.S. lost the Vietnam War. His *Triumph Forsaken* is the latest book in the long line that seeks to create a positive image of America's defeat. Moyar cites new scholarship and data that only became accessible after the Cold War ended, as well as Vietnamese sources. *Triumph Forsaken* is clearly the best expression of conservative scholarship on the Vietnam War in years. For some, this work is an act of *sartori*; for others, a case of angina. But whatever the reaction, his opinions cannot be swept under the rug since they reflect the latest neoconservative intellectual reaction to the defeat in Vietnam.

Moyar's arguments are actually old wine packaged in new bottles, with whipped cream and cherries sprinkled on top. His opinions about the nature of Vietnamese communism, his portrayal of Ngo Dinh Diem's regime, and his account of Johnson's war escalation in 1965 will generate much contention. In my opinion, Moyar overestimates the ability of military force to alter a complicated political environment. Moyar's examination of the American attempt to save the beleaguered French garrison at Dien Bien Phu during their occupation of Indochina is such a case. He writes that the use of U.S. airpower during the battle of Dien Bien Phu against the Vietminh "almost certainly would have thwarted their attack . . . and left them with sharply reduced capacity for large-unit warfare throughout Indochina." There is no doubt that such a bombing campaign would have disrupted and possibly lifted the Vietminh siege of the French forces at Dien Bien Phu. But then what? One of the greatest opponents of bombing at Dien Bien Phu was U.S. Army Chief of Staff Matthew Ridgway. In his memoir, *Soldier*, Ridgway looks back on his opposition with pride: "[T]he thing that I would be most humbly proud of was having fought against, and perhaps contributing to preventing the carrying out of some harebrained tactical schemes which would have cost the lives of thousands of men. To that list of tragic incidents that fortunately never happened I would add the Indochina intervention."

I disagree emphatically with Moyar's positive view of Diem, a centerpiece of his argument. As Moyar points out, it is clear that Diem, an anti-communist nationalist, was a highly complicated figure. Like some American allies in the Cold War, his power stemmed largely from U.S. support. Moyar decouples Diem from the long history of Vietnamese anti-colonialism by reducing Vietnamese communism to merely a tool of international communism. He then valorizes what other historians for decades have seen as Diem's weakness: his narrow basis of legitimacy.

Moyar arduously reconstructs the progress of the war on the ground. He argues that the war had been turned around by 1962 and that Diem's ill-timed demise accelerated the subsequent turn for the worse. Others view this period differently. In *JFK and Vietnam*, John Newman documents disputes over the order of battle of the Viet Cong that began in the Kennedy period. At the conference held in Honolulu in February 1962, Robert McNamara asked: "What happened to the V.C.; in July they were reported to have a strength of 12,300, in December 17,000, in January 20–25,000. Have they increased or have we been miscounting?" He then was told that there were also 100,000 militia and local self-defense forces, which prompted Chairman of the Joint Chiefs of Staff Lyman Louis Lemnitzer to say: "The apparent growing strength of the V.C. makes it look like we are losing." This resulted in an intense effort to ascertain what the actual V.C. order of battle was. Led by George Allen, it produced an estimate of V.C. main and local force battalions that amounted to 40,000 active troops. Newman recounts how General Paul Harkins hacked this figure down to the point at which the first official order of battle published on April 15, 1962, listed the V.C. as 16,305 regular troops. These details raise serious questions concerning Moyar's depiction of the war from 1960 to Diem's coup as being a march of progress.

Moyar downplays the threat of Chinese intervention in 1965. We have much to learn about this subject, but what we do know tends to differ from Moyar's interpretation. U.S. policymakers viewed Mao's China as an aggressive, Stalinist dictatorship, willing to use force massively to expand its aims. The fact that China was on the verge of building nuclear weapons prompted both the Kennedy and Johnson administrations to explore the issue of preemptive attacks against Chinese nuclear facilities. China openly supported "people's wars" around the world. The situation was perilous, and miscalculations between the U.S. and China could have led to a general war.

The Gulf of Tonkin incident and the U.S. reaction took the Democratic Republic of Vietnam (D.R.V.) and the Chinese by surprise. China reacted quickly. Fearful of a general war with the U.S., the Chinese moved key industries from vulnerable eastern China to the western and central provinces. The D.R.V. asked immediately for their newly equipped 921st Jet Fighter Regiment currently training in China to redeploy to Vietnam. China doubled their air defenses in southern China. Moyar cites several statements by Mao to support his claim that Mao wanted the Vietnamese to wage war alone against the U.S., and was hesitant to give support. Mao told the North Vietnamese in early October 1964 that if the Americans invade, "you must not engage in a head to head confrontation and must well maintain your main force." In January 1965, Mao said to Edgar Snow, "only if the United States attacked China would the Chinese fight ... the Vietnamese can cope with their own situation." According to Moyar, these comments show that China would not have intervened outside its borders, even if the U.S. had invaded the D.R.V.

But later events provoked an altogether different response from China. Indeed, Mao's comments were made before the beginning of the U.S. bombing campaign and the landing of U.S. ground troops in February–March 1965. At the time Mao made these remarks, the Chinese were urging the D.R.V. to wage a more intensified ground war in order to finish off the South Vietnamese before further reinforcements arrived from the U.S.

Moyar plays down the possibility of Chinese ground intervention and maintains that a Sino-Vietnamese conventional offensive of twenty divisions could have been rebuffed by five to eighteen U.S. divisions. All of this presumes a U.S. will to mobilize and fight a major war of this magnitude with China in Southeast Asia. But this was precisely what President Johnson was seeking to avoid. Furthermore, Moyar does not address the practicalities of mobilizing and logistically supporting a force of this size in Southeast Asia. The temptation to use tactical nuclear weapons would have been difficult to restrain and could easily, dangerously, have spilled into a general war with China.

When the U.S. began bombing North Vietnam and sent ground troops in March 1965, China responded in kind. On April 12, 1965, the country issued a general order to mobilize for war, and China gave immediate support to North Vietnam. Zhou Enlai made it clear that a U.S. ground assault on the North would be met with an overwhelming Chinese response. China immediately sent three reinforced divisions, designated the "Corps of Chinese Rear Services," to build up the Vietnamese defense and transportation networks. In addition, two Chinese antiaircraft divisions were sent to North Vietnam by the summer of 1965. Between 1965 and 1969, the Chinese sent 320,000 troops to North Vietnam, of which 150,000 were in antiaircraft units.

It is hard to come to definite conclusions about the Vietnam War. There are gaps in our knowledge of the decision making on both sides. Moyar does not accept these crucial ambiguities. Moreover, the United States and its allies were defeated, and this had serious and far-reaching implications for historiography. We did not capture the archives of our foes or employ their senior officers in writing accounts of their activities as we did, so extensively, after World War II. The German Military History Program produced accounts of all the war theaters where the Wehrmacht had fought. These narratives, famously known as the Green Book Series, were used to prepare the official histories of the U.S. Army. Nothing like this exists for the Vietnam War. Until scholars have unfettered access to the archives of China, the U.S.S.R., Vietnam, and the U.S., controversies will continue to be fought over limited evidence, overladen with interpretative schema.

CHAPTER 7
Fighting Stories

CHARLES HILL

Herodotus was a hedgehog. The "One Big Thing" he knew was that the stories we tell about ourselves will shape our political community. At some point, the accepted, dominant narrative will have to defend itself against another version in the Herodotean phenomenon of "fighting stories."

The Vietnam War's "master narrative" locked onto the national mind after Tet '68. Books, articles, films, and documentaries produced after that date almost invariably covered events up to and including 1968, but almost nothing of what happened during the years that followed until the fall of Saigon in 1975. The success of the post-Tet "one war" strategy pursued by General Creighton Abrams and Ambassador Ellsworth Bunker, and the striking achievements of the Army of the Republic of Vietnam in throwing back the huge North Vietnamese invasion of April 1972 went unchronicled. It is not too much to say that the South Vietnamese government and armed forces, with strong air support by the U.S., won the Vietnam War on the ground in the early 1970s until the U.S. abandoned its ally after the 1973 Paris Agreement.

While studiously avoiding the post-Tet '68 period, the storytellers of the war probed back into every detail of American and South Vietnamese policies and actions since the 1954 French defeat at Dien Bien Phu. Their narrative ran something like this: the U.S., out of arrogance, ignorance, and lust for imperial dominance, was pulled—or pushed itself—into an insignificant civil war between admirable, anti-colonialist nationalists and reactionary authoritarians. America took the side of the authoritarians against the will and interests of "the people." The U.S. fought this war with foolish strategy and brutish tactics. Although the American record in the war was one of failure upon failure, presidents nonetheless prolonged the devastation and string of defeats in a feckless attempt to preserve "credibility." (The only exception, according to this story, was President Kennedy who, had he not been assassinated, would have closed out America's involvement.) The story concludes in a dishonorable, deceptive, and disgraceful defeat.

But not a few who served in Vietnam knew that there was something wrong with this master narrative. It had its source in the layers of domestic American cultural revolutions of the late 1960s and early 1970s, and was infected by the importation of a European New Left ideology that saw all aspects of the American polity through the lens of "late capitalism," doomed but dangerous in the throes of its final stage of existence.

Tellers of this story only recently have sensed that another version has entered the ring. The entrenched narrative still holds 90 percent of the battlefield, but a contest of "fighting stories" is at hand. Mark Moyar's *Triumph Forsaken* tells the Vietnam War's history from the ground up and from a perspective untrammeled by 1960s doctrine.

Scholars, reporters, and analysts have hurried to excoriate Moyar and his book, and to insist once again on adherence to the master narrative, energized by the belief that it is a truth generally acknowledged that a story told interminable times becomes a truth generally acknowledged. But *Triumph Forsaken* reveals that what has been called "truth" should more accurately be recognized as "truthiness"—a story that its tellers want to be true.

Moyar's book is of larger significance than even the important matter of getting the Vietnam War story straightened out. *Triumph Forsaken* delves into an array of categories that may be observed across a larger pattern of American warfare since the end of the Second World War. From that time to this, the U.S. has fought at least ten wars—in the Cold War context, the post-Cold War decade, and at the opening of the twenty-first century—against terror-using enemies of the international system. In one way or another, all have been limited wars and, in one way or another, nearly all have been lost or abandoned by the U.S.

All across *Triumph Forsaken*'s 500 pages (with hefty notes) are the elements of a strange, larger epic of America's struggle to maintain international peace and security under severely debilitating, often self-imposed handicaps.

First is the threat to the established international state system from a revolutionary ideology aimed at destroying and replacing it. Starting with the Marxist–Leninist doctrine that the state itself must be destroyed, communist ideology comprehensively opposed the world order invented at Westphalia in 1648 and developed, extended, and accepted in every part of the world in subsequent centuries. Moyar makes it clear that Ho Chi Minh and his regime were utterly convinced communist ideologues. No American president could have stayed aloof from Hanoi's moves into South Vietnam any more than Truman could have acquiesced in Acheson's signal that North Korea's attack on the South need not be a cause for U.S. response. The international communist challenge, the American doctrine of containment, the need to maintain Cold War "credibility," as felt so strongly by President Kennedy, all made the Vietnam War a world-historical event.

Second, Moyar takes us to the starting point of the American media's rapid shift from overly compliant reporting to relentlessly adversarial involvement. Many in the media ceased to function as a "medium" between political–military–governmental action and the public, and began to engage as outcome-driven players in the war. Those of us around East and Southeast Asia at the time may recall the strange feeling as though a heavy, opaque curtain had fallen between officials and reporters. The late David Halberstam, praised for his scathing *Time* reports in the mid-1960s, slavishly emulated by virtually every reporter who followed him in Vietnam, and canonized at eulogies at the time of his recent tragic death, is redrawn by Moyar as the tendentious journalist many recognized at the time, particularly in his coverage of what journalists should have sensed as a concocted, politicized, and probably communist-instigated Buddhist campaign against President Ngo Dinh Diem. The reporter Marguerite Higgins made devastating critiques of Halberstam and his ilk at the time, "bringing to light glaring factual and analytical errors in their coverage of the Buddhist crisis and the military situation." As Assistant Secretary of State Robert Manning wrote, Halberstam and his reporter buddies "seem for the most part to be given to quick-rising emotionalism, and they unquestionably are severely afflicted with localitis, the disease which causes newsmen long assigned to the confines of one given situation to distort perspective by over-concentration on their own irritations, adventures and opinions." Moyar's history of Halberstam in Vietnam is an account of "the birth of a culture." That culture is still with us, as revealed in a 2006 Lehrer *NewsHour* segment in which correspondents interviewed each other on the topic of "Reporting the Iraq War," a colloquy that revealed not reporting on the war, but reporting on "the horrors of war."

Third is the strained relationship between Americans and our allies or partners in the fight against a common enemy. Often, the cacophonous dialogue among the Americans involved is filled with cross-cutting confusions. Our intellectuals consider the enemy to be "authentic," the understandable product of their land, heritage, and culture. Our partners are depicted as reactionary, elitist, out of touch, senselessly brutal, and corrupt. Moyar's look at President Diem's travails emerges as one of the most stupid and self-defeating episodes in twentieth-century American foreign policy. It was the communist side that was ruthlessly modern, disciplined, and mobilized (the ideologically indoctrinated V.C. would show up on schedule as ordered; the A.R.V.N. farm boys would not). Diem was succeeding in moving a traditional society towards a contemporary level of capacity to defend itself. As he did so, Washington—and, in the field, the obtuse Ambassador Henry Cabot Lodge—prodded him toward "democratic reforms" that in context made no sense. As Moyar quotes the President of the Republic of Vietnam, Diem lamented that, "I cannot seem to convince the embassy that this is Vietnam—not the United States of America." JFK sensed that Lodge was blundering into disaster, but had put him in Saigon to take him out of the picture as a potential rival for the presidency. The American ambassador's desire to be rid of Diem, along with the American reporters' drumbeat of renunciation led to the hideous overthrow and murder of the South Vietnamese president. The 1963 coup opened a time of one incompetent South Vietnamese government—and coup—after another, pulling the U.S. involvement ever further into matters that Diem had been managing in a way that might be called "Vietnamization" before the fact of Nixon's invention of that policy. Across America's many late-twentieth-century wars, we would never quite learn the value of focusing on defeating the enemy more than badgering our friends.

Then there is the grand strategic puzzle: why has the U.S. fought one regional war after another so ineffectively, at such length, and with so apparently dismal results? Three reasons stand out. Moyar points to the "rational actor" theory of Harvard professor Thomas Schelling, certainly one of the most bone-headed and deleterious concoctions to emerge from academia in modern times. LBJ "chose to follow the prescriptions of his civilian advisors, who advocated an academic approach that used small doses of force to convey America's resolve without provoking the enemy." The fear of a Chinese military intervention as in the Korean War was influential here. But the "signal," as received in Hanoi, was that the U.S. lacked resolve and staying power.

Other analysts recently have reviewed the decades-long list of America's self-limited and usually lost regional wars and suggested that these were "spoiler" conflicts, deliberately conducted so as to derail the objectives of a variety of adversaries. This seems "overdetermined," as political scientists might say. Still, at least some of these wars eventually did achieve a positive strategic outcome for large American ends. The Korean War showed that the policy of "containment" was more than a slogan; it took over three decades of direct American commitment there before Korea became a democracy and a world-class economic power. The Vietnam War bought time for key Southeast Asian countries to strengthen their anti-communist stance and start economic growth. (I heard Lee Kuan Yew deliver a diatribe about this to an astounded group of anti-Vietnam War Harvard professors in 1971.)

The U.S. ignominiously pulled out of the Lebanon War in 1983 when 241 Marines were killed by a suicide bomb attack, but the overall American role, based on Ambassador Philip Habib's diplomacy to rid Lebanon of the P.L.O. may be seen as the start of a still ongoing attempt to help Lebanon regain its full sovereignty as an independent state. "Desert Storm" in 1990 reversed the "international murder" of Kuwait, a strong action in support of the integrity of the international state system, even though in retrospect it can be seen as "Saddam War I." Other wars of the 1990s had mixed results. The U.S. failed to act against "ethnic cleansing" in Bosnia; it failed in its "humanitarian intervention" in Somalia in 1993; it failed to act to stop the Rwanda genocide of 1994; it launched a 1999 air war against Serbia that protected the Kosovars but undermined U.N. authority and produced, years later, a legal assault on Serbia's integrity as a legitimate sovereign state. Yet in the aftermath of all of these campaigns, the U.S. nonetheless persevered in trying to revive and support the international state system while shoring up the institutions of international law and the U.N. as the world organization of its Member States.

The real reason for this strange un-Clausewitzian series of wars may be found in "a dirty little secret": that no American president going back to and including LBJ has believed that the American people any longer possess the national character to take a long and painful war. So every war has been fought in a partial, tentative way. This seems to be the reason why the American strategy in Iraq from 2003 through 2006 was to train a new Iraqi army rather than secure the territory with U.S. forces.

Moyar's description and analysis of the American military in Vietnam does more than other studies to clarify the uniquely difficult challenges of warfare waged by an enemy ideologically, and tactically, almost totally at odds with a Geneva Convention–Laws of War-trained professional military. How can an army educated in something like "the purity of arms" deal with an adversary that is not in uniform, does not carry weapons openly, burrows into and fires from civilian populations, and does not hesitate to carry out mass terrorist slaughter of civilians? In Moyar's account of Diem's Strategic Hamlet program can be discerned the starting point of what would eventually be refined by General Abrams (and sure to be covered in Moyar's next volume) as a network of fortified lines of communication inside which populations could feel secure and start to build socio-economic ways capable of fending off the communists. One of the more bizarre aspects (of many) of the Iraq war was the revelation that these "lessons" of the Vietnam War were not incorporated into U.S.

military doctrine and training in the decades between that war and the Iraq War. America's strategic hesitancy and distancing from the task was the main reason why the U.S. did not succeed in Iraq until a "new" strategy of "clear, hold, and build" ("the Surge")—just another way of describing the Abrams approach 1969–1973—had to be conjured up in 2007 as though out of nothing.

And along with Moyar's overall recasting of the Vietnam War narrative, *Triumph Forsaken* refutes years of denigration of General William Westmoreland. Instead of a commander too dumb to know that "search and destroy" sweeps could never succeed because U.S. forces would return to base, Moyar explains the imperative of big unit warfare. The critics who would have had American forces forget the major conventional conflict in order to focus on small-scale counterinsurgency tactics overlooked one great danger: that in the absence of big U.S. conventional operations, North Vietnamese main force units would simply have conquered South Vietnam blitzkrieg style.

Out of this seemingly contradictory and mutually incompatible array of overlapping policies can be found a clear and simple Vietnam War storyline. In the late 1960s, the U.S. defended South Vietnam against big-unit, conventional North Vietnamese military attack. At the same time, the U.S. and the Republic of Vietnam sought frantically to find ways to combat Vietnamese communist tactics of terror, intimidation, and subversion, which the laws of war and long-entrenched definitions of warfare as state-to-state combat by professional armies did not comprehend and apparently could not manage. With the arrival of Abrams and Bunker, however, and their "one war" approach, increasingly larger areas of South Vietnam were made secure for the population until, by 1972, it could fairly be said that the war for the survival of the Republic of Vietnam had been won. Then, with American combat forces out of Vietnam, Hanoi, having no other option, launched the conventional blitzkrieg that General Westmoreland, years before, had blocked. By this time, the policy of Vietnamization had produced an Army of the Republic of Vietnam capable of relatively effective ground combat operations. When the 1972 "Easter Offensive" was launched by the North, the A.R.V.N., with strong American air support, won that battle on all three fronts, most notably at An Loc, north of Saigon.

In this flow of decisions, adjustments, actions, and resolve can be found factors of signal importance to the defense of world order today when the various forms of warfare coming out of the Arab-Islamist world—terrorist, rogue state, theocratic—all combine as a deadly threat to the international state system and the world order it supports. An accurate account of what the U.S. achieved, and failed to achieve, in Vietnam in the post-Tet '68 years may hold lessons for this new and larger threat to civilization. So the current "revisionist" controversy—this time with the Left as the entrenched establishment—has significance beyond the questions about whether the Vietnam War should have been fought, whether it was fought at all well, or whether, near the end, the U.S. won or lost the war on the ground.

The Vietnam War provides a foundation for a set of principles essential to the preservation of world order in the twenty-first century.

- *First*, a grand strategic understanding of the threat and how to deal with it.

In the Cold War, ideological communism sought to overcome the international state system. The critical frontlines were drawn in divided states: Korea, China, Germany, and Vietnam. The communist side attempted to wreck the doctrine of containment in each case. The U.S. stood up to the challenge at the thirty-eighth parallel, in the Taiwan Strait, and Berlin, and could not have won the Cold War had a series of American presidents not recognized the imperative of fighting for South Vietnam.

Today, there is a world-spanning ideological challenge to the international state system from Islamism. Within the state system itself there are "rogue" states that play the system against its own principles, there are state-governing regimes seeking "spheres of influence", and there are well-meaning intellectuals who hopefully argue that the era of sovereign statehood is, or should be, over. All of these must be countered by a well-understood strategy of saving failed states and shoring up legitimate states in distress. The Vietnam example is illuminating.

- *Second*, we must continue to seek effective tactics to suppress and defeat enemies—insurgents, guerillas, terrorists, gangs—that violate every law of war on every occasion in an intellectual and cultural context that gives non-state actors immense leeway to ignore the civilizational and legal norms against deliberately targeting civilians.

The Abrams system of civilian population protection neutralized the Viet-Cong. Reborn in 2007 as "clear, hold, and build," it produced success in Iraq. Reworked for different conditions in Afghanistan and elsewhere, it can succeed again. Along with this there must be a more coherent intellectual and legal effort to reform and redesign the international state system's laws and procedures to comprehend the unique challenge posed by adversaries who situate themselves entirely outside the system and dedicate themselves to its destruction. Important efforts since 2001 have been made by the courts, the Congress, the military, and the Executive Branch, but the results so far are far from workable, primarily because excessive lawyering has worked to treat unlawful combatants within the civilian justice system, an obvious impossibility and one that in some areas has given illegal combatants more protection than professional soldiers receive under the law of war.

And in this same category comes nation-building, or "stability operations" in recent parlance. "Clear, hold, and build" may succeed, but will not endure without a sustained endeavor to consolidate its gains through institutionalization and reformed political, social, and economic systems. Part of this process must be Vietnamization-like policies to train effective and respected national military and police forces.

- *Third*, the larger conventional dimension of defense cannot be neglected. General Westmoreland's Vietnam War involved fighting off the threat of conventional military victories by North Vietnamese main force battalions in the South. When General Abrams's counterinsurgency war defeated the Viet Cong in the first years of the 1970s, driving Hanoi to launch its conventional army invasion of the south across three international borders, the U.S., albeit with no American troops on the ground, was prepared through air power to support the A.R.V.N. in throwing back the communist assaults. But when the North invaded again, in 1975, the U.S. did nothing, for all of the key consolidation requirements had been abandoned for political reasons.

The U.S. in 1972 had the resolve to join in South Vietnam's defense against the conventional military attack coming on the heels of the communists' loss of their unconventional insurgent strategy. Today's military experts have pointed out how terror-using guerrilla movements have, in many cases, taken on the characteristics of regular military forces and must be dealt with as such. The Hezbollah militia in Lebanon is an example. Here, again, the Vietnam War example is more relevant than earlier believed.

Against this background, it is worth reviewing what happened in that last successful U.S.–R.V.N. operation in 1972. In doing so, we return to the first concern of this essay: how do we describe what is happening at any given moment? How do we get the narrative right? What happens when the story we tell ourselves is wrong? So today's battle for the Vietnam War is a matter ranging far beyond that one now-long-ago conflict. Our current debate, if it reveals one thing indisputably, shows that few, if any, Americans at the time of the Vietnam War could comprehend its meaning in the largest sense.

This was Tolstoy's aim in *War and Peace*, the monumental novel and a sustained diatribe against all those who see chains of causation in history or believe in "the great man" theory of history's shaping. For Tolstoy, as Isaiah Berlin put it in "The Hedgehog and the Fox," the wisdom of statecraft, if any there be, resides not in scientific knowledge, but in "a special sensitiveness to the contours of the circumstances in which we happen to be placed . . ."

During the 1972 Battle of An Loc, Tolstoy's *War and Peace* came often to mind. Field Marshall Mikhail Illarionovich Kutuzov—played exquisitely by Oscar Homolka in the film—was commander in chief of Russian forces as Napoleon crossed into Russia. In the tradition of Rome's Fabius Maximus Cunctator (the "delayer") who stayed just out of reach of Hannibal, Kutuzov retreated as Napoleon thrust on. Kutuzov abandoned Moscow before Napoleon took the Kremlin on September 14, 1812. The city, nearly deserted, was soon in flames. Kutuzov moved his army to the countryside; Napoleon deployed a force to counter a Russian move, which would not come. After a mild fall, the first snow fell on October 13; on October 19, the *Grande Armée*—in defeat—began its retreat.

What if Napoleon's Moscow campaign had been ignored by journalists and historians and left almost unknown to the public because the intelligentsia had written off Russia after the Battle of Austerlitz in 1805? Something like that happened to the R.V.N.–U.S. achievements of the early years of the 1970s.

The "one war" strategy of Bunker and Abrams had erased the Viet Cong movement; North Vietnam's revolutionary strategy had failed. Recognizing that Nixon and Kissinger were shifting America's geostrategic relationships with China and the Soviet Union, Hanoi, in desperation, launched its major, multipronged conventional military invasion of the Republic of Vietnam—the "Easter Offensive." In April 1972, North Vietnamese forces smashed through the demilitarized zone in the north, crossed the Laos–Vietnam international border in the Central Highlands, and moved from Cambodia to drive an assault aimed at Saigon.

The invading communist army far outpowered the Army of the Republic of Vietnam in tanks and long-range artillery. Fierce fighting raged for weeks. North Vietnam, General Abrams said, was "holding nothing back." On the D.M.Z. front, President Thieu installed Lieutenant General Ngo Quang Truong, South Vietnam's best field commander, and the enemy push was broken. In the Central Highlands, American air power pounded the approaches to Kontum as the twenty-third A.R.V.N. Division inflicted heavy casualties on North Vietnamese troops, and the V.N.A.F., South Vietnam's air force, had been "magnificent, absolutely magnificent."[1]

But on the most politically dangerous and dramatic front, An Loc, thirty miles north of Saigon, the situation seemed desperate in what was "probably the single most important battle in the war."[2] South Vietnamese troops, having retreated to An Loc before the communist advance, were apparently doing nothing. Bunker had served as a top American ambassador in many roles and places: Argentina, the Dominican Republic,

Yemen, and India. He had established a list of key principles of diplomacy over the years, and one of them was "Sometimes the best thing to do is nothing." Kutuzov would have understood. But this was too much even for Bunker. In growing frustration, the American ambassador went to the presidential palace again and again, to urge Thieu to order his troops to take offensive action. Thieu was calm, polite, and reassuring. Bunker, who liked and admired Thieu, found him impossible to understand on these occasions. Clearly, Thieu was stalling for time, Bunker thought. Now it was Thieu who was asking Bunker to see the wisdom, in this situation, of "doing nothing," and Bunker found the advice hard to take.

Thieu was right. He had a feel for the situation akin to Marshall Kutuzov's in 1812. His A.R.V.N. forces at An Loc were doing nothing. They were not moving forward to engage the enemy, but they were not moving backward either. They were the anvil, and U.S. and South Vietnamese air power were decimating the communist forces as they hammered them against the A.R.V.N. anvil. Soon Hanoi's troops, at the end of a long logistics line, were in dire straits, and the battle of An Loc was won, by U.S. and V.N.A.F. air power, and by courageous and stubborn A.R.V.N. ground forces. Hanoi's Easter Offensive had failed.

But politically it was too late. Although Henry Kissinger negotiated at Paris an agreement that could have solidified the military achievements of 1972, the political world of Washington would have none of it. When, after the Paris Peace Accords were signed in 1973, the foreign minister of the Republic of Vietnam, Tran Van Lam, visited Washington to consult on the next steps, no one in the Congress would meet with him. From that point on, the outcome was fated. The South Vietnamese army ran short of ammunition. Even so, the defeat inflicted by the South on the invading forces of the North in 1972 had been so severe that it took the North two years to be able to mount the 1975 invasion that brought the fall of Saigon.

Did Nguyen Van Thieu have some Tolstoyan–Kutuzovian sense of history? I think he did. To think of it in Tolstoy's terms, there are infinite, multifarious atoms of causation that sweep across time, creating a "labyrinth of concatenations."[3] To think in "great man" terms of "Kennedy's War," "Johnson's War," "Nixon's War" may illuminate, yet never reveal larger forces in play.

"The Hedgehog and the Fox," Isaiah Berlin's classic essay on Tolstoy's philosophy of history, offers an angle of vision. The Vietnam War, about which we are still battling, can only be understood as one vital part of an epic struggle carried out across the past 200-plus years: between ideological concepts of world order and the procedural order that is the established international state system. Every major world war has been about this.

Ideologies are hedgehogs: they understand—only understand—one big thing. The international state system is part hedgehog, but its one big idea is that there must be many foxes—and this is the American idea as well, as set forth in *Federalist* 10.

So fighting over the Vietnam War story has just begun. One thing seems clear: the narrative established in the late 1960s will not hold up.

The monuments on the Washington D.C. Mall visually represent the nation's story in symbols. As they originally took shape, they represented the wars of the American polity—the Washington Monument for the Revolution that formed the nation; the Lincoln Memorial for the Civil War that saved it; the Lee mansion across the Potomac representing the South's secession and its reincorporation. There seemed to be an unwritten rule that no foreign war, however important, should ever encroach upon this domestic set of symbols.

The Vietnam Veterans Memorial (V.V.M.) changed that. For America, the war had been traumatic—a word in close accord with the original master narrative that Vietnam had been a profound failure and moral shame. But something else was sensed, if unspoken, as the V.V.M. was designed and built: that Vietnam was, and is, a war that affected the national character and, at the same time, had been vital in the defense of the international state system and world order. Along with the Civil War, Vietnam may take its place as the most consequential of all of America's wars.

Notes

1. A U.S. Air Force advisor quoted in Lewis Sorley, *A Better War: The Unexamined Victories and Final Tragedy of America's Last Years in Vietnam* (New York: Harcourt, Brace & Company, 1999), 338.
2. Douglas Pike, *PAVN: People's Army of Vietnam* (Novato, CA: Presidio Press, 1986), 225.
3. Lydia Ginzburg in Leo Tolstoy, *War and Peace*, ed. George Gibian (New York: Norton, 1996).

CHAPTER 8

Imperial Revanchism
Attempting to Recover a Post-war "Noble Cause"

SCOTT LADERMAN

The survey results could not have been pleasing to proponents of an imperial foreign policy. With the 20th century coming to a close, and nearly 25 years having elapsed since the U.S. evacuation from Saigon, 63 percent of Americans in 1998, according to the Chicago Council on Foreign Relations, still agreed that the Vietnam War was "more than a mistake; it was fundamentally wrong and immoral."[1] This was in spite of Jimmy Carter's outlandish attempt to obliterate the reality of the war's asymmetry by arguing that the "destruction [in the United States and Vietnam] was mutual," or Ronald Reagan's effort to rewrite the history of that conflict as a "noble cause" in which "we did have victory"; or a virtual barrage of Hollywood films that demonized the Vietnamese revolutionaries while celebrating the fictional Americans (John Rambo, Col. James Braddock, and others) who fearlessly confronted these sadistic primitives.[2] For champions of American militarism, this memory of the war in Southeast Asia—one so closely tied to the post-1975 "Vietnam syndrome"—represented an unfortunate encumbrance. American political leaders had failed to smite it, and so had the culture industries. Now, perhaps, it was scholarship's turn.

The problem here, however, was that the preponderance of historians did not share this revanchist desire. Indeed, concluded Fredrik Logevall,

> "[t]hat the American decision for war was the wrong decision is today taken as axiomatic by a large majority of both lay observers

and scholars ... who see the U.S. intervention as, at best, a failure and a mistake, at worst a crime."[3]

To be sure, it is not that *no* scholars sympathized with Reagan's "noble cause" narrative. The works of various academics and journalists could in important ways be said to accord with the former President's right-wing views. Still, what the revanchists lacked was a young, assertive, impeccably credentialed historian who was willing to undertake a major new study that would fundamentally revise (or at least seek to revise) the academy's basic Vietnam War narrative. Into this vacuum stepped Mark Moyar. As a product of elite institutions on both sides of the Atlantic (bachelor's degree at Harvard, doctoral degree at Cambridge), Moyar seemed ideally suited to the task.[4] Publishing his work with a major university press as the United States found itself enmeshed in an increasingly unpopular gamble in Iraq, Moyar would emerge as a popular engagé intellectual, extracting lessons from his history of the intervention in Vietnam that could be applied to America's 21st-century crusade in the Middle East. For him, consideration of the internal Cold War-era dynamics of the former conflict could, it was hoped, help to "save" the latter.[5]

In politically committing to *Triumph Forsaken*—and its authorship *was* a political commitment—Mark Moyar thus came to embody the aspirations of an imperial school furious about most historians' rejection of Cold War ideology. Displeased with the extant literature on the Vietnam conflict, which he broadly characterized as "shoddy and biased" and rife with "discredited interpretations," Moyar sought to correct what he saw as the inaccuracy of previous accounts that, as he wrote in his 2006 monograph, considered the U.S. involvement in the war to have been "wrongheaded and unjust."[6] He would, instead, situate his work among those that consider the intervention to have been a "noble but improperly executed enterprise."[7] For this, Moyar suggested, he could expect "rebellio[us]" undertakings such as his to be "suppressed" by "Big Academia and Big Media."[8] The first of two volumes, *Triumph Forsaken* admirably distinguished itself from many other syntheses of the war in its pursuit of a broad international focus. It is evident to readers, moreover, that Moyar did extensive research in both primary and secondary sources, and this is to be commended. Yet, having said that, *Triumph Forsaken* remains a deeply-flawed study. Certainly, the book is not flawed because it challenges much of the "orthodox school" of Vietnam War scholarship, as Moyar designated the bulk of the post-1975 literature. Challenges to the orthodoxy can in fact be quite healthy, and they—including what Moyar called his "multifront offensive against the conventional wisdom"—should generally be encouraged.[9] But when the end product is a monograph as tendentious, unpersuasive, and selective in its use of evidence as is *Triumph Forsaken*, this reflects poorly on the "revisionist school" project in which Moyar has firmly placed his work.[10]

Although peppered with a number of new interpretive insights, the largest arguments framing *Triumph Forsaken* are not especially original: the book maintains that Ho Chi Minh and his comrades were dedicated agents of international Communism. Likewise, Ngo Dinh Diem has been misunderstood, the American press contributed to the American defeat, the domino theory was valid, and so on. Most of these positions were advanced by the war's proponents decades ago and, after the American withdrawal, they were rehashed in various permutations by authors ranging from Guenter Lewy and Robert F. Turner to Peter Braestrup and Michael Lind.[11] The novelty of Moyar's contribution is its broad narrative scope and, crucially, the scholarly garb that more than 80 pages of endnotes lend it. In the end, however, *Triumph Forsaken* has proved no more convincing than its predecessors.

Consider Moyar's treatment of Ho Chi Minh. Dismissing Ho's nationalism as qualified—he was "a nationalist in the sense that he had a special affection for Vietnam's people and favored Vietnamese unification and independence"—Moyar suggested that Ho was, above all else, a willing tool of the Soviets and Chinese, "firmly adher[ing] to the Leninist principle that Communist nations should subordinate their interests to those of the international Communist movement."[12] Moyar therefore saw in Ho's professions of global solidarity not Vietnam's placement at the forefront of a vast wave of anti-colonialism and revolutionary nationalism but, rather, machinations in pursuit of collapsing dominoes. The Vietnamese revolutionaries' gestures towards the Soviets and Chinese were thus viewed invariably in *Triumph Forsaken* as genuine and nefarious, while their gestures towards the United States were dismissed as duplicitous and insincere.[13] It is apparently inconceivable to Moyar that Ho could simultaneously have been both a nationalist and a Communist, or that he or his comrades could have been shrewd individuals willing to make pragmatic accommodations in pursuit of larger national objectives.

Ngo Dinh Diem, on the other hand, was a "very wise and effective leader."[14] Moyar is not the first historian to have claimed that Diem was not an American puppet—and this argument, while by no means original, is one of *Triumph Forsaken*'s strongest—but Moyar went much further than other scholars by positing not only his independent mindedness but also his general effectiveness. There may be areas in which this was true, but Moyar overreached. It strains credulity, for example, to characterize Diem's early land reform program as a "significant achievement."[15] The argument that Moyar unfolded on this issue—his conclusion contravenes those of nearly all other scholars, including the far more detailed treatment by one of Moyar's sources, Philip Catton, who found Diem's record to be "dismal" on this account—is not compelling.[16] Indeed, given that, as noted by Moyar, Diem's program would have entailed breaking up only holdings larger than 100 hectares, while 44 percent of the peasantry in the Mekong Delta remained landless, the case presented in *Triumph Forsaken* would seem to warrant the opposite conclusion.[17]

As for the widespread repression exercised by the Diem government, it is true, Moyar conceded, that Diem was authoritarian. But, whereas Ho's heavy-handedness was a contemptible illustration of the Communist threat, for Diem it was an asset to be celebrated. This was because "Vietnamese culture" was "imbued with authoritarianism," Moyar claimed. Indeed, Vietnam was, as a whole, an "authoritarian country." Moyar failed to cite any credible evidence for this view. When he did attempt to marshal sources in his favor, they were invariably self-serving: U.S. officials and Diem or his brother, Ngo Dinh Nhu. Moyar casually dismissed those Vietnamese who did not subscribe to these cultural norms as a "very small urban elite" that was "severed philosophically from the rest of Vietnamese society" and who "resented Diem for taking away privileges or possessions" bestowed on them by the French. This "intellectual class"—driven, it seems, by little more than scorn for the threat to its class station—lacked "inherent worth," he wrote. Real Vietnamese, according to Moyar, were not interested in "ideas," "democracy," or "civil liberties," and "liberal governance" was clearly "unsuitab[le]" for such people. The masses cared only for power, craving a "strong and charismatic leader" who, while treating them "justly," would "protect them" and "shield them from subversives." They were, in essence, unthinking automatons, who accepted "the judgment of the elites without question or complaint" or, in his description of peasants recruited by the revolutionaries, just "given weapons and ordered to attack." These simpletons "accepted and expected one-man rule as part of the natural order of the world," while the "best officials . . . operated as kindly despots, treating the people as their children."[18] Such reductionism, which echoes much too closely the racist suppositions of American policymakers in earlier decades, is not useful.[19] If Moyar's contention was broadly accurate then, to cite one obvious example, why did Diem employ democratic discourses in campaigning for the October 1955 referendum in an effort to appeal to these same Vietnamese masses?[20]

Moyar's argument is also internally inconsistent. He rendered his judgments about "Vietnamese culture" in an effort to demonstrate how Vietnamese differed from Americans, a difference that he used to criticize U.S. officials' concerns with Diem's authoritarianism—concerns that, incidentally, Moyar greatly overstated in ascribing them to these officials' democratic principles. Yet Moyar did not hesitate to note elsewhere how Americans responded positively to first the threat and then the reality of U.S. bombing of Vietnam—a clear demonstration of power, even if Moyar thinks the United States should have hit the Vietnamese harder—or address how Americans respected anti-Communist leaders who promised to most-effectively protect them from the alleged subversives imperiling the country.[21] His numerous references to the importance to Vietnamese of "prestige" and "losing face," furthermore, sound quite similar to well-explored U.S. concerns about "credibility."[22] Assuming one is willing to speak in broad terms about national political cultures, Vietnamese, in other words, turn out to have seemed, at least in this respect, not so very different from Americans.

Like a number of scholars, I examined some of the sources cited by Moyar in *Triumph Forsaken* to assess his use of primary and secondary materials. A full examination would have required far more time and space than I had at my disposal, so my analysis is necessarily limited. But already the findings of other reviewers had raised serious questions. James McAllister, for example, showed how the only documentary evidence cited by Moyar for his claim that some "high-ranking" U.S. officials were concluding in 1964 that "Tri Quang himself was a Communist" said nothing of the sort.[23] Gareth Porter, commenting on Moyar's explication of the domino theory's validity, accused the author of "violat[ing] the basic norms of scholarship" by, among other things, alleging that the Malay Communist insurgency "never really stopped" when, according to Porter, the allegation is "contradicted flatly by the very source [Moyar] cites."[24] Edwin Moïse, addressing the alleged attack during the Tonkin Gulf incident of August 4, 1964, expressed his annoyance with "the way Moyar carefully [sic] selects from my own book only those facts that support" *Triumph Forsaken*'s argument that the available contemporaneous evidence "strongly supported the reality of the attack"—a point Moïse disputed and said was "very strongly contradicted" elsewhere in his same book.[25] And William Stueck, commenting on Moyar's claims regarding the battle at Dien Bien Phu and the 1954 Geneva Conference, wrote that while Moyar cited for "some specifics" what are arguably the leading sources on Vietnamese relations with China and the Soviet Union, he "ignore[d] other details" in these sources that weakened his position "as well as these authors' conclusions."[26]

My own brief examination only further reinforced the concerns expressed above. To cite one easily confirmable example, Moyar wrote that "[i]n Vietnamese Communist parlance, the label 'reactionary' was applied to anyone who was not a Communist. Many more 'reactionaries' would suffer death during the remainder of 1946, bringing the toll of civilians killed by the Communists during the period of Communist rule into the tens of thousands." Moyar then provided an endnote in which he added that "[i]ntra-Vietnamese killings, which the Communists perpetrated in greater numbers than everyone else combined, came to a total of as high as 50,000 in this period, according to recent estimates."[27] In support Moyar cited Shawn McHale's *Print and Power: Confucianism, Communism, and Buddhism in the Making of Modern Vietnam*. Yet McHale did not write that "the Communists" killed "tens of thousands," nor did he write that they perpetrated killings "in greater numbers than everyone else combined." In fact, he did not mention "the Communists" at all; his discursion was, rather, about the Viet Minh (a "front organization . . . led by the communists") and its opponents "assassinating each other." Moreover, McHale was careful to "underline" that the "Viet Minh was not . . . responsible for all of the deaths, as other nationalist and religious groups contributed to the carnage," for which he cited an estimate by François Guillemot (5,000 to 50,000 killed) and added his own belief that "at least ten thousand were killed in intra-Vietnamese violence" though the death toll was "probably much higher."[28] At no point did McHale seek to apportion the level of responsibility of the various groupings. As is true of a number of damning statements in Moyar's book, the claims noted above therefore lack a citation to evidentiary support—something especially important in a work that seeks to challenge nearly the entire corpus of Vietnam War scholarship. The point is not that Moyar is wrong; he may very well be correct. But in a book that consistently attempts to portray the Viet Minh in the most negative possible light, this lack of substantiation for his empirical claims only exacerbates the concerns raised by Moyar's problematical use of evidence elsewhere.

In other instances, Moyar leveled charges that require far more support than he provided. Take, for example, the case of the northern land reform executions of the mid-1950s—a record that was crucial to Moyar's assertion that the revolutionaries were responsible for the most reprehensible atrocities against noncombatants "in recent memory," which in turn helped to justify his full-throated defense of the Diem regime.[29] It would seem necessary, after all, to have established some rational or moral basis for his support of Diem other than rank anti-Communism. Moyar wrote that, according to "a former Communist land reform cadre who is the most well-informed and trustworthy source on the subject," approximately 32,000 people lost their lives "over the course of [the land reform campaign's] five phases."[30] Who was this apparently unimpeachable source? What made him or her so "well-informed and trustworthy"? What was the basis for his or her enumeration? Moyar did not say.

Without providing any clarifying information, his endnote simply cited a November 1973 dispatch—that is, a document drafted nearly two decades after the land reform campaign ended—from the United States Embassy in Saigon to the State Department. My analysis of the document reinforces why scholars would do well not to blindly trust what they read in *Triumph Forsaken*.

The embassy dispatch summarizes an interrogation by an unnamed "reporting officer" of an unnamed "former communist cadre who rallied to the GVN in the summer of 1973." The "reporting officer," the author of the document conceded, was "not an experienced interrogator"—an interesting and potentially revelatory statement—though the author added that the "rallier" was believed to have responded truthfully and candidly to "most" of the questions he faced. Of course, this implies that the rallier was not truthful or candid in responding to at least some of the questions posed to him. Which questions? The document is silent on this matter. When the dispatch provides an enumeration of executions during the land reform, the enumeration is attributed to "figures" the rallier "saw" when heading a "Correction Group" nearly 20 years prior to the interrogation. Where did he see these figures, who compiled them, and by what method were they calculated? Again the document is silent. The rallier, moreover, refused to "be drawn out regarding the extent of blood-letting in the district for which he was responsible," though he added, according to the document's author, that the sort of "Correction Group" on which he would later serve was composed of "better cadres" in the land reform campaign (that is, "those who served in districts where abuses and excesses during land reform were relatively infrequent").[31]

Readers get no sense from Moyar's uncritical account that the dispatch might be problematical. Some of the potential problems are noted above. But the context in which the information cited in *Triumph Forsaken* was imparted by this "former Communist land reform cadre," as Moyar innocuously described him, deserves special consideration. At no point did the book disclose that the figure of 32,000 executions was offered during a "rallier" interrogation, the details of which are uncertain. This is significant. Commenting, for instance, on the interrogation program in which RAND Corporation analysts participated, the historian David Hunt noted how, given the "power-laden context" in which the interviews were conducted, "transparency was impossible" and informants "could not be counted on to speak truthfully."[32] With torture frequently employed against them and with built-in incentives for their perceived cooperation, the informants, Hunt cautioned, "testified under duress." The interviewees, he added, "could not have been unaware that they were being prodded to choose between competing party lines."[33] The political scientist

David Elliott similarly acknowledged the potential problems with rallier testimony. There was a "frequently encountered tendency of defectors to embellish the revolution's problems, both to justify their own decision and to ingratiate themselves with the new authorities who controlled their destiny," Elliott wrote.[34] To be sure, this does not mean that ralliers' testimony should be dismissed out of hand. It does, however, suggest the need to use such testimony carefully. At the very least, the potential problems with statements offered by those surrendering to the Saigon government should be acknowledged. Moyar, however, not only failed to note any potential problems with such sources; he offered an unequivocal endorsement of them, concluding that the rallier he cited was "the most well-informed and trustworthy source on the subject."[35]

Yet the significance of Moyar's uncritical use of the embassy dispatch lay not merely in his failure to qualify it. The example also conveys how Moyar conveniently, and unpersuasively, dismissed the leading scholarship on the land reform issue. The same endnote in which Moyar cited the November 1973 document relates Bernard Fall's earlier estimate of 50,000 land reform executions, adding that Fall "was conducting research in Vietnam during this period"—a statement presumably meant to suggest, without actually saying so, that Fall's figure is more credible than the one other published source Moyar addressed in the endnote. That other source is the one generally considered most reliable by Vietnam specialists: Edwin Moïse's *Land Reform in China and North Vietnam*. Moïse, in his 1983 study, estimated that the total number of executions during the land reform "was probably in the rough order of 5,000 and almost certainly between 3,000 and 15,000."[36] More recently, he wrote that "probably fewer than 8,000 landlords and would-be opponents of the regime were put to death."[37] While the executions were horribly brutal whatever the actual figure, Moïse's conclusions nevertheless represent an estimate that, even at its highest, is still less than half of that provided by the unnamed source upon whom Moyar relied. If Moïse's probable estimate is accurate, the number of executions would represent only one-fifth to one-quarter of what Moyar asserted. But a number higher than Moïse's would be necessary if Moyar, judging only by the body count, wished to represent Hanoi as more ruthless and contemptible than Saigon. After all, other scholars had concluded that, to cite William Turley, the "number of politically motivated executions in the South during the 1950s probably exceeded the number in the North."[38] Alexander Kendrick offered an estimate for the south of "as many as 75,000 persons," though Turley added that figures for the south, as with the north, were "impossible to verify."[39]

Moyar thus dismissed Moïse's work on the executions in a single sentence. Fall, who covered the issue in less than a page and explained his estimate of approximately 50,000 people killed by citing simply "the best-educated guesses"—of whom, and on what basis, Fall did not say—was not directly challenged by Moyar.[40] But not so Moïse, who devoted seven full pages to his treatment of the land reform atrocities.[41] "Moïse contended that some of Fall's evidence was unreliable," wrote Moyar, "but his alternative approach of extrapolating from incomplete data provided by the Communists rested on the dubious assumption that the Communists would show accurate figures to outsiders." And that's it. To be sure, it is certainly possible that Moïse is incorrect. Yet Moyar's characterization of his methodology is misleading, and it is certainly the case that an author wishing to overturn the operative consensus on a historical issue will need to offer a far more effective critique than does *Triumph Forsaken*.

The example appears typical of Moyar's style. Favorable evidence was marshaled in framing the monograph's arguments, while inconvenient evidence was ignored, downplayed, or dismissed. It is, of course, necessary for scholars in evaluating sources to make subjective decisions about which evidence seems credible and which evidence does not. But given how often Moyar used seemingly incriminating details from sources authored by leading specialists while concomitantly overlooking the many other details that lend these specialists' work a nuance that *Triumph Forsaken*, for the most part, does not possess, readers would be well advised not to pick up the tome in isolation.

For reasons that are hardly surprising, Moyar's book has found an enthusiastic audience among proponents of a militaristic foreign policy. They find in its pages an assertive revisionist account in which, it turns out, Ronald Reagan was right after all. It *was* a "noble cause" that the United States fought in Southeast Asia, just as it *is* a "noble purpose" being fought now in Iraq (and Afghanistan).[42] If assessments of *Triumph Forsaken* from Vietnam and Vietnam War specialists have been decidedly cooler than those of the general public, it is largely because scholars have had the time and the inclination to closely examine the evidentiary foundation on which the book rests. The results have, to say the least, been deeply troubling thus far, particularly for a study that purports to have been driven by the pressing need for "[h]istorical accuracy."[43]

Notes

1. John E. Rielly, "Americans and the World: A Survey at Century's End," *Foreign Policy* 114 (Spring 1999): 100.
2. Jimmy Carter, "The President's News Conference of March 24, 1977," *Public Papers of the Presidents of the United States: Jimmy Carter, 1977* (Washington, DC: Government Printing Office, 1977), I: 501; Reagan, who referred to the war as a "noble cause" while campaigning in August 1980 and as one in which "we did have victory" nearly five years later, quoted in Howell Raines, "Reagan Calls Arms Race Essential to Avoid a

'Surrender' or 'Defeat,'" *New York Times*, August 19, 1980; and Ronald Reagan, "Remarks and a Question-and-Answer Session with Regional Editors and Broadcasters," April 18, 1985, *Public Papers of the Presidents of the United States: Ronald Reagan, 1985* (Washington, DC: Government Printing Office, 1988), I: 454.
3. Fredrik Logevall, *Choosing War: The Lost Chance for Peace and the Escalation of War in Vietnam* (Berkeley, CA: University of California Press, 1999), xiii.
4. Examples of Moyar's academic pedigree being highlighted by right-wing supporters are legion: see, for example, Guenter Lewy, "The War That Could Have Been Won," *New York Sun*, November 24, 2006; John Hinderaker, "You Think You Know About Vietnam? Think Again," *Power Line*, December 18, 2006, at <http://www.powerlineblog.com/archives/2006/12/015981.php> (accessed May 1, 2009); Mackubin Thomas Owens, "A Winnable War: The Argument Against the Orthodox History of Vietnam," *Weekly Standard*, January 15, 2007; "Van Helsing," "Prof Mark Moyar Rejected for Not Being a Moonbat," *Moonbattery*, June 7, 2007, at <http://www.moonbattery.com/archives/2007/06/prof_mark_moyar.html> (accessed May 1, 2009); and Wheeler Frost, "History at Iowa Was History at Duke for Mark Moyar," *Campus Report Online*, November 1, 2007, at <http://www.campusreportonline.net/main/articles.php?id=1942> (accessed May 1, 2009).
5. See, for example, Mark Moyar, "An Iraqi Solution, Vietnam Style," *New York Times*, November 21, 2006.
6. Mark Moyar, "Vietnam: An Overview," Hillsdale College, September 9, 2007, at <http://fora.tv/2007/09/09/Vietnam_An_Overview_with_Mark_Moyar> (accessed April 27, 2009); Mark Moyar, *Triumph Forsaken: The Vietnam War, 1954–1965* (Cambridge, UK: Cambridge University Press, 2006), xi.
7. Moyar, *Triumph Forsaken*, xi.
8. Moyar, "Vietnam: An Overview." In addition to the present volume, *Triumph Forsaken* has, as of April 2009, been the focus of a March 2007 conference at Williams College, a July 2007 roundtable on H-Diplo, a December 2007 roundtable in *Passport: The Newsletter of the Society for Historians of American Foreign Relations*, and has, considering only media outlets, been reviewed or mentioned in the *Wall Street Journal*, the *Sunday Times* (London), *The Australian*, *The Nation*, the *Christian Science Monitor*, the *American Spectator*, and the *National Review*, among others. (The book has also been reviewed in numerous professional journals including, significantly, as a "featured review" in the February 2008 issue of the American historical profession's flagship journal, the *American Historical Review*.) While Moyar may be unhappy with the judgment of his work that these assessments produced, they nevertheless amount to an extraordinary level of attention for an academic monograph.
9. Moyar, "Vietnam: An Overview."
10. Moyar, *Triumph Forsaken*, xi.
11. Guenter Lewy, *America in Vietnam* (Oxford, UK: Oxford University Press, 1978); Robert F. Turner, *Vietnamese Communism: Its Origins and Development* (Stanford, CA: Hoover Institution Press, 1975); Peter Braestrup, *Big Story: How the American Press and Television Reported and Interpreted the Crisis of Tet 1968 in Vietnam and Washington*, Volumes I and II (Boulder, CO: Westview Press, 1977); and Michael Lind, *Vietnam, the Necessary War: A Reinterpretation of America's Most Disastrous Military Conflict* (New York: Free Press, 1999).
12. Moyar, *Triumph Forsaken*, 9.
13. While American leaders were capable of "merely telling [people] what they wanted to hear," according to Moyar, the same was evidently not true of the leaders of the Vietnamese revolution. Ibid., 277.
14. Ibid., xiv. Moyar elsewhere wrote that Diem was "a highly effective national war leader." Moyar, "An Iraqi Solution, Vietnam Style."
15. Moyar, *Triumph Forsaken*, 72.
16. Philip E. Catton, *Diem's Final Failure: Prelude to America's War in Vietnam* (Lawrence, KS: University Press of Kansas, 2002), 54.

17. Moyar, *Triumph Forsaken*, 73.
18. Ibid., 36–37, 40, 43, 71, 73, 75, 94, 428 (nn. 11 and 13).
19. See, for example, Seth Jacobs, *America's Miracle Man in Vietnam: Ngo Dinh Diem, Religion, Race, and U.S. Intervention in Southeast Asia, 1950–1957* (Durham, NC: Duke University Press, 2004).
20. Jessica M. Chapman, "Staging Democracy: South Vietnam's 1955 Referendum to Depose Bao Dai," *Diplomatic History* 30:4 (September 2006): 671–703.
21. Moyar, *Triumph Forsaken*, 314, 330.
22. Ibid., 43, 81, 231, 236, 239–240, 279–280, 316, 346.
23. Ibid., 317; James McAllister, "H-Diplo Roundtable on *Triumph Forsaken*," H-Diplo, July 8, 2007. Moyar's response to McAllister was disingenuous. Moyar wrote that the CIA document in question "says what I stated that it said, that there were 'objective and well-informed U.S. official observers' who believed Tri Quang to be a Communist." Mark Moyar, "H-Diplo Roundtable on *Triumph Forsaken*," H-Diplo, July 10, 2007. Yet this elided McAllister's criticism and misrepresented what Moyar originally claimed. Moyar did not write in *Triumph Forsaken* that U.S. "official observers" believed this of Tri Quang; rather, he wrote that some "high-ranking" U.S. officials believed it, which is quite different.
24. Gareth Porter, "Did South Vietnamese President Ngo Dinh Diem Get a Bad Rap, and Were the Dominos Really Ready to Fall?" *Vietnam* 20:1 (June 2007): 60.
25. Edwin Moïse, "A Glance at Moyar's Book," Comment No. 99133, *History News Network*, October 8, 2006, at <http://hnn.us/readcomment.php?id=99133&bheaders=1#99133> (accessed June 4, 2007). The book in question is Edwin E. Moïse, *Tonkin Gulf and the Escalation of the Vietnam War* (Chapel Hill, NC: University of North Carolina Press, 1996).
26. William Stueck, "*Triumph Forsaken* Roundtable Review," H-Diplo, July 2, 2007, 24, at <http://www.h-net.org/~diplo/roundtables/PDF/TriumphForsaken-Roundtable.pdf> (accessed July 11, 2007).
27. Moyar, *Triumph Forsaken*, 19, 425 (n. 42).
28. Shawn Frederick McHale, *Print and Power: Confucianism, Communism, and Buddhism in the Making of Modern Vietnam* (Honolulu, HI: University of Hawai'i Press, 2004), 35–36, 193.
29. Moyar, *Triumph Forsaken*, 62.
30. Ibid., 62.
31. U.S. Embassy, Saigon, to Department of State, November 21, 1973; Airgram A-268; Folder: POL 2 VIET N, 3–14–72; Box 2801; Subject Numeric Files, 1970–1973, Political & Defense; Record Group 59; National Archives II, College Park, Maryland.
32. David Hunt, *Vietnam's Southern Revolution: From Peasant Insurrection to Total War* (Amherst, MA: University of Massachusetts Press, 2008), 225, 228.
33. David Hunt, "Revolution in the Delta," *Critical Asian Studies* 35:4 (2003): 599.
34. David W.P. Elliott, *The Vietnamese War: Revolution and Social Change in the Mekong Delta, 1930–1975* (Armonk, NY: M.E. Sharpe, 2003), 761. On the "caution" that Elliott counsels should be employed in relying on interrogation testimony whose "constraints" are "obvious," see ibid., 7–8.
35. Moyar, *Triumph Forsaken*, 62.
36. Edwin E. Moïse, *Land Reform in China and North Vietnam: Consolidating the Revolution at the Village Level* (Chapel Hill, NC: University of North Carolina Press, 1983), 222. See also Edwin E. Moïse, "Land Reform and Land Reform Errors in North Vietnam," *Pacific Affairs* 49:1 (Spring 1976): 70–92.
37. Edwin E. Moïse, "Land Reform," in Spencer C. Tucker, ed., *Encyclopedia of the Vietnam War: A Political, Social, and Military History* (Oxford, UK: Oxford University Press, 2000), 219.
38. William S. Turley, *The Second Indochina War: A Short Political and Military History, 1954–1975* (Boulder, CO: Westview Press, 1986), 18. In the revised edition of his book published in 2009, Turley replaced "probably" with "may have." William S. Turley, *The*

Second Indochina War: A Concise Political and Military History, 2nd edn (Lanham, MD: Rowman and Littlefield Publishers, 2009), 33.
39. Alexander Kendrick, *The Wound Within: America in the Vietnam Years, 1945–1974* (Boston, MA: Little, Brown and Company, 1974), 112; Turley, *The Second Indochina War*, 2nd edn, 50 (n. 25).
40. Bernard B. Fall, *The Two Viet-Nams: A Political and Military Analysis*, 2nd rev. edn (New York: Frederick A. Praeger, Publishers, 1967), 155–156.
41. Moïse, *Land Reform in China and North Vietnam*, 216–222.
42. George W. Bush, "Remarks to National Veterans Organizations," March 28, 2003, *Public Papers of the Presidents of the United States: George W. Bush, 2003* (Washington, DC: Government Printing Office, 2006), I: 308.
43. Moyar, *Triumph Forsaken*, xi.

CHAPTER 9

Triumph Forsaken as a Path to Setting the Record Straight

ROBERT F. TURNER

Anyone who cares seriously about the realities of the Vietnam War or wishes to learn its key lessons owes a great debt of gratitude to Mark Moyar, whose new volume is a landmark contribution to the subject. Indeed, it should be mandatory reading for any serious scholar seeking to understand that conflict, as well as any politician or senior aide who seeks lessons for the current conflict in Iraq or future armed conflicts.

These are not new issues to me. I wrote my undergraduate honors thesis on the war forty-three years ago, before volunteering for the army and for duty in Vietnam. Indeed, the day Dr. Moyar was born, I was an army captain four months into my second tour of duty attached to the North Vietnam/Viet Cong Affairs Division of Joint United States Public Affairs Office, a component of the U.S. embassy in Saigon. During five visits to Indochina between 1968 and the final evacuation in April 1975, I visited forty-two of South Vietnam's forty-four provinces, traveled extensively in Cambodia, and briefly visited Laos as well.

Triumph Foresaken is often described as a "revisionist" history of the war. Moyar himself asserts that he is carrying on "a relatively small, but strong, tradition of revisionist literature that dates back to the mid-1970s." In an accompanying footnote, he identifies nine volumes as "the most significant of the early revisionist books," of which my *Vietnamese Communism* (1975) is the oldest. I am not sure it matters, but I have always viewed my own scholarship on the war as "counter-revisionist," on the theory that the original orthodoxy was the support for "containment" that led to America's involvement in Vietnam. There were a number of books supporting this view, among the best being Frank N. Trager's *Why Vietnam* (1966), Dennis Duncanson's *Government and Revolution in Vietnam* (1968), and Wesley Fishel's *Vietnam: Anatomy of a Conflict* (1969). But the modern verdict seems unanimous that the views of my late friend Bill Colby (*Lost Victory*, 1989) and Guenter Lewy (*America in Vietnam*, 1978) are "revisionist," and in that spirit I am honored to be in their company.

Moyar has taken advantage of resources that were simply not available when I wrote *Vietnamese Communism* thirty-five years ago, and by skillfully applying his considerable research and writing talents has given us the first volume of what truly must be viewed as an extraordinary contribution to the history of the Vietnam War. He has wisely drawn from the labors of those who went before him, but a great deal of this volume results from his own original research. From my perspective as a scholar who has been working in this field for more than four decades and teaching seminars on the war at both the graduate and undergraduate level since the 1980s, he has most of it right.

Take, for example, the issue of Ngo Dinh Diem, South Vietnam's controversial president, who was assassinated on November 1, 1963. Moyar views American encouragement of the anti-Diem coup as the greatest blunder of the war, and I could not agree more. War critics were fond of noting that Diem had served in the early 1930s in the French colonial administration and had lived in New Jersey during the final years of the French–Viet Minh war. They failed to appreciate what Bernard Fall in *The Two Viet-Nams* called Diem's "reputation for 'all-or-nothing' integrity." Because of his unparalleled reputation for competence and integrity, Diem was admired even by his political rivals and sought as a figurehead leader by Bao Dai, the French, the Japanese, and even Ho Chi Minh's Viet Minh. But he refused to be anyone's lackey, and his unwillingness to take instructions from the arrogant American proconsul, Ambassador Henry Cabot Lodge, helped seal his ultimate fate.

In 1968, a friend in the embassy arranged for me to have dinner with Dr. Tran Van Do, who had represented Vietnam at the 1954 Geneva Conference. Knowing he had later feuded with Diem, I sought his candid opinion on the former president. Yes, he acknowledged they had had their differences, but like most of the Vietnamese I spoke with, Dr. Do still held Diem in high esteem as a great Vietnamese patriot and effective national leader.

Perhaps my most revealing experience on this issue resulted from a casual remark I made to Bui Cong Tuong, one of the most senior defectors in the war who had served as director of propaganda, education, culture, and training for what the Viet Cong called Ben Tre Province and we called Kien

Hoa. He told me that when they heard on the radio that Diem had been killed, they thought it was some sort of American trick, because surely the Americans would not be so foolish as to allow anything to happen to Diem.

Tuong explained that senior party officials viewed Diem as a great patriot—in the same league as Ho Chi Minh—but because Diem would not follow the party's leadership they had to try to destroy his reputation with the people by branding him an American puppet and traitor. And surely if there is one clear message from the Pentagon Papers it is that Diem was far less willing to take instructions from the Americans than Ho was to follow instructions from Moscow and Beijing. I certainly share Moyar's view—one also shared by Bill Colby and other leading experts—that promoting the coup that overthrew Diem was America's greatest blunder in the war.

Moyar's book is of tremendous importance, not just to historians, but also to anyone interested in current U.S. policy in places like Iraq. Much of the current debate is driven by mythology—such "lessons" as: America should never go to war without the support of the people and the approval of Congress. In reality, the Gallup Polls show that President Johnson's approval rating shot up 58 percent (an increase of thirty percentage points) between July and August of 1964, and Gallup attributed this to LBJ's decision to bomb some military bases in North Vietnam. Polls consistently showed strong support for the war in Indochina, with those favoring escalation greatly outnumbering those favoring immediate withdrawal. As Lesley Gelb and Richard Betts observed in their excellent Brookings Institution volume, *The Irony of Vietnam*, a plurality of the people who voted for Eugene McCarthy in the 1968 New Hampshire primary went on to support Governor George Wallace and retired Strategic Air Command Commander General Curtis "Bomb Hanoi back to the Stone Age" LeMay in the November election. These were protest voters who supported the Vietnam War, but objected to LBJ's and McNamara's "no win" strategy. As for Congress, long before LBJ sent U.S. combat units to fight in South Vietnam, the Congress, by a vote of 504–2 (a 99.6 percent majority), passed the August 1964 Southeast Asia Resolution. The Resolution declared as a matter of law that the president was authorized to use force to defend the Protocol states (South Vietnam, Laos, and Cambodia) to the Southeast Asia Treaty Organization Treaty against communist aggression. During the Senate floor debate on this statute, Foreign Relations Committee Chairman J. William Fulbright was asked by ranking Republican Senator John Sherman Cooper whether by enacting the joint resolution the Congress would be empowering the president to take the country into "war." And Fulbright responded: "That is the way I would interpret it."

Another major myth is that the Vietnam War was "unwinnable."

Writing in the January/February 2005 issue of *Foreign Affairs*, Yale Professor John Lewis Gaddis—regarded by many as the dean of American diplomatic historians—observed: "Historians now acknowledge that American counter-insurgency operations in Vietnam were succeeding during the final years of that conflict; the problem was that support for the war had long since crumbled at home." Many of America's most experienced observers made the point that the war had been effectively won by the spring of 1972 if not earlier, including the C.I.A.'s William E. Colby in his *Lost Victory*, my old embassy colleague Douglas Pike, and journalist Robert Elegant in his superb essay, "How to Lose a War," in the August 1981 issue of *Encounter*. Perhaps even more interestingly, former Viet Cong official Truong Nhu Tang—who served as minister of justice for the "Provisional Revolutionary Government"—and People's Army of Vietnam Colonel Bui Tin have echoed this view. In an interview excerpted in the *Wall Street Journal* on August 3, 1995, the former deputy editor of Hanoi's major daily *Nhan Dan* ("The People") acknowledged: "[The anti-war movement] was *essential* to our strategy . . . Every day our leadership would listen to world news over the radio at 9 a.m. to follow the growth of the American antiwar movement. Visits to Hanoi by people like Jane Fonda . . . gave us confidence that we should hold on in the face of battlefield reversals."

The campus debates about Vietnam in the 1960s were filled with mythology and misinformation. The United States did not violate its commitments under the 1954 Geneva Accords—as the Pentagon Papers document, we refused to sign or verbally agree to anything at Geneva. Along with the noncommunist "State of Vietnam," we opposed partition and expressly declared that reunification elections should be supervised by the United Nations to ensure that they were conducted fairly. (In contrast, Molitov and Pham Van Dong objected to international supervision as interference in the internal affairs of Vietnam and insisted upon "locally supervised" elections—the kind that routinely gave Ho Chi Minh 99.9 percent of the votes in the more populous North Vietnam.

As reprinted on pages 570–571 of volume 1 of the Gravel edition of the Pentagon Papers, at the final session of the Geneva Conference on July 21, 1954, U.S. delegate Walter Bedell Smith declared:

> As I stated on July 18, my Government is not prepared to join in a declaration by the Conference such as is submitted. However, the United States makes this unilateral declaration of its position on these matters . . . In connection with the statement in the declaration concerning free elections in Viet-Nam my Government wishes to make clear its position which it has expressed in a declaration made in Washington on June 29, 1954, as follows: "In the case of nations

now divided against their will, we shall continue to seek to achieve unity through free elections supervised by the United Nations to insure that they are conducted fairly.["]

One of the most common assertions in the more than one hundred debates, teach-ins, and other programs I took part in between 1965 and entering the Army three years later was that even President Eisenhower had admitted that Ho Chi Minh would have defeated Ngo Dinh Diem in a free election had the United States and South Vietnam not refused to permit the July 1956 elections required by the Geneva Agreements. Critics would routinely quote from page 449 of Eisenhower's *Mandate for Change*, but from my experience they never even finished the sentence—much less the full contextual quotation. I have set in italics the language quoted time and again by anti-Vietnam critics:

> *I have never talked or corresponded with a person knowledgeable in Indochinese affairs who did not agree that had elections been held as of the time of the fighting, possibly 80 percent of the population would have voted for the Communist Ho Chi Minh as their leader* rather than Chief of State Bao Dai. Indeed, the lack of leadership and drive on the part of Bao Dai was a factor in the feeling prevalent among Vietnamese that they had nothing to fight for.

As is apparent from the full quotation, Eisenhower is not discussing a possible 1956 election between Ho and Diem, but rather an election "as of the time of the fighting," which ended in 1954, between Ho and the hated French puppet Bao Dai, whom Diem easily defeated by a far greater margin. His message was not that Ho Chi Minh was the preference of most Vietnamese, but rather that "the feeling prevalent among Vietnamese" was that "they had nothing to fight for"—they did not want communism or French colonial rule.

As the Pentagon Papers later observed (vol. 1, pp. 246–247):

> It is almost certain that by 1956 the proportion which might have voted for Ho—in a free election against Diem—would have been much smaller than 80%. Diem's success in the South had been far greater than anyone could have foreseen, while the North Vietnamese regime had been suffering from food scarcity, and low public morale stemming from inept imitation of Chinese Communism—including a harsh agrarian program that reportedly led to the killing of over 50,000 small scale "landlords" . . .
>
> [T]he basis for the policy of both nations [South Vietnam and the United States] in rejecting the Geneva elections was . . . convictions that Hanoi would not permit "free general elections by secret ballot,"

and that the International Code Council would be impotent in supervising the elections in any case.

In the belief that he was being misquoted, around the end of 1967, I sent a letter to President Eisenhower attaching a copy of a two-page circular I had prepared entitled: "Vietnam Cliché Series: Eisenhower Admitted that Had the 1956 Elections Been Held, Ho Chi Minh Would Have Won by 80% of the Vote." The circular sought to rebut the assertion that the quotation addressed the likely outcome of a 1956 election between Ho and Diem. An individual named Samuel S. Vaughan, from Doubleday & Company (publisher of *Mandate for Change*), responded on behalf of President Eisenhower on February 16, 1968, that my reading of the passage was correct and President Eisenhower was addressing only the issue of a possible election between Ho and Bao Dai: "No further great conclusion should be drawn from the statement."

On March 5, 1956, the *New York Times* featured an editorial supporting South Vietnam's decision not to participate in unsupervised elections, declaring: "To attempt to settle the fate of the free Vietnamese without even consulting them is monstrous. To suggest a 'free' election in a Communist territory is to presume the possible existence of conditions and safeguards for which there is neither assurance nor precedent." On April 11, the *Times* noted that the government of Great Britain had the previous day sent a diplomatic note to the Soviet Union—the other co-chair of the 1954 Geneva Conference—"recognized that South Vietnam was not legally bound by the armistice agreements since it had not signed them and had protested against them at the Geneva Conference."

Many of the most effective arguments against the war pertained to alleged "human rights" abuses. Like virtually every Third World country, South Vietnam had serious corruption problems and its human rights record was far from perfect. But when contrasted with what the communists were offering (and what they later imposed on South Vietnam), there was no comparison. There were hundreds of bookstalls around Saigon where I found writings of Ho Chi Minh, Vo Nguyen Giap, and even Chairman Mao himself. (That is not to say selling communist literature was legal, only that the booksellers did not live in apparent fear of government repression.) As *Christian Science Monitor* Bureau Chief Daniel Sutherland observed in a September 18, 1970, article:

> Under its new press law, South Vietnam now has one of the freest presses in Southeast Asia, and the daily paper with the biggest circulation here happens to be sharply critical of President Thieu.... [S]ince the new press law was promulgated nine months ago, the government has not been able to close down *Tin Sang* or any

other newspaper among the more than 30 now being published in Saigon.

In 1974, I personally interviewed lawyer Ngo Ba Thanh and Father Chanh Tin about their allegations of 200,000 political prisoners, and it was apparent there was no basis to the claim—which had first appeared in Hanoi's *Vietnam Courrier*. Mrs. Thanh declared that by her definition of "political prisoner," Sirhan Sirhan—the man convicted of assassinating Senator Robert Kennedy—was one, because "his motive was political." Thus, Viet Cong terrorists who threw grenades into buses would be included in her count. Father Tin told me he came up with his figure by talking with former prisoners and their relatives and asking for their estimates—hardly a scientific method. In reality, the American Embassy did an actual count of the populations of each of the South Vietnamese prisons and came up with a total figure of about (if my memory serves me well after so many years) 35,000—of which about 6,000 were classed as "Communist criminals." And, interestingly, when the communists took over and Chi Hoa prison in Saigon was opened up, the prisoner count was within a few percentage points of the Embassy's earlier figure.

The so-called "tiger cages" were another propaganda victory for Hanoi, and at least some of the American anti-war activists who made frequent reference to them apparently knew the story was false. When I informed friends in the anti-war movement that I would be allowed to visit Con Son Prison during a May 1974 congressional staff delegation to South Vietnam, they immediately downplayed that option and suggested that instead I insist on visiting Chi Hoa Prison. (I actually measured the so-called "tiger cages," which were 3 meters tall, 3 meters long, and 1.5 meters wide—roughly 10 × 10 × 5 feet in size. And the widely repeated assertion that they were too short for Vietnamese prisoners to stand erect in was preposterous—I'm 6′ 4″ and I could not come close to reaching the ceiling with my arm fully extended.)

Perhaps the greatest myth about Vietnam is that there was no reason to go to war in the first place. Moyar does a great job of puncturing part of this argument—namely, the allegation that Ho Chi Minh was in reality but a Vietnamese "nationalist" who accepted communist assistance when the United States refused to help him free his country from French occupation. Had we simply permitted him to unite Vietnam, it is often alleged, he would have been an "Asian Tito" and a barrier to further Chinese expansion into Southeast Asia. This is an issue I addressed at some length in my 1975 book *Vietnamese Communism*, in which I observed that Ho spent thirty years outside Vietnam between 1911 and 1941, most of it in the paid service of the Communist International (Comintern). Indeed, numerous

Hanoi publications note that when Ho Chi Minh was present at the founding of the Indochinese Communist Party in 1930, he was there as the official Comintern representative.

Ho's Viet Minh radio repeatedly denounced Tito as an American spy during the late 1940s, and even when Khrushchev made peace with Tito, Hanoi media continued to denounce him. At the Third Party Congress in 1960, for example, First Secretary Le Duan stated:

> The modern revisionists represented by the Tito clique in Yugoslavia are trumpeting that the nature of imperialism has changed... [I]f we want to lay bare the aggressive and bellicose nature of imperialism ... the Communist ... parties must necessarily direct their main blow against revisionism ... It is precisely the Chinese Communist Party, headed by Comrade Mao Tse-tung, which has most brilliantly carried into effect the teachings of the great Lenin.

Vietnam was tremendously important because it represented a test case of whether the United States could effectively resist the tactic of "people's war" or "national liberation warfare." Eisenhower had effectively deterred Khrushchev after Korea with threats of massive retaliation, but by concentrating on the strategic nuclear triad and cutting back on ground forces, Ike left America unprepared to deal with low-intensity aggression. As the communists developed nuclear weapons of their own, the idea of defending Saigon with a nuclear strike lost credibility. America was not going to bomb Moscow to protect Saigon with the knowledge that Soviet missiles would soon fall on New York, Los Angeles, and Washington, D.C.

Mao declared the "imperialists" to be in reality but "paper tigers," since fierce-looking nuclear weapons were useless against guerrillas who lived among the people. In 1965, China was actively supporting guerrilla movements throughout Indochina, Thailand, Indonesia, the Philippines, and as far away as Mozambique; Chinese Communist Party Central Committee Vice Chairman Lin Biao declared that a victory in Vietnam would show other Third World countries that what the Vietnamese could do, they could do, too. Ché Guevara declared that the reason Latin American communists raised the Viet Cong flag was "because that battlefront is most important for the future of all America."

Had the United States simply walked away from Vietnam in 1965, we would have proven Mao and Castro right and perhaps even persuaded Moscow to support national liberation movements more vigorously. Within two or three years, we likely would have been faced with a dozen or more such struggles—and we could not have won a dozen "Vietnams" without resort to nuclear weapons. By delaying the loss of South Vietnam until 1975, we bought time for basket cases like Thailand and Indonesia to strengthen themselves, and watched China turn inward as it struggled through the Great Proletarian Cultural Revolution that left Lin Biao dead and saw an end to massive Chinese support for revolutionary movements around the globe. The Cold War might have turned out very differently had we been perceived in 1965 as being unwilling or unable to resist low-intensity Leninist aggression.

In a very real sense, we lost the war in Vietnam politically but not militarily (although the results were the same and our enemies gained victory). My old friend Harry Summers, in his landmark book, *On Strategy*, included this epigram on page 1:

> "You know you never defeated us on the battlefield," said the American colonel.
> The North Vietnamese colonel pondered this remark a moment. "That may be so," he replied, "but it is also irrelevant."

I submit that both men were correct. And the question arises, how were we beaten politically? I think the answer is complex and there is a great deal of responsibility to spread around. First, Hanoi and Moscow ran a brilliant political warfare program designed to mislead and swell the ranks of anti-war protesters around the globe. This is a classic element of Leninism. (See Lenin's *"Left-Wing" Communism: An Infantile Disorder.*) For reasons I do not fully understand, our government did little to engage the critics on the merits, and gradually more and more people began to doubt the moral foundations to our commitment.

There were scholars within the academic community who could have helped set the record straight, but to do so would alienate radical colleagues and perhaps result in charges of being a "warmonger," "baby killer," or "war criminal"—and few seemed willing to risk not being invited to the annual faculty holiday party by standing up to the radicals. Many apparently viewed it the job of "the government" to defend its actions.

A great deal of responsibility, I believe, falls on President Johnson and especially Defense Secretary Robert S. McNamara, whose refusal to listen to the advice of their military and intelligence advisors led to horrible mismanagement of the conflict and the pursuit of an incredibly flawed strategy they should have realized would not maintain the support of the public. While I do not question their constitutional right to ignore military advice, by essentially ignoring the advice of the Joint Chiefs of Staff and the Director of Central Intelligence they betrayed the civil–military partnership that dated back to the earliest days of our nation.

I think the American media deserves a great deal of responsibility for misleading and often incompetent coverage of the war. (It is not by chance that public opinion polls show that Vietnam veterans support the war by more than twice the level of the American public—we saw what was going on without it being filtered through the news media.) I strongly concur in the analysis of prize-winning journalist Robert Elegant, whose article "How to Lose A War: The Press and Viet Nam," was published in *Encounter* magazine in August 1981. It is available online at http://www.wellesley.edu/Polisci/wj/Vietnam/Readings/elegant.htm, and I highly recommend it to anyone who has not yet read it.

My first trip to Vietnam in 1968 was with press credentials (although, in fairness, I was more of a tourist with a press card), and that permitted me to stay for a few dollars a night at the various military press centers around the country. And I recall a rather heated exchange I had one evening after dinner in the DaNang Press Center with a journalist who had published a series of articles I felt did not fairly reflect the character of most of our armed forces in the country. He listened patiently to my complaint, acknowledged that I was correct in my perception that most U.S. forces were behaving very honorably in Vietnam—but added that the American people knew that, and that I simply did not understand the business of journalist. If he wanted to get his stories on page 1 and get prizes and pay rises, he had to do something more than just write puffery pieces about the good deeds of American soldiers. As he put it, he had to write "man bites dog" stories rather than "dog bites man" stories. But sadly, after a number of such stories, his readers back in the States began to assume that men biting dogs was the norm in South Vietnam.

I have already given Hanoi credit for a very extensive and effective political warfare campaign that provided tons of propaganda to so-called "peace" groups around the globe. I should also acknowledge their effectiveness in sending agents into the bars and restaurants frequented by Western reporters to plant stories and provide "information" that often made its way into print back home. Perhaps the most effective of these agents, but certainly not the only one, was Pham Xuan An—who, among other things, spent ten years as the senior Vietnamese correspondent for *Time* magazine and earlier worked for Reuters news agency. He was perhaps the most trusted Vietnamese journalist by such American journalists as David Halberstam and Morley Safer; in reality, he was a colonel in the North Vietnamese Army. The recent book *Perfect Spy: the Incredible Double Life of Pham Xuan An*, tells his story. Perhaps the most telling evidence of the gullibility of much of the American press in Vietnam is the fact that, even after An was exposed as a communist agent from the start, American journalists accepted his claim that he merely gathered military intelligence for Hanoi and never tried to influence a news story.

Understanding what actually happened in Vietnam is important, and there really are "lessons" that can be learned and applied to other conflicts.

Today, gullible Americans are told that George W. Bush invented the idea that Saddam Hussein had weapons of mass destruction in order to justify going to war to help his Texas oil buddies or gain revenge for Saddam's plot to kill his father. But this ignores the reality that in 1998—years before then-Governor Bush moved from Texas to Washington, D.C.—a unanimous Senate and more than 90 percent of the House of Representatives approved the "Iraq Liberation Act" that declared: "It should be the policy of the United States to support efforts to remove the regime headed by Saddam Hussein from power in Iraq and to promote the emergence of a democratic government to replace that regime."

The lies about "lying" continue to divide and weaken our country in a time of national crisis, just as misperceptions about "Vietnam" lead us astray. It is imperative that this record be corrected, and Dr. Moyar's book provides valuable insight and ammunition for that struggle.

CHAPTER 10

Governing the Vietnamese "Masses"
The United States, Ngo Dinh Diem, and the Notion of Triumph Forsaken

JESSICA CHAPMAN

The country was torn asunder by years of bloody warfare. It emerged politically and culturally divided with a tremendous rift between north and south. The war freed millions of people from years of oppression and domination by whites, who justified their dominion on the grounds that the dark-skinned people they subjugated had yet to develop the cultural, and perhaps even the biological, capacity for self-rule. The oppressors claimed that their strict regime of discipline and control served to protect the oppressed from their own worst tendencies and, even more critically, it was necessary to maintain social and political order. Once the people were liberated, their former masters insisted that granting them the full rights of citizens in a democracy would encourage chaos, violence, and disorder, and ultimately undermine the country's political processes. Such arguments justified the creation of a new social order for the post-war era that ensured the ongoing political disenfranchisement of the recently freed population. This description of American slavery and the rise of Jim Crow after the Civil War bears striking resemblance to postcolonial Vietnam in the wake of the First Indochina War.

Since the 1860s, Vietnam had been subject to French colonial rule under the rubric of *mission civilastrice*, through which colonizers justified their subordination of Indochinese peoples on the grounds that racial inferiority—both cultural and biological—rendered them unfit for self-rule.[1] After the Second World War, the communist Viet Minh led a bloody eight-year struggle to expel the French, and in the process they brutalized and alienated large segments of Vietnam's population, especially in the South. In 1954, the Geneva Accords ended the French War and divided Vietnam in half at the seventeenth parallel, leaving the country's political future up in the air. Newly appointed South Vietnamese Prime Minister Ngo Dinh Diem and his American patrons contended that the people of Vietnam remained unprepared for and uninterested in self-government, and that above all they needed an authoritarian leader who could protect them from internal and external threats. More than fifty years later, historian Mark Moyar agrees.

Moyar writes that Diem, "a man deeply dedicated to the welfare of his country ... governed in an authoritarian way because he considered Western-style democracy inappropriate for a country that was fractious and dominated by an authoritarian culture."[2] In Moyar's assessment, Diem had it right, because society both north and south of the seventeenth parallel reflected "the prevailing Vietnamese belief that whoever had actual military and political power was legitimate."[3] By extension, then, methods like oppression, violence, and intimidation would only enhance political legitimacy if they led to the successful consolidation of authority and maintenance of order.[4] Such claims are nothing new, as they echo official U.S. justifications for support to Ngo Dinh Diem put forth in the 1950s and 1960s. However, they run counter to recent scholarly trends that call into question those official perceptions, and merit close consideration since Moyar relies upon this interpretation of Vietnamese culture to justify his claim that the United States forsook triumph in Vietnam when it withdrew support from Diem in 1963. How well, then, does Moyar's assessment reflect a well-substantiated, nuanced understanding of Vietnamese politics, culture, and society in the mid-twentieth century?

Sophie Quinn-Judge, a historian of modern Vietnam, remarks, "If one looks beyond the narrow confines of [Moyar's] assumptions about the Vietnamese people ... his reconstruction of the events of 1954–1965 loses much of its power."[5] Even William Stueck, one of Moyar's more sympathetic reviewers, writes, "I find suspect the glowing description by Moyar of Diem's leadership and his downplaying of the issue of land distribution. Moyar is certainly correct to rebut orthodox portrayals of Diem as an unthinking reactionary and to emphasize security as a primary concern of the peasants, but the extent to which he goes in these directions strikes me as excessive."[6] Recent studies by Philip Catton and Edward Miller, both of whom have brought extensive training in Vietnamese history and language as well as U.S. diplomatic history to their research on Ngo Dinh Diem's administration, lend support to Stueck's hunch. Miller, whom some have mischaracterized as an apologist for Diem and for the American War due to his efforts to restore agency to the South Vietnamese leader, has taken issue with suggestions that "Ngo Dinh Diem was a sagacious and shrewd leader who was on the verge of 'stabilizing' South Vietnam when he was killed in 1963." He contends instead that Diem was "motivated by a distinctive vision of how South Vietnam could and should become a modern nation," which proves that the South Vietnamese leader was more independent than orthodox scholars often recognize, but also "more responsible for the ultimate failure of his government" than revisionist scholars acknowledge.[7] Philip Catton, in his study of Diem's land reform and nation-building project, claims, "While [Diem] was no hopeless reactionary, neither did he appear capable of building a nation south of the Seventeenth Parallel." According to Catton, Diem's failings were most evident in the implementation of the Strategic Hamlet program—an undertaking that, in the name of security, displaced and alienated many of the Vietnamese peasants that Moyar claims remained loyal to Diem up to his assassination.[8]

Miller and Catton's conclusions are far from the final word on the nature of Diem's government, its relationship to South Vietnamese society, and its political viability. Historians have just recently begun to tap into Vietnamese sources to address these issues with attention to the "other side."[9] At the very least, though, any convincing challenge to their well-documented assertions that Diem's own oppressive and at times brutal policies contributed to his administration's crisis of legitimacy (and thereby to the failure of the joint U.S.–R.V.N. nation-building project) would require compelling evidence to support an alternative view of South Vietnam's political sphere in the 1950s and early 1960s. Moyar makes an attempt, arguing that "the Vietnamese masses of the mid-twentieth century were not seeking a leader whose ideas appealed to them, but a strong and charismatic leader who would organize the people, protect them, and treat them justly."[10] He claims that assumptions held by Edward Lansdale and other American officials that the Vietnamese people could be won over by promises of democracy and civil liberties were based on an inaccurate understanding of Vietnamese culture.[11] On the contrary, Moyar argues, the success or failure of both Ho Chi Minh and Ngo Dinh Diem's governments rested strictly on their ability to control the population, and by this metric, Diem's administration was successful to the very end. However, one cannot help but question his reading of Vietnamese culture, because it rests exclusively upon contemporary British and American commentary as well as some of Ngo Dinh Diem's own utterances.[12]

Moyar's reliance on Ngo Dinh Diem's own judgment about the futility of democracy in Vietnam as evidence that democratic reforms had no appeal to Vietnamese people is bizarre.[13] It hardly seems sensible to rely upon a dictator for an accurate assessment of his subjects' desire and capacity for democratic participation, especially since several of Ngo Dinh Diem's contemporaries vociferously demanded that he broaden his government and implement democratic reforms, only to come under governmental persecution. While Moyar admits that a small, urban elite advocated Western-style democracy and civil liberties, he explains away the Ngo brothers' decision to ignore these demands and exclude those who made them from South Vietnam's political sphere with the following claim:

> No ideology that Diem could have chosen would have both satisfied the intellectuals and permitted his anti-Communist government to survive, for the liberal methods that appealed to the Westernized intelligentsia were the opposite of the authoritarian methods needed to control the masses and shield them from subversives.[14]

As evidence that these authoritarian methods were necessary and successful in legitimizing Ngo Dinh Diem's government, Moyar writes, "The real proof of the people's support for the government could be found in the establishment of well-led armed forces and administrations in the villages, and in the elimination of organized opposition."[15] While one could take issue with the assertion that the Army of the Republic of Vietnam (A.R.V.N.) was well led, it is even more curious that Moyar provides no evidence to support the rather odd claim that Ngo Dinh Diem's ability to suppress opposition somehow proved that popular support for his government existed.

To justify his claim that dictatorial methods were the key to legitimacy in Vietnam, Moyar writes, "The unsuitability of liberal governance would be amply demonstrated by subsequent events during the years 1963 to 1965, when toleration and conciliation of opposition groups led to political disintegration."[16] But might it be possible instead that the very persistence of this opposition throughout Ngo Dinh Diem's rule, silenced in 1955 and revived in the early 1960s, disproves Moyar's contention that the Ngo brothers' suppression of organized opposition fostered popular support? Arguably, opposition to Diem was always lurking and perhaps growing beneath the surface of South Vietnamese society, and might well have overpowered the government at some point, with support from North Vietnam, regardless of whether Diem and his brother remained in power to organize suppression efforts.[17] Moreover, we must ask ourselves whether it is reasonable to assume, as Moyar does, that an increase in political dissent and a corresponding decrease in social order following a period of reform reflects Vietnam's unique political tradition, or even Asian culture more generally. This contention loses its bite when you consider similar phenomena that took place in Soviet bloc countries such as Hungary, Poland, and Czechoslovakia during the Cold War, and indeed the entire process by which the Soviet bloc crumbled in 1989. Historical cases such as these demonstrate that political reform programs involving increased "toleration and conciliation of opposition groups" frequently lead to challenges to the status quo and chaos that might be characterized as political disintegration. To take this chaos as evidence that dictatorship was the only viable option in a given society, and therefore a highly desirable one, is a logical fallacy. Arguing that Vietnamese people, by dint of their traditions, required dictatorial leadership is at best a reassertion of the white man's burden used to justify European colonialism and the United States' related doctrine of Manifest Destiny.

The tendency among U.S. officials to deem other peoples culturally and politically unprepared for or incompatible with democratic government, and thereby more responsive to force than civil liberty and political inclusion, was nothing new in the 1950s and was not applied uniquely to Asia, much less Vietnam. Historian David Schmitz has identified a consistent pattern in twentieth-century U.S. foreign policy of support for right-wing dictatorships throughout the globe as a means of promoting political stability and combating the allure of communism in places that were destabilized by the century's geopolitical tumult. This pattern emerged in the 1920s and intensified with the onset of the Cold War in the mid-1940s. Schmitz argues that, throughout the twentieth century, American policymakers, casting their support for right-wing dictators as the lesser of two evils, developed rhetorical justifications "based on a paternalistic racism that categorized non-Western European peoples as inferior, vulnerable to radical ideas and solutions, and, therefore, in need of a firm government to maintain order."[18] U.S. officials applied this assessment indiscriminately across the globe without full consideration for the nuanced political traditions and circumstances at work within individual countries, Vietnam included. As Schmitz puts it, "Policymakers viewed and understood Vietnam primarily as a symbol of the Cold War, not as a real and distinct place with a history and people who were acting on their own local needs and desires."[19]

Recent studies by Mark Bradley, Seth Jacobs, and others on Americans' mid-twentieth-century perceptions of the Vietnamese people have ably demonstrated that the broad pattern of justifying support for dictatorships in the racialized terms that Schmitz identifies was indeed a critical factor in U.S. policymaking towards Vietnam. In his work on Vietnamese and Americans' mutual perceptions between 1919 and 1950, Mark Bradley notes, "American diplomatic reporting was refracted through the prism of unfavorable assumptions about the Vietnamese and the French that denied any real agency to the Vietnamese."[20] Reportage literature published in the United States during the Great Depression cast Vietnamese people as "primitive," "lazy," "cowardly," "vain," "dishonest," "unclean," and "somnolent," all of which helped explain why "expressions of Vietnamese nationalism were dismissed as the work of external, often Soviet, agents."[21] Bradley notes that American assumptions about the unfamiliar Vietnamese people were based not on first-hand observation or cultural study, but almost exclusively upon the writings of French scholars, colonial officials, and journalists.[22] And those French figures viewed the people of Vietnam through the very particular lens of their colonial project. American commentators who derided the Vietnamese as racially inferior drew upon environmental theories of racial inequality that came in vogue to explain the supposed deficiencies of non-white people in the interwar years—not coincidentally the same years in which the United States inaugurated its consistent pattern of support for right-wing dictatorships. Bradley argues that this early, racialized reporting provided the framework for U.S. officials' ongoing "unfavorable assumption of the Vietnamese capacity for self-government."[23]

Seth Jacobs, in his work on the early years of Ngo Dinh Diem's administration, builds upon Bradley's research to argue that the men in Eisenhower's administration who designed America's policy of support for Diem, "grew up in a culture shaped by more than a century of stereotypical depictions about Asians, and when they looked at Vietnam in the 1950s, they saw what their background had conditioned them to see."[24] What they saw was a people unprepared for self-government and in need of a strong dictator to save them from themselves. In the mid-twentieth century, social scientists updated this racialized perception, predicated on older justifications for Western colonialism and Manifest Destiny, into an ideological framework known as modernization theory. According to Jacobs, modernization theory "portrayed nonwhite people as primitive, untutored in the ways of democracy, and incapable of uplifting themselves without the help of a Western mentor."[25] Historian Michael Latham argues, "Because modernizers typically evaluated foreign, 'undeveloped' societies almost entirely in terms of their relative position on a unitary, abstract scale of progress, they frequently paid little attention to specific historical conditions or distinct cultural features."[26] Modernization theory, with its inherent assumptions about racial and cultural hierarchies, and its universal predictions about political and economic development, seemed to absolve American officials of the responsibility to formulate a policy suited to Vietnam's unique political environment. It enabled them to accept Diem's oppressive government as a necessary step on the way to political maturity and democratic self-government. As Jacobs writes,

"American racism explained away his more disturbing traits—paranoia, violent temper, and vainglory—as being customary in Asia."[27] Meanwhile, despite their own ignorance of and inattention towards Vietnamese tradition and culture beyond superficial, second-hand stereotypes inherited from the French, Diem's supporters in the United States often silenced those who criticized him for his violations of human rights by accusing them of being insensitive to Asian ways of thinking.[28] Moyar's conclusions about Diem's popularity and success seem to rest on the same patterns of thinking as those held by American policymakers in the mid-twentieth century, and he poses no new evidence to suggest that they are any less problematic than Schmitz, Bradley, Jacobs, Latham, and others claim.

Historical scholarship on Vietnamese culture and politics during the colonial and wartime periods is just beginning to emerge and remains sparse, especially compared to the enormous body of literature on the American side of the war. Nonetheless, extant literature suggests that Vietnamese culture at large and the South Vietnamese political sphere in particular was much more complex than Moyar claims. As Moyar suggests, there is ample historical evidence to support the claim that Vietnamese political customs and sensibilities operated quite differently from the liberal democratic traditions embraced by the post-Enlightenment West.[29] But there is also abundant evidence that Vietnamese anti-colonialists in the first half of the twentieth century not only studied Western political thought, but also infused peasant-centered movements with those ideas in ways that subtly but significantly revised peasants' and villagers' attitudes towards and expectations of their leaders.[30] As anti-colonial figures sought to build grassroots support for competing movements against French colonial rule, they devised political programs that appealed to Vietnamese traditions while also incorporating foreign ideas about modernization and representative government.[31] This process not only spread the influence of Western political thought among the peasantry, but it also generated competing loyalties to groups like the Viet Minh, the Vietnam Quoc Dan Dang (V.N.Q.D.D.), the Hoa Hao, and the Cao Dai, to name some of the most influential nationalist organizations.[32]

By the time Diem came to power, he faced a country transformed by the colonial and revolutionary experience that was no longer "traditional," nor was it fully remade by modernizing ideas from the West. Below the seventeenth parallel, he confronted a regionally divided countryside fraught with mixed loyalties, and he contended with an ever-present grassroots communist movement that disputed his claims to legitimacy from the outset. Recent scholarship on Diem's own attempts at nation-building reveal his own awareness of the fact that a well-run military and police force capable of suppressing political opponents alone would not be sufficient to establish his legitimacy. Rather, as Matthew Masur argues, Diem sought to "appropriate the historical narrative of Vietnam's long resistance to outside invaders," and to establish his government as the entity most capable of representing the country's past while modernizing it into a strong and independent state for the future.[33] Although Diem certainly convinced a small minority of South Vietnamese constituents of his legitimacy in these terms, his efforts at cultural nation-building were far less successful than his program of institution-building, especially with regards to the military and police forces.[34]

In sum, historians are beginning to uncover the complexity of Vietnamese society during the years of U.S. involvement, but we still have much to learn. What we do know belies the simplified image of Vietnamese "masses" in need of a strong-man dictator that Moyar depicts. This undermines his core argument that there was a triumph to forsake in Vietnam in the final days of Diem's life. Moyar's insistence that Diem was a legitimate and effective leader rests on the assumption that the Vietnamese people would and did lend their allegiance to him who forced them into line, and the literature discussed here provides ample cause to question that premise. With the benefit of Vietnamese archives and published materials, historians are now well positioned to improve our understanding of the multiple Vietnamese sides of this story. While fleshing out the complexities of Vietnamese history during this critical period poses no small challenge, it is incumbent upon historians to meet it in order to determine the true significance of American involvement in Vietnam to both Vietnamese and American history.

Notes

1. See Nicola Cooper, *France in Indochina: Colonial Encounters* (Oxford: Berg, 2001); Robert Young, *White Mythologies: Writing History and the West* (New York: Routledge, 1990).
2. Mark Moyar, *Triumph Forsaken: The Vietnam War, 1954–1965* (Cambridge: Cambridge University Press, 2006), xiv; Moyar cites Diem's 98.2 percent victory over Chief of State Bao Dai in 1955 as evidence for "the people's lack of interest in democratic procedures and their willingness to follow the dictates of government" (55). For another view, see Jessica M. Chapman, "Staging Democracy: South Vietnam's 1955 Referendum to Depose Bao Dai," *Diplomatic History* 30, 4: 671–703.
3. Moyar, 58.
4. Moyar writes, "The Vietnamese tended to look favorably upon a government that suppressed public demonstrations, so long as they were not among the demonstrators and the crackdowns were carried out effectively" (216).
5. Sophie Quinn Judge, "Review of Mark Moyar, *Triumph Forsaken: The Vietnam War, 1954–1965*" in the *Journal of Contemporary History* 44 (2009), 175.
6. Stueck *H-Diplo* review, July 2, 2002, 5.
7. Edward Miller, "War Stories: The Taylor–Buzzanco Debate and How We Think about the Vietnam War," *Journal of Vietnamese Studies* 1: 1–2 (Fall 2006), 463–464; see also

Edward Garvey Miller, "Grand Designs: Vision, Power and Nation Building in America's Alliance with Ngo Dinh Diem, 1954–1960" (Ph.D. Dissertation, Harvard University, 2004).
8. Philip E. Catton, *Diem's Final Failure: Prelude to America's War in Vietnam* (Lawrence: University Press of Kansas, 2002), 3.
9. Fredrik Logevall, "Bringing in the 'Other Side': New Scholarship on the Vietnam Wars," *Journal of Cold War Studies* 3:3 (2001), 77–93). Since Logevall published this article, new scholarship based in Vietnamese sources has appeared, much of which is discussed here.
10. Moyar, 37.
11. Moyar, 40.
12. For example, Moyar cites as evidence for his position the following statement by Robert Thompson, of the British Advisory Mission to Diem, issued in October 1963: "Western thought is overly influenced by phrases such as 'lack of public support' which have little relevance in the Asian, still less the Vietnamese context. In my view, all this is wasteful and wishful thinking" (245); Moyar cites Diem's February 18, 1963, comment, "All the underdeveloped countries are under authoritarian or dictatorial regimes, which is a historical and general phenomenon having nothing to do with individuals or government and which corresponds to a historical need for centralization of power to wipe out the age-old poverty and humiliation of the people ... The governments which have tried to establish Western-style democracy from the top down in an underdeveloped country have all been liquidated by military coups d'état" (37, note 11). While this provides interesting evidence of Diem's own teleological view of history, and of his justifications for ruling South Vietnam as a dictatorship, it hardly proves that such a course was necessary or inevitable. To counter claims by Robert McNamara and others that "the United States suffered from an utter lack of expertise on Vietnam," Moyar points to General Samuel T. Williams, Kenneth T. Young, Sterling Cottrell, Williams Colby, Theodore Heavner, Fredrik. E. Nolting, General Paul Harkins, and John H. Richardson (38, note 13). However, he does not account for the fact that these individuals gained their understanding of Vietnamese society during the course of their efforts to preserve Ngo Dinh Diem's government and with it a non-communist South Vietnam. This no doubt colored their understanding of Vietnam and their perceptions should be re-evaluated in light of additional evidence from the wide variety of Vietnamese perspectives represented during the 1950s and 1960s. While Moyar does employ some primary and secondary Vietnamese sources in translation for this book, he cites none of them to support his reading of Vietnamese culture.
13. Moyar, 428, notes 9 and 11.
14. Moyar, 36–37.
15. Moyar, 58.
16. Moyar 37.
17. See James C. Scott, *Domination and the Art of Resistance: Hidden Transcripts* (New Haven: Yale University Press, 1990). Scott, based on comparisons between structurally oppressed groups such as slaves, serfs, the colonized, and untouchables, argues that the powerless often feign deference in public out of necessity while working under the surface to criticize, resist, and in many cases subvert existing power structures. Their external deference, then, cannot be construed as support for and approval of those who hold power. For evidence of widespread dissatisfaction amongst South Vietnamese people with Ngo Dinh Diem's political oppression and land reform policies, and the communists' ability to capitalize on that dissatisfaction to build support for their revolutionary aims in the South, see Carlyle A. Thayer, *War by Other Means: National Liberation and Revolution in Vietnam 1054–60* (Sydney: Allen & Unwin, 1989); David W.P. Elliott, *The Vietnamese War: Revolution and Social Change in the Mekong Delta 1930–1975* (Armonk, NY: M.E. Sharpe, 2003); Jeffrey Race, *War Comes to Long An: Revolutionary Conflict in a Vietnamese Province* (Berkeley: University of California

Press, 1972); Catton, *Diem's Final Failure*; Truong Nhu Tang, *A Viet Cong Memoir: An Inside Account of the Vietnam War and its Aftermath* (New York: Vintage Books, 1985); David Lan Pham, *Two Hamlets in Nam Bo: Memoirs of Life in Vietnam* (London: McFarland, 2000).
18. David F. Schmitz, *Thank God they're on our Side: The United States and Right Wing Dictatorships, 1921–1965* (Chapel Hill: University of North Carolina Press, 1999), 5.
19. Schmitz, 209.
20. Mark Philip Bradley, *Imagining Vietnam and America: The Making of Postcolonial Vietnam, 1919–1950* (Chapel Hill: University of North Carolina Press, 2000), 185.
21. Bradley, 46.
22. Bradley, 47.
23. Bradley, 185.
24. Seth Jacobs, 14.
25. Jacobs, 94; see also Michael E. Latham, *Modernization as Ideology: American Social Science and "Nation Building" in the Kennedy Era* (Chapel Hill: University of North Carolina Press, 2000). Latham writes, "Nation building in Vietnam, official and public sources claimed, would inspire a primitive people to and bring out the best of the United States in the process ... The Strategic Hamlet program revised older ideologies of imperialism and Manifest Destiny to suit the demands of the Cold War" (153).
26. Latham, 213.
27. Jacobs, 15.
28. Jacobs, 16.
29. For sources that emphasize the traditional Vietnamese penchant for unanimity in politics, and the tendency to follow based on loyalty and duty rather than the "right to decide" between competing political platforms, see Frances FitzGerald, *Fire in the Lake: The Vietnamese and the Americans in Vietnam* (New York: Vintage Books, 1972); John T. McAlister, Jr. and Paul Mus, *The Vietnamese and Their Revolution* (New York: Harper and Row Publishers, 1970).
30. See David G. Marr, *Vietnamese Anticolonialism, 1885–1925* (Berkeley: University of California Press, 1971). Marr has demonstrated the arduous process by which anticolonial figures like Phan Boi Chau, Phan Chu Trinh, and their followers disseminated their arguments to villagers across Vietnam and, by 1945, gained widespread support for their goal of expelling the French oppressor and establishing an independent Vietnamese state using ideas borrowed from the West. See also William J. Duiker, *The Rise of Nationalism in Vietnam, 1900–1941* (Ithaca: Cornell University Press, 1976); William J. Duiker, *The Communist Road to Power in Vietnam* (Boulder, CO: Westview Press, 1981).
31. See David G. Marr, *Vietnamese Tradition on Trial, 1920–1954* (Berkeley: University of California Press, 1984); Shawn Fredrick McHale, *Print and Power: Confucianism, Communism, and Buddhism in the Making of Modern Vietnam* (Honolulu: University of Hawaii Press, 2004). On the role of the colonial prison system in spreading anticolonial ideas, see Peter Zinoman, *The Colonial Bastille: A History of Imprisonment in Vietnam, 1862–1940* (Berkeley: University of California Press, 2001).
32. See Hue-Tam Ho-Tai, *Millenarianism and Peasant Politics in Vietnam* (Boston: Harvard University Press, 1983); Hue-Tam Ho-Tai, *Radicalism and the Origins of the Vietnamese Revolution* (Boston: Harvard University Press, 1992); Neil L. Jameson, *Understanding Vietnam* (Berkeley: University of California Press, 1995); Jayne Susan Werner, *Peasant Politics and Religious Sectarianism: Peasant and Priest in the Cao Dai in Vietnam* (New Haven: Yale University Southeast Asia Studies, 1981).
33. Matthew Masur, "Exhibiting Signs of Resistance: South Vietnam's Struggle for Legitimacy, 1954–1960," *Diplomatic History* 33:2 (April 2009), 294; see also Matthew B. Masur, "Hearts and Minds: Cultural Nation Building in South Vietnam, 1954–1963" (Ph.D. Dissertation, Ohio State University, 2004); Jessica M. Chapman, "Debating the Will of Heaven: South Vietnamese Politics and Nationalism in International

Perspective, 1953–1956" (Ph.D. Dissertation, University of California at Santa Barbara, 2006); Edward Miller, "Grand Designs."
34. Even joint U.S.–R.V.N. institution-building projects were limited in their successes. See Robert K. Brigham, *ARVN: Life and Death in the South Vietnamese Army* (Lawrence: University Press of Kansas, 2006); James Carter, *Inventing Vietnam: The United States and State Building, 1954–1968* (Cambridge: Cambridge University Press, 2008).

CHAPTER 11
Triumph Forsaken as Military History

ANDREW J. BIRTLE

In 2006, Dr. Mark Moyar unveiled a fresh interpretation of the Vietnam War with the publication of *Triumph Forsaken, The Vietnam War, 1954–1965*, in which he argued that South Vietnamese President Ngo Dinh Diem was winning the battle against the Viet Cong until the United States undermined the war effort by engineering his overthrow. Three years later, Dr. John Prados rejected the "fevered conjecture that Diem could have won the war," and reasserted the traditional view of the Diem years as ones of failure, in *Vietnam, The History of an Unwinnable War, 1945–1975*.[1] In the battle of the book titles, who is right? Was triumph forsaken, or was the war truly unwinnable? In this essay, I will shed light on part of this question by examining some of the military aspects of the Diem years. I will focus on two issues, the organization of South Vietnam's military forces, and the performance of those forces in the field.

Organization and Training

"The most valid criticism of the [South Vietnamese] Army . . . was that it was overly conventional in its organization, equipment, and tactics." So wrote the commander of the U.S. Military Assistance Command, Vietnam (M.A.C.V.), General William C. Westmoreland, about the army he found when he arrived in Vietnam in 1964.[2] Other prominent U.S. officials shared this sentiment, as have many historians and some Vietnamese veterans, who have asserted that the United States set Vietnam up for failure by organizing and training Saigon's army for conventional rather than for counterguerrilla warfare.³ Moyar joins George C. Herring in postulating that much of this criticism is exaggerated and unfair, and I agree.⁴

In 1958, one of America's leading authorities on counterinsurgency, Colonel Edward G. Lansdale, dismissed the "wrong war" thesis on the grounds that the threat from North Vietnam necessitated that the United States prepare the South Vietnamese Army for conventional warfare.⁵ Just like North Korea during the Korean War, North Vietnam was willing to employ any means to conquer the South, and in the late 1950s, it set out to build a large conventional army for just this purpose. The North Vietnamese Army was not only larger than the South's, but its divisions were as heavily armed as Southern divisions, a situation that remained true throughout the period covered by *Triumph Forsaken*. The North's deployment of these conventional forces into the South beginning in 1964, and its eventual use of tanks and heavy artillery that were often more powerful and more numerous than those possessed by South Vietnam demonstrated the correctness of Lansdale's analysis.⁶

The "wrong war" thesis reflects a common misperception that conventional forces cannot defeat guerrillas. This view overlooks the fact that, throughout history, conventional forces have defeated insurgencies, including those that were contemporaneous with the Indochina War in places such as Greece, Korea, the Philippines, and Malaya. In Vietnam, U.S. advisors generally found that "conventional" tactics and procedures were readily adaptable to the conflict.⁷ Anyone doubting the utility of "conventional" training need look no further than the Viet Cong, whose success was based largely on the professionalism provided by cadre trained by the North Vietnamese Army. The thoroughly "conventional" nature of Viet Cong military administration, battle plans, and after-action reports would have made instructors at Forts Benning or Leavenworth beam in admiration. Organizational factors can facilitate or hinder operations, but the key factor to success is what one does with the forces that one has. An accurate appraisal of the nature of the conflict and the enemy, the intelligent adaptation of "conventional" structures and techniques to the situation, flexibility, and leadership—these are, and were, far more important than organizational structure per se in producing an effective counterguerrilla force.

Although the United States fashioned the Vietnamese military establishment in its own image, it was not unmindful of the need to adapt American forms to Vietnam's needs. "Don't try to do everything the Western way," recommended one advisor to his colleagues, advice that the Military Assistance Advisory Group (M.A.A.G.) officially embraced and reiterated frequently.⁸ It is worth noting that the first force structure designed by M.A.A.G. was decidedly light and largely tailored for providing internal security. As the internal security situation seemed to stabilize and the North's army grew, M.A.A.G. Chief Lieutenant General Samuel T. Williams (1955–1960) reorganized the army along more "conventional" lines in 1958.[9] It nonetheless remained a light infantry force devoid of the numbers and types of vehicles, tanks, and artillery found in U.S. divisions. There was nothing inherent in this structure that would make it incapable of fighting guerrillas. True, the bulk of U.S. instruction during the 1950s was "conventional," but much of that advice pertained to matters of administration, logistics, communications, and other areas that any newly created army needs if it is to be an effective organization. With regard to tactics, training focused on basics that were largely applicable to any form of warfare. That the South Vietnamese Army of the late 1950s and early 1960s was no more effective at conventional operations than it was at unconventional ones adds further doubt over the alleged harmful effects of early U.S. training. Building an army from scratch is a daunting task under the best of circumstances and regardless of the mission(s) for which it is intended. Unfortunately, conditions in Vietnam were far from ideal. Given the situation, I doubt the South Vietnamese Army would have performed any more effectively against the insurgency than it would have if the advisory group had designed it purely for unconventional warfare—a luxury that the allies did not have.

One reason why U.S. military advisors oriented the South Vietnamese Army primarily for "conventional" warfare was the existence of police and paramilitary forces whose sole mission was internal security. M.A.A.G. chiefs Williams and Lieutenant General Lionel C. McGarr (1960–1962) fully supported the organization and training of these forces, but as Moyar points out, they were thwarted by bureaucratic obstacles, funding constraints, and by U.S. Ambassador Elbridge Durbrow's stubborn refusal to prepare these elements for a counterinsurgency—as opposed to a peacetime—environment. Durbrow, the U.S. Agency for International Development, and Michigan State University, to which the United States entrusted the initial training of the police and Civil Guard, bear responsibility for the unpreparedness of South Vietnam's front-line internal security forces at the outbreak of active rebellion in 1959–1960.[10]

Another common yet incorrect assumption of the "wrong war" school is that the military advisory group completely ignored counterinsurgency issues in the 1950s and early 1960s. As Moyar indicates, General Williams had given Diem sound counterinsurgency advice based on U.S. Army doctrine as early as December 1955. Subsequently, Williams made information on counterguerrilla warfare available on a number of occasions, and both he and McGarr amplified this advice after the outbreak of open insurrection in 1960. By 1962, the advisory group had recast the

South Vietnamese Army's training program to focus heavily on counter-guerrilla warfare.[11]

Representative of the advice that the U.S. Army gave the South Vietnamese was M.A.A.G.'s *Tactics and Techniques of Counter-Insurgent Operations*. First published in March 1961 and updated periodically thereafter, it was the bible for U.S. advisors. The manual asserted that "the fundamental factor in meeting and defeating the ... Communist insurgency is the absolute necessity to separate the people from the Viet Cong."[12] Protecting the population from the guerrillas through area security measures was essential to this task, but so too were political initiatives, for "there is seldom a 'purely military' answer to the domestic unrest in which guerrilla action flourishes, and without eradication of the *cause*, guerrilla actions historically drag on for years."[13] "The solution," the manual instructed,

> ... lies in the coordinated use of additional military, political, social, economic and psychological power or actions with the objective of *truly* winning over and motivating the population down to the hamlet level with a *common purpose*—thereby gaining their active support ... not merely apathetic acquiescence or neutrality. For the assistance and cooperation of the population is as *necessary* to overall success against the Communist threat as is breath of life itself.[14]

Recognizing that it was engaged in a politico-military struggle, M.A.A.G. became an early champion of integrated, multiagency actions based on comprehensive, well-coordinated politico-military plans. Both McGarr and subsequent M.A.C.V. chiefs Generals Paul D. Harkins (1962–1964) and William C. Westmoreland (1964–1968) closely adhered to this approach. Unfortunately, both the U.S. and Vietnamese governments had significant difficulty achieving the necessary integration. In the meantime, by 1962, M.A.A.G., as well as many civilian observers, had come to the conclusion that the insurgency had reached the point at which force needed to take precedence over the other tools in the counterinsurgent's kit bag, for without security, meaningful progress was unlikely on the political and socio-economic fronts.[15] Nevertheless, the military advisory group never lost sight of the importance of nonmilitary factors, and every M.A.A.G. and M.A.C.V. chief stressed the necessity of counterinfrastructure, administrative, psychological, public relations, and civic actions through all phases of military operations, as well as the desirability of implementing longer-ranged socio-economic and political initiatives to solidify the gains made on the battlefield.[16]

Operationally, *Tactics and Techniques* prescribed the "progressive pacification of selected areas," a concept derived from the French "oil spot" (*tache d'huile*) method in which government forces radiated out from secure to insecure areas. The Army based many of the techniques of such area security campaigns—dubbed "clear and hold" operations—on methods the British used in Malaya. Working in close conjunction with civil authorities, government forces would secure the population, preventing it from helping the guerrillas or from being intimidated by them. While militiamen guarded the villages, small-unit patrols would scour the area day and night backed by more heavily armed mobile reaction forces that could be called in when the patrols detected the enemy—a method McGarr termed "net and spear" tactics.[17] Small hunter-killer groups would keep the enemy on the move, while larger formations would perform "search and clear" operations to destroy known enemy bases and major units. Once an area was secured, officials would raise local defense forces, reinstitute government administration, and initiate beneficial socioeconomic programs as the regular forces moved on to repeat the process in another area. Noting that "the only orthodoxy is success," the manual stressed the need for experimentation, warning soldiers that they must avoid the "mental crutch" of sticking to the traditional prescriptions found in either conventional or unconventional warfare doctrine.[18]

The guidance found in *Tactics and Techniques* formed the basis of U.S. military advice from 1961 to 1965. M.A.A.G. advisors relayed this doctrine to South Vietnamese soldiers through countless documents, training courses, and conversations with counterparts. Of course not all advisors were adept at adjusting to Vietnam conditions. Part of the reason for this was that few advisors in the early 1960s had had any experience in counterguerrilla warfare before deploying to Vietnam. Moreover, the Army had only begun to introduce counterinsurgency into its educational and training system in 1961. Nevertheless, advisors at all levels generally understood the basic thrust of U.S. Army counterinsurgency doctrine and attempted to implement it. The comment that journalist David Halberstam made about the M.A.A.G. personnel he met in I Corps in the fall of 1962 was equally applicable to U.S. soldiers throughout the country: "The advisers are aware that the primary job in winning this war is to win the support of the peasants and that such support will only come if the peasants believe the government will protect them against the Vietcong."[19]

Performance in the Field

If U.S. soldiers understood the nature of the conflict and provided appropriate advice, whence did the South Vietnamese Army's well-known dysfunctional behavior stem? The answer lay with the Vietnamese themselves. As the Australian counterinsurgency advisor to M.A.A.G.,

Colonel Francis P. "Ted" Serong, put it, the root of the problem was not the nature of U.S. advice, but of getting South Vietnamese officers "off their collective bottoms."[20]

There were many legitimate reasons for the shortcomings exhibited by the South Vietnamese Army in the early 1960s. Moyar notes that Saigon's security forces were too small and woefully understaffed. Junior officers and noncommissioned officers were in such short supply as to seriously disrupt almost any military organization.[21] Just as important as the inevitable growing pains, however, was the fact that the Vietnamese were not anxious pupils who hung on their mentor's every word. Rather, they exhibited a formidable talent for ignoring, twisting, or miscarrying U.S. advice in virtually every area of endeavor, from organization, administration, and training to command and control, leadership, soldier welfare, civil affairs, and pacification.

Sometimes, resistance to U.S. advice was justified—after all, the Vietnamese had extensive experience in irregular warfare since 1945 and knew both the enemy and their own people far better than Americans. U.S. mistakes, such as the one Lieutenant Colonel John Paul Vann made when he ordered helicopters to land too close to enemy lines at Ap Bac, contributed to battlefield defeats and further eroded Vietnamese confidence in their mentors.[22] All too often, however, Vietnamese resistance stemmed from institutional malaise and personal insecurity, incompetence, or indifference. Sensitivity to foreign interference born from national pride, the politicization of the officer corps, and a military culture that discouraged field duty, aggressiveness, and initiative likewise contributed to the uneven performance of the South Vietnamese Army. Ten years of assistance by thousands of U.S. personnel was only partially effective in overcoming these obstacles prior to 1965.

The realm of tactics provides an example of how the South Vietnamese Army resisted U.S. advice. Many authors have assumed that the South Vietnamese fought the way they did—using large formations to make what often turned out to be overly grandiose, but often fruitless, sweeps of the countryside—because U.S. soldiers told them to do so.[23] This assumption overlooks Vietnamese autonomy. First, M.A.A.G. had virtually no influence over Vietnamese field operations during the early years. It functioned mostly at the upper administrative level, had no clear operational authority, and had a mere handful of men in the field—men whom Vietnamese commanders generally ignored. Not until 1962, when President John F. Kennedy put advisors into Vietnamese battalions and provided U.S. aviation support, did the United States begin to exercise direct influence over field operations. Even then, advisory reports indicate that Vietnamese commanders routinely ignored U.S. advice, withheld information, or executed operations with little or no input from their American counterparts.[24] In units in which relations between the senior Vietnamese and American officer were good, consultation was frequent and in-depth, yet commanders still tended to act without, or in disregard of, U.S. advice. If relations were less than ideal, the commander might not inform his counterpart about an operation until the night before it was scheduled to begin. The best advisors could do at that point was to propose marginal fixes to plans they believed were flawed.

U.S. advisers believed that the tenacious affinity that Vietnamese commanders exhibited for large-unit sweeps stemmed from their desire to minimize casualties, to maximize their control over subordinates, and last but not least, from their initial training by the French. If the last factor was true, it was not unusual, for U.S. advisory efforts worldwide have found that soldiers who have had prior military experience are often the most difficult to influence. Until a younger generation could rise to command, the advisory group had no choice but to work with individuals who, in the words of M.A.A.G. Chief Major General Charles J. Timmes (1962–1964) "were fixated on 'big tactics,'" and who did not understand or show much interest in the pacification programs pushed by the military advisory group.[25]

The result of this predicament was that frustration became the most common emotion experienced by U.S. advisors.[26] This is not to say that the U.S. government's efforts were problem-free. Nor should we overlook the fact that South Vietnam's Army contained many talented and dedicated officers and an even larger number of courageous rank-and-file soldiers. As in any army, there were good units and bad units, effective leaders and ineffective ones. Generally speaking, however, during the 1950s and early 1960s, U.S. advisors and Vietnamese reformers alike found themselves caught in a web created by weaknesses in Vietnam's political, social, and military culture, not to mention the unfavorable situation in which the country found itself.

The Question of Progress

Given what has been written up to this point, what are we to make of Moyar's claim that the South Vietnamese Army was not only making progress during the Diem years, but was also actually winning the war? Before going further, we should acknowledge that it is always difficult to judge progress in frontless wars, and Vietnam was no exception. Guerrilla conflicts are heavily influenced by local factors, so that it is frequently true that, at any given time, a war might be going well in one region and poorly in another. Drawing conclusions from just one or two geographical areas—as Moyar argues some U.S. officials did in 1963—can easily yield a skewed view.[27] Finally, the documentary record, then and now, is often incomplete and contradictory, making a definitive judgment difficult.

That U.S. soldiers in 1964 and 1965 complained about many of the same institutional, operational, and tactical shortcomings noted by advisors in 1960 and 1961 weakens Moyar's position.[28] So too does the fact that the communists shared American perceptions. According to a Central Office for South Vietnam (C.O.S.V.N.) document prepared in 1964 entitled "Preliminary Study of RVNAF Combat Potential up to March 1964," enemy analysts identified many of the same weaknesses that M.A.A.G. had been harping about for years: inadequate troop numbers; overdispersion; cumbersome operations; low morale; passivity; inflexibility; weak leadership; and a reluctance to operate at night. C.O.S.V.N. also observed that South Vietnamese regulars had become so "bogged down in their pacification missions" that they had difficulty mounting effective offensive actions. The enemy added, however, a shortcoming that heretofore had not been on M.A.A.G.'s list of complaints—"weak in firepower." Thanks to the infusion of modern arms from the North, by 1964, C.O.S.V.N. could report that "the equipment of an enemy infantry platoon is less than that of our infantry platoons."[29] This development, when combined with the South's perennial shortcomings and the commitment of North Vietnamese conventional combat formations, created a truly perilous situation for the government by early 1965.

The continuity in institutional shortcomings, when combined with an ample number of battlefield setbacks, leads one to question Moyar's assertion that, in 1962, the South Vietnamese began "a steady ascent that was to continue for the remainder of Diem's time in office."[30] On the other hand, reports from U.S. military advisors at all levels in 1962 do indeed contain stories of battles won and positive changes made. That these same reports also contain admissions of lost engagements and unsatisfactory performance indicate that their authors were neither unrealistic nor biased in their reporting. Some progress, then, was real. If *Triumph Forsaken* paints too rosy a picture, claims by historians such as John M. Newman that the South Vietnamese were actually losing the war in 1962 and that M.A.C.V. deliberately and successfully deceived Washington officials about the true state of affairs do not bear up against the weight of evidence.[31] As Moyar points out, Harkins' self-confessed optimism stemmed from a desire to motivate rather than to deceive, and there is plenty of evidence that officials in Washington and Saigon had a fairly good understanding of the South's many shortcomings despite Harkin's alleged obfuscation.[32] Many people and institutions provided information and analysis, and while officials often disagreed over the extent to which forward momentum had occurred, few doubted by the end of 1962 that there had been some progress. Most, in fact, expressed cautious optimism about the future. Victory was not yet in sight, but the specter of imminent defeat likewise no longer clouded most officials' vision.[33]

Triumph Forsaken cites enemy documents to confirm the perception of progress among U.S. officials in 1962.[34] More evidence could be added. For example, according to a C.O.S.V.N. report written in 1964, South Vietnamese military operations in 1962 had led to "heavy attrition" in some units and "many awkward difficulties."[35] Communist authorities conceded that they had lost control of significant numbers of people living in both the highlands and along South Vietnam's northern and central coasts. Further south, the situation was just as serious, as a combination of government military operations, population resettlement, and the spread of strategic hamlets had begun to test the insurgents' hold on the countryside, with C.O.S.V.N. reporting that "nearly all the lowland liberated areas suffered some occupation, and some areas were narrowed and nearly lost."[36] A communist history about the war in the upper Delta likewise observed,

> The situation was developing too quickly for us ... in many aspects of operations our capabilities had not kept up with the requirements for this war. Our armed forces, and especially our massed, full-time units at the province level and main force units at the region level, were still too small, were poorly equipped, had not been adequately trained to meet the requirements of this new type of war, and had not been prepared to deal with the modern equipment, tactics (helicopter assault operations, armored personnel carrier operations, "casting the net and then throwing the spear," and rapid mobility of the U.S.—puppet forces).[37]

During the first half of 1963, many allied officials continued to report positive developments, and communist sources once again corroborate this impression.[38] C.O.S.V.N., for example, reported that "the enemy used military forces to carry out attacks to annihilate the revolutionary armed forces while fully promoting the pacification plan on a large scale."[39] It further conceded that the Strategic Hamlet program "was able to control the masses in some" areas, and that "the mass movement was weak in many locations. The more the enemy concentrated his efforts to vigorously expand the strategic hamlets and resettlement in all areas, the more difficulties the movement encountered and in some locations by May 1963, the situation had still not favorably changed."[40] In fact, in many places, the situation remained bleak for months thereafter. Thus the National Liberation Front in Lam Dong Province reported that the revolutionary movement could not gain traction because:

... the enemy pressed it by herding the people into strategic hamlets. From June 1963 to August 1963, our agents were annihilated in large number. The base area was harassed and the corridors widened. Cadre encountered many difficulties in their activities. The masses' movement was lowered. The forces suffered losses. The living was hard and food was insufficient. Pessimism spread in the ranks and among the people ... our cadre were afraid of enemy new tactics and did not believe that they can defeat the enemy.[41]

The Buddhist crisis and growing enemy activity clouded the picture in the fall, but Moyar is correct that the political storm that was about to engulf the Diem regime had little effect on the prosecution of the war in the field. According to the enemy, the government mounted over twice as many operations in 1963 than it had in 1961.[42] Even after the turmoil that occurred in the last months of 1963, C.O.S.V.N. reported:

the revolutionary base areas are not yet strong, the balance of forces has not yet tilted in a manner favorable to us, we have not yet fought battles inflicting heavy casualties on the enemy, and the enemy still continues to carry out large-scale and fierce sweep operations in an attempt to block the movement and annihilate the revolutionary forces.[43]

Not only did the Saigon government "still control thousands of strategic hamlets and dominate an entire one-half of the people of the South," but getting Vietnamese youth "to join the [insurgent] army, participate as guerrillas, carry out corvée labor, resist [government] conscription, and participate in combat was done with much difficulty."[44]

The status of South Vietnam's most important economic product—rice—supports the thesis that the South's fortunes did not truly begin to decline until after Diem's death. The following chart illustrates developments in South Vietnam's rice economy between 1959 and 1966. As can be seen, the amount of cultivated rice land under government control fell in 1960 when the insurgency erupted. Thereafter, it grew steadily. By 1962, South Vietnam had more rice land under cultivation than in 1959, the year before the insurgency had begun. The amount of land put into production under government control continued to expand through 1964. The reversal did not occur until 1965, and not until 1966 did the government have less land under cultivation than before the insurgency began. Paddy production showed similar trends, with production peaking in 1962 and 1963, before starting to decline in 1964. Finally, the chart indicates that South Vietnam was a net exporter of rice through the end of 1964. Thereafter it became one of the world's largest importers of rice.[45]

South Vietnamese Rice Production and Trade

Year	Cultivated Area (in 1,000 hectares)	Paddy Production (in 1,000 tons)	Rice Exports (in 1,000 tons)	Rice Imports (in 1,000 tons)
1959	2,400	5,092	249	4
1960	2,318	4,955	346	14
1961	2,353	4,607	156	2
1962	2,479	5,205	86	42
1963	2,538	5,327	338	0
1964	2,557	5,185	49	0
1965	2,429	4,822	0	130
1966	2,295	4,336	0	434

Since rice cultivation occurred in those parts of the country that were the most populated, the statistics provide insight into the state of population security. They support the argument that government security forces and the Strategic Hamlet program were making progress in 1962 and 1963, and that it was not until after Diem's demise that the situation took a serious turn for the worse.

Taking Stock

The dueling titles *Triumph Forsaken* and *Vietnam, The History of an Unwinnable War* stake out two extremes in Vietnam War historiography. As is often the case, the truth lies somewhere between these polar opposites. Moyar has done a service by bringing to our attention the fact that the South Vietnamese enjoyed some important successes in 1962 and 1963. Thanks in large part to U.S. assistance, South Vietnam stopped the hemorrhaging that had characterized 1960 and 1961 and began taking the war to the enemy. As the enemy himself concedes, the government's successes during the last two years of Diem's tenure were real and not the figment of Harkins' imagination, as Newman and others would have us believe.

Where *Triumph Forsaken* goes too far is in claiming that the South Vietnamese were actually winning the war in 1962 and 1963. The government was no longer losing, but progress was spotty, incremental, and easily reversible—facts that the book tends to gloss over. Many serious and deeply rooted obstacles remained, and there was no guarantee that Diem would have been able to overcome them had he lived. Moreover, as Army Chief of Staff General Earle G. Wheeler cautioned in January 1963, one should never forget that "the enemy has something to say about this."[46] And indeed he did. As the government increased its efforts, so did the communists, producing what the Central Intelligence Agency termed "a slowly escalating stalemate."[47] Ultimately, the answer to the question "who was winning in 1962–1963" is "no one." C.O.S.V.N.'s characterization of those years as being a "see-saw situation" is most apt.[48] Both sides enjoyed successes and suffered reverses, but the outcome by the time of Diem's death was still very much in doubt.

Moyar correctly notes that the deterioration experienced in South Vietnam's fortunes in 1964 and 1965 were due to the turmoil that descended over the government after Diem's death and the North's decision to exploit that turmoil by escalating the conflict.[49] The fact that North Vietnamese policymakers specifically cited the opportunity created by Diem's death when they decided to escalate the war in December 1963 supports this view. The thesis that the South Vietnamese Army was holding its own during 1962 and 1963 is likewise bolstered by the fact that Northern leaders further justified their decision to shift to conventional warfare on the grounds that experience had shown that political agitation and guerrilla warfare were incapable of producing victory.[50] But the escalation that occurred in 1964 and 1965 was not simply the result either of the need to overcome the South's unexpectedly strong resistance or of the desire to exploit the opportunity provided by Diem's overthrow. Rather it was just one more step in the execution of North Vietnam's long-range plan to conquer the South. In 1961, the Politburo had decided to infiltrate 30,000–40,000 trained soldiers into South Vietnam by the end of 1963, with the goal of having ten to fifteen main force regiments in the South by the end of 1965.[51] By the time of Diem's death, the North had achieved the first goal and was well along toward meeting the second—an objective that it actually exceeded in 1965.[52] What the North might have done had Diem not been overthrown is impossible to say, but its determination to prosecute the war almost regardless of cost is not a matter of conjecture.

Perhaps a better title for Moyar's book than "Triumph Forsaken" would have been "Opportunity Lost," for while a proclamation of victory seems unwarranted, it seems equally speculative to conclude that the war was either lost or unwinnable by the time of Diem's removal. The deck may have been stacked against the South from the start, but human affairs are full of decisions that can shift events in a different direction. Moyar rightly highlights three strategic decisions made by President Kennedy and his successor, Lyndon B. Johnson, that made it very difficult for South Vietnam to preserve its independence.

The first major error was in allowing North Vietnam to continue to use Laos as an infiltration route. In 1961, the Joint Chiefs of Staff warned President Kennedy that South Vietnam would be in a strategically untenable situation if the communists were allowed to dominate southeastern Laos. Kennedy rejected their advice because he did not want to risk becoming embroiled in a ground war in Laos—an understandably unappealing prospect. But by failing to treat the conflict in South Vietnam as a regional phenomenon, Kennedy hammered a large nail into South Vietnam's coffin. President Johnson tried to negate the ill effects of this decision through bombing, but he never attempted to pull the nail out—something that could only be accomplished by troops on the ground. Consequently, the allies failed to isolate the battlefield, a key principle of both conventional and counterguerrilla warfare. Ironically, the counterinsurgency doctrine Kennedy so vigorously promoted during his presidency played a role in this fundamental error, for some civilian policymakers, such as the Director of the State Department's Bureau of Intelligence and Research, Roger Hilsman, justified their opposition to taking decisive action against Northern infiltration on the premise that counterinsurgency theory held that the key to resolving an insurgency was inside the affected country itself, in its villages and among its people, rather than along its borders or on the battlefield. In the case of Vietnam, the doctrinaire application of this theoretical principle proved disastrous.[53]

The second strategic error of the pre-1965 era was Kennedy's decision to support the overthrow of Diem. As I have indicated, the North's escalation of the war in 1964 was not simply a reaction to the opportunity presented by post-Diem instability. Yet that instability did severely undermine the South's efforts. Diem and his family were far from perfect, but they had held the state together. The sudden elimination of the Ngo family apparatus opened up a Pandora's Box of political intrigue that sent the government into a tail spin from which it nearly did not recover. As General Westmoreland observed, "none of our efforts had any chance of success in the periods during which the government was weak, divided, and thus ineffective."[54] Indeed, there is no better example of the importance of politics in war in general, and in counterinsurgency specifically, than the turmoil that roiled South Vietnam's political, military, and intelligence structures in 1964 and 1965. There were plenty of warnings that removing Diem would prove counterproductive, but the anti-Diem cabal in the administration blithely ignored them, encouraging the coup without having a plan for the installation of a more effective replacement. The elimination of Diem and the subsequent era of instability banged a second nail in the South Vietnam's coffin. Once again, counterinsurgency theory played a role in this error, for the doctrine held that political reform was the key to defeating an insurgency, and it was Diem's reluctance to embrace Western-style reforms that provided the primary rationale for the administration's support of the coup. Ironically, the change did not lead to the substantial enactment of any of the major political reforms that Americans somewhat erroneously believed were indispensible for victory.[55]

The final strategic error occurred at the end of the period covered in *Triumph Forsaken*, when President Johnson embraced the academic concepts of limited war and gradual escalation—concepts that ultimately proved bankrupt as war-fighting doctrine.[56] Together with the decisions to unseat Diem and to close neither North Vietnam's ports nor its access to the South via Laos, the United States had indeed gone far toward making the Vietnam War unwinnable. But none of these decisions was inevitable. A different action on any one of them might have altered the flow of historical events to produce a more favorable outcome for the allies. These truly were opportunities lost.

Notes

1. John Prados, *Vietnam, The History of an Unwinnable War, 1945–1975* (Lawrence: University Press of Kansas, 2009), 74.3.
2. C.I.N.C.P.A.C. and C.O.M.M.A.C.V., Report on the War in Vietnam (as of June 30, 1968), 210, Military History Institute (MHI), Carlisle Barracks, PA.
3. Memo, Major General E. L. Rowny for Deputy Chief of Staff for Military Operations, Jul. 30, 1963, sub: Debriefing of Officers Retuning from Field Assignments, 3, Center of Military History (C.M.H.), Washington, D.C.; Cao Van Vien and Dong Van Khuyen, *Reflections on the Vietnam War* (Washington, D.C.: U.S. Army Center of Military History, 1980), 10, 37; Tran Van Don, *Our Endless War* (San Rafael, CA: Presidio Press, 1978), 149–150; Department of Defense, *United States–Vietnam Relations* (Washington, D.C.: Government Printing Office, 1971), book 2, IV.A.4, 18–20, 24–31.
4. George C. Herring, *America's Longest War: The United States and Vietnam, 1950–1975* (New York: John Wiley, 1979), 58; Moyar, *Triumph Forsaken*, xv, 69, 100.
5. Questions and Answers, December 3, 1958, Edward G. Lansdale Papers, National Security Archives, George Washington University, Washington, D.C.
6. The Military History Institute of Vietnam, *Victory in Vietnam, The Official History of the People's Army of Vietnam, 1954–1975*, trans. Merle L. Pribbenow (Lawrence: University Press of Kansas, 2002), 28–29, 93–95; Martin Loicano, "Military and Political Roles of Weapons Systems in the Republic of Viet Nam Armed Forces, 1966–1972" (Ph.D. Dissertation, Cornell University, 2008).
7. Moyar, *Triumph Forsaken*, 70, 99–100.
8. Ralph W. Shelton, "Advice for Advisers," *Infantry* 54 (July–August 1964): 12 (quotation); Bryce Denno, "Advisor and Counterpart," *Army* 15 (July 1965): 28; Memo, Lt. Gen. Lionel C. McGarr, Ch. M.A.A.G. for M.A.A.G. Advisors, Nov. 10, 1960, sub: Information, Guidance and Instructions to M.A.A.G. Advisory Personnel, 2–3; Memo, McGarr for M.A.A.G. Advisors, Nov. 15, 1960, sub: Implementing Actions for Anti-Guerrilla Operations, 3–4. Both at C.M.H.
9. Ronald H. Spector, *Advice and Support, The Middle Years* (Washington, D.C.: U.S. Army Center of Military History, 1983), 296.
10. Moyar, *Triumph Forsaken*, xv, 69–70, 81, 91, 99, 101; Andrew J. Birtle, *U.S. Army Counterinsurgency and Contingency Operations Doctrine, 1942–1976* (Washington, D.C.: U.S. Army Center of Military History, 2006), 312–313.
11. Moyar, *Triumph Forsaken*, 69; Birtle, *Counterinsurgency Doctrine*, 308–314.
12. M.A.A.G., *Tactics and Techniques of Counter-Insurgent Operations*, Feb. 10, 1962, I-2, M.H.I. (hereafter cited as *Tactics and Techniques*).
13. Ibid., II-1.
14. Ibid., I-6.
15. Ibid., II-1.

16. Ibid., I-2, II-3, III-A-5, III-B-1, III-B-3, III-B-7, III-B-8, III-B-12, IV-C-13, IV-C-14, IV-D-2; "To Liberate from Oppression," *Time Magazine* 79 (May 1962): 28; *Foreign Relations of the United States, 1961–1963, Vol. II, Vietnam 1962*, 528–529 (hereafter cited as *F.R.U.S., Vietnam, 1962*); *Foreign Relations of the United States, 1961–1963, Vol. III, Vietnam, January–August 1963*, 39 (hereafter cited as *F.R.U.S., Vietnam, Jan.–Aug. 63*); Report on the War in Vietnam, 105; M.A.C.V. Directive 525–4, Sep. 17, 1965, sub: Tactics and Techniques for Employment of US Forces in the Republic of Vietnam, 1–2, History Files no. 1, William C. Westmoreland Papers, C.M.H.
17. Tactics and Techniques, II-2, II-12 (quotation), II-17, II-18, III-A-1–III-A-3, III-B-1–III-B-9, IV-F-5, V-H-2.
18. Ibid., I-2, II-D-1 (quotation).
19. *New York Times*, Sep. 23, 1962 (quotation), and Oct. 21, 1962; David Halberstam, Keynote Address, Vietnam and the Presidency Conference, JFK Presidential Library, March 2006; Forrest K. Kleinman, "Report from Vietnam," *Army* 13 (September 1962): 24, 31–32.
20. Report, Col. Francis P. Serong, Special Advisor to General Paul D. Harkins, C.O.M.U.S.-M.A.C.V., Oct. 1962, sub: Current Operations in South Vietnam, 47–50, 51 (quotation), C.M.H.
21. Moyar, *Triumph Forsaken*, 100.
22. Ibid., 195–196.
23. Prados, *Vietnam*, 70–71.
24. For a typical experience, see Martin J. Dockery, *Lost in Translation, Vietnam, A Combat Advisor's Story* (New York: Balantine Books, 2003).
25. Remarks by Lt. Gen. Lionel G. McGarr, Senior Advisors Conference, June 17, 1961, 8; Letter, McGarr to Maj. Gen. John J. Hennessy, Commandant, Command & General Staff College, Mar. 22, 1972; Interviews, Charles Von Luttichau, C.M.H. with Maj. Gen. Charles J. Timmes, former M.A.A.G. chief, 1962–1964, Apr. 27, 1967, Oct. 12 and 16, 1967 (quote). All at C.M.H. *F.R.U.S., Vietnam, 1962*, 531; Cao Van Vien et al., *The U.S. Adviser* (Washington, D.C.: U.S. Army Center of Military History, 1980), 73–74; Hoang Lung, *Strategy and Tactics* (Washington, D.C.: U.S. Army Center of Military History, 1980), 84–85.
26. Denno, "Advisor and Counterpart," 30.
27. Moyar, *Triumph Forsaken*, 248–253, 283.
28. For the continuity in complaints, see M.A.C.V. Command History, 1964, 121–122; Debriefing Report, Maj. Gen. Charles J. Timmes, Jun. 10, 1964; Report, Office of the Deputy Chief of Staff for Operations, Apr. 1, 1965, sub: Analysis of the Military Effort in South Vietnam, 22; message, Westmoreland to Wheeler, Sep. 6, 1964, Westmoreland Message Files, Jan. 1–Dec. 31, 1964; Complete Report to the Chief of Staff United States Army on the U.S.–G.V.N. Effort, Mar. 21, 64, A-4, C-1, D-1–D-9. All of the above at C.M.H. Memo, M.A.C.V. Military History Branch for Distribution, 1965, sub: Report on Interview Program of U.S. Army Advisors in Vietnam, 8–9, box 63, MACJ03, Military History Branch, Historians Background Material Files, RG 472, NARA.
29. Report, M.A.C.V., Sep. 9, 1964, sub: Analysis of V.C. Document entitled: Preliminary Study of RVNAF Combat Potential up to March 1964, 2, 3 (quotation), 6, C.M.H.
30. Moyar, *Triumph Forsaken*, 153.
31. John M. Newman, *JFK and Vietnam: A Deception, Intrigue, and Struggle for Power* (New York: Warner Books, 1992), 294, 300; Prados, *Vietnam*, 72.
32. Moyar, *Triumph Forsaken*, 167, 203–205; McNamara, *In Retrospect, The Tragedy and Lessons of Vietnam* (New York: Random House, 1995), 47–48; *F.R.U.S., Vietnam, 1962*, 627, 761; *F.R.U.S., Vietnam, Jan.–Aug. 63*, 70, 118, 121; "To Liberate from Oppression," *Time Magazine*, 79 (May 1962): 28.
33. For examples of appraisals of the situation at the end of 1962, see Memo, Senior Advisor III Corps for Ch. M.A.A.G., Jan. 23, 1963, sub: Information for Army Chief of Staff, 3; Memo, Senior Advisor II Corps for Ch. M.A.A.G., Jan. 22, 1963, sub: Signs of

Progress in the Vietnam Effort to Bring the Viet Cong Under Control. Both in MACJ03, Military History Branch, Policy and Precedent files, RG 472, NARA. Message, Saigon 597 to State, Dec. 15, 1962, sub: TF/Saigon Weekly Progress Report for Week Dec. 7–13; Message, Senior Advisor I Corps to Ch. M.A.A.G., Jan. 23, 1963. Both at C.M.H. *F.R.U.S., Vietnam, 1962,* 650, 655–656, 693–695, 740, 764; *F.R.U.S., Vietnam, Jan.–Aug. 1963,* 265.
34. Moyar, *Triumph Forsaken,* 182–84.
35. Report, C.O.S.V.N., Apr. 20, 1964, sub: A C.O.S.V.N. Standing Committee Account of the Situation in South Vietnam from the end of 1961 to the beginning of 1964, 16, C.M.H. (hereafter cited as C.O.S.V.N. Standing Committee Account).
36. Ibid., 37.
37. *Military Region 8: Thirty Years of Resistance War (1945–1975)* (Hanoi: People's Army Publishing House, 1998), 423, 425, 427, 428, 429 (quotation).
38. See, for example, Memo, Col. Bryce F. Denno for Deputy Chief of Staff for Military Operations, Jul 19, 1963, sub: Report of Duty Tour in a Country Confronted with Insurgency, 10, C.M.H.; *F.R.U.S., Vietnam, Jan.–Aug. 63,* 257, 439–440; Peter Busch, "'Killing the Vietcong': The British Advisory Mission and the Strategic Hamlet Programme," *Journal of Strategic Studies* 25 (2002): 152.
39. C.O.S.V.N. Standing Committee Account, 5.
40. Ibid., 27.
41. Lam Dong Propaganda and Training Meeting, Feb. 27, 1964, M.A.C.V. J2 Translation 12-139, Jan. 28, 1965, 21, C.M.H.
42. C.O.S.V.N. Standing Committee Account, 6.
43. Ibid.
44. Ibid., 33.
45. Hiroshi Tsujii, "Rice Economy and Rice Policy in South Vietnam up to 1974," *South East Asian Studies* 15 (December 1977): 264, 268.
46. Transcript, C.I.N.C.P.A.C., J.C.S. Team Debrief, Jan. 29, 1963, 23, C.M.H.
47. *F.R.U.S., Vietnam, Jan.–Aug. 63,* 22.
48. C.O.S.V.N. Standing Committee Account, 6.
49. Moyar, *Triumph Forsaken,* 283–284.
50. Ang Cheng Guan, "The Vietnam War, 1962–1964: The Vietnamese Communist Perspective," *Journal of Contemporary History,* 35 (October 2000): 611–612; Tai Sung An, *The Vietnam War* (Madison, WI: Teaneck, 1998), 61–62; Lt. Gen. Phan Hong Son, *The Vietnamese National Art of Fighting to Defend the Nation,* vol. II: *A Scientific Study* [Nghe Thuat Danh Giac Giu Nuoc cua Dan Toc viet Nam, Tap II: Cong Trinh Khoa] (Hanoi: Senior Level Military Studies Institute [Hoc Vien Quan Su Cao Cap] of the Ministry of Defense, 1990), 75.
51. *Victory in Vietnam,* 12, 118.
52. By December 1965, M.A.C.V. estimated that there were a total of nineteen North Vietnamese and Viet Cong regiments inside South Vietnam, plus many independent battalions: Paul E. Suplizio, "A Study of the Military Support of Pacification in South Vietnam, April 1964–April 1965" (Master of Military Art and Science Thesis, Army Command and General Staff College, 1966), ch. 4, table 2, Combined Arms Research Library, Ft. Leavenworth, KA.
53. *F.R.U.S., Vietnam, 1962,* 74–75, 113–114; Moyar, *Triumph Forsaken,* xv; Norman B. Hannah, *The Key to Failure: Laos and the Vietnam War* (Lanham, MD: Madison Books, 1987).
54. Report on the War in Vietnam, 71 (quotation), 83, C.M.H.; Jeffrey J. Clarke, *Advice and Support: The Final Years, 1965–1973* (Washington, D.C.: U.S. Army Center of Military History, 1988), 81.
55. Moyar, *Triumph Forsaken,* 303, 305.
56. Moyar, *Triumph Forsaken,* 306, 324–325; Richard Betts, "Misadventure Revisited," in Peter Braestrup, ed., *Vietnam as History* (Washington, D.C.: University Press of America, 1984), 7–8.

CHAPTER 12
Section II Response

MARK MOYAR

According to James Dingeman, numerous polls have shown that the majority of Americans believe Vietnam to have been an unjust, unnecessary, and unwinnable war. I have not seen polls in which the majority of Americans asserted that Vietnam was unjust, and I do not believe that the majority of Americans have ever felt that way. Whether the war was unnecessary or unwinnable are trickier questions. Many Americans will state that the war was a mistake, but if one probes further, it turns out that many of them believe that the war was fought for the right reasons but in the wrong way. Many who say that it was unwinnable believe it was unwinnable only because of America's self-imposed restraints, not because it was wholly impossible to win. Most important, American citizens opining about the merits of Vietnam often base their conclusions on the misinformation with which the war's opponents have deluged them in print and on television.

Dingeman asserts that Diem owed his power primarily to U.S. support and that he lacked legitimacy with many Vietnamese. Diem, however, was not installed by the United States as is often believed, but was chosen by Bao Dai because of Diem's popularity among Vietnamese nationalists (33). Enough of South Vietnam's elites supported Diem that he could run the country effectively. Most intellectuals did not like Diem, but the same could be said of Ho Chi Minh (and every Republican President of the United States in recent memory). In both halves of Vietnam, the peasants did not think about legitimacy in Western terms. They knew nothing of national politics, and generally equated the legitimacy of a political entity with its physical power. Both Diem and Ho Chi Minh did owe much of their power to foreign nations, for as countries with little modern industry, neither South Vietnam nor North Vietnam could mass-produce the implements of twentieth-century warfare. At the same time, neither Diem nor Ho could have fielded viable armed forces without the ability to induce hundreds of thousands of men to take up arms.

Dingeman uses a controversy about the size of the Viet Cong armed forces in early 1962 to argue that I was mistaken in asserting that the war went well from 1960 to early 1962. Actually, *Triumph Forsaken* states that the war was going poorly in 1960 and 1961 and did not turn around until early 1962 (87–101, 124, 146–147, 153–159). In discussing enemy strength figures, one must keep in mind that those figures were driven not only by casualties suffered, but also by local recruitment and infiltration from North Vietnam. The communist armed forces suffered heavy combat losses in 1962 and 1963, but their overall size changed little because North Vietnam sent many thousands of replacements from the North to the South via the Ho Chi Minh Trail (211).

Dingeman questions the feasibility of using five to eighteen U.S. divisions to stop a Chinese and North Vietnamese offensive of twenty divisions in Southeast Asia. The number I provide is actually five to eight U.S. divisions (321). The feasibility would be deserving of discussion if eighteen divisions were at issue, but not with eight divisions, which is why I did not mention it in the book. The documents I cited do state explicitly that a troop deployment of this magnitude was feasible (480, note 59). Dingeman's claim that there would have been a great temptation for the United States to use nuclear weapons is unpersuasive. U.S. military planners believed that the five to eight divisions would be enough to stop the enemy without nuclear weapons (321). The United States avoided using nuclear weapons when confronted with huge Chinese and North Korean forces during the Korean War, before the communist bloc had developed strong nuclear capabilities.

Scholars' lack of access to most Chinese, Soviet, and Vietnamese archival materials, says Dingeman, sharply limits their ability to draw conclusions about the Vietnam War. My first response is that supporters of the orthodox narrative of Vietnam have not expressed such reservations about histories of the war that support their views, including works written decades ago. It is particularly ironic that they would begin by leveling this charge against the history that draws on a wider range of Vietnamese communist sources and other sources than any other. Certainly there are numerous documents still hidden in foreign archives that will change how we view Vietnam in one way or another. But we do know a great deal already, especially from foreign publications and from documents captured during the war. Very extensive and consistent documentation is available on all of the major North Vietnamese decisions during the war, and on most of the big military operations.

Charles Hill, a diplomat with forty years of experience in Vietnam and many of the world's other countries, skillfully places *Triumph Forsaken* within the broader context of American history and international history. Hill makes the crucial point that our political community is formed by the narratives we tell about ourselves. Professional historians, with their preference for focused analysis over large narrative, often lose sight of this point, but academic historians have kept it in view in the case of Vietnam, for unlike most stories in American history, the Vietnam narrative was central to the lives of today's senior academics and now can be wielded as a club in the debates over Iraq, Afghanistan, and other foreign conflicts. As foreseen by Herodotus, Americans across the political spectrum are fighting over the Vietnam narrative in an effort to move the political community in their preferred direction.

Hill is right to lament America's tendency in the wars of the late twentieth century to miss "the value of focusing on defeating the enemy more than badgering our friends." One of the most startling features of American officials like Averell Harriman, George Ball, and Roger Hilsman is the contrast between their deferential posture toward America's enemies and their inflexible, and at times devious, strong-arming of allies like Ngo Dinh Diem. They overestimated the adverse consequences of getting tough with enemies, and underestimated the adverse consequences of getting tough with friends. During the last years of the Diem period, those officials sought accommodation with the Soviets and countenanced North Vietnamese violations of Laotian sovereignty, while they leaked negative remarks on Ngo Dinh Diem to the press, tried to compel Diem to impose American political solutions on South Vietnam, and, when Diem did not comply, helped orchestrate his overthrow. The result was encouragement and facilitation of enemy aggression, and the destruction of a powerful ally. In 1964, South Vietnamese chief of state Nguyen Khanh and allied leaders in other countries like Taiwan and South Korea recommended striking the North Vietnamese hard, while the prospects for deterrence were still high, but Johnson rejected their advice in favor of avoiding provocation of North Vietnam and China, leading to the North Vietnamese decision in November 1964 to send North Vietnamese Army regiments into South Vietnam.

As Hill stresses, combating an enemy that does not abide by recognized rules of warfare poses enormous challenges. Finding such an enemy requires superior intelligence collection capabilities, and it is much easier for indigenous forces than for foreign forces because of linguistic, cultural, and familial commonalities. Decisions on whether and how to engage enemy forces that choose to intermingle with the civilian populace requires excellent leaders on the ground, who will need to make snap decisions without recourse to hard-and-fast rules. Later in the war, the North Vietnamese increasingly relied on the tactic of staying near the population to discourage American use of air and artillery. I will cover that subject more thoroughly in the next volume of *Triumph Forsaken*. In Vietnam, as in Iraq and Afghanistan today, American concerns about excessive and indiscriminate uses of force are much higher when American troops are using force rather than indigenous troops, both friendly and enemy, so there will be much more documentation to cover in the 1965–1972 period. Unfortunately, Americans too often remain unaware that their adversaries deliberately intermingle with the civilian populace and that this practice frequently precludes the defeat of those adversaries without civilian casualties.

I also appreciate Hill's situating Vietnam within the context of grand strategy, for far too much of what has been written on Vietnam has ignored this context. Countries like Indonesia, Thailand, Japan, and the Philippines are completely absent from most accounts, egregious omissions not only because the U.S. government counted those countries among the principal stakes in Vietnam, but also because, as I argue in *Triumph Forsaken*, they were indeed at stake. Vietnam was a key front in the Asian Cold War, rather than a country of minor importance that the United States sought to protect because of abstract notions of credibility or Lyndon Johnson's concern about his masculinity or the various other causes that have been advanced.

Hill's discussion of the Vietnam Veterans Memorial offers another example of the Left's use of the orthodox narrative of Vietnam as a political weapon. The orthodox portrayals of the war's American veterans as victims/baby killers, America's allies as worthless, the strategic stakes as minimal, and the strategic alternatives as unfeasible have been invoked regularly to justify reduced American involvement in the world, lower defense spending, and contempt for Western civilization. The American Right has disputed this characterization of the war and has tried to use Vietnam to show the perils of abandoning allies, limiting the use of force, and appearing exceedingly eager to negotiate, in order to preserve national solidarity and justify the use of the military. *Triumph Forsaken* generally supports the claims of the Right. It shows that cunning adversaries view eagerness to negotiate as weakness and are much more likely to be restrained by threats and force than by professions of goodwill and desire for dialogue. It demonstrates the soundness of America's purpose in Vietnam and the existence of viable alternatives for winning the war.

On the other hand, certain of the book's points have been welcomed by elements of the Left and have unsettled elements of the Right, which is not surprising given that the Left and Right both contain a diversity of viewpoints. Some on the Left have long been convinced that the United States instigated the overthrow of Diem and cited it as proof of nefarious American meddling in other countries' affairs, while many on the Right have tried to deny American complicity in that event, viewing it as another left-wing attempt to besmirch the United States. *Triumph Forsaken* shows conclusively that the United States instigated the coup and that the South Vietnamese generals had wanted to keep Diem until the Americans insisted that Diem and Nhu had to go. In addition, the neoconservatives, who in recent years have tried to impose democracy and other Western practices on Afghanistan and Iraq, do not care for my argument that Ambassador Lodge and others in the U.S. government erred in trying to impose Western reforms on a non-Western country in wartime because this non-Western culture could not be changed so easily and because the reform efforts undermined vital antisubversive activities. Paleoconservatives, on the other hand, will see in Diem's overthrow the folly of liberal disregard for culture and tradition, and those on the Left who chafe at American disrespect for foreign cultures will also find therein some validation for their views.

The ranks of those on the Left concerned about Western erosion of foreign cultures do not include Scott Laderman, because he does not acknowledge the presence of great cultural differences between Vietnam and the West. Laderman states that I present no evidence of an authoritarian political culture in Vietnam. He overlooked a great deal. For instance, in the elections held in both North Vietnam and South Vietnam, almost everyone voted as the government told them to vote, and very few became upset when the government's preferred candidates won by overwhelming margins or when nonpreferred candidates were allowed to win but relegated to meaningless offices (17, 54–55, 75–76). The Communists and Diem's nationalists both mobilized the peasantry effectively without holding democratic elections in the villages (71, 158). No one would claim that these same behaviors were prevalent in the United States during the mid-twentieth century.

The book also shows that most Vietnamese differed from Westerners by choosing their political allegiance on the basis of the armed strength, prestige, and charisma of a political leader or group, rather than political ideology or political programs (16–18, 43–44, 52–55, 62–63, 80–81, 93–94, 136, 152–153, 160, 169, 209, 216, 232–233, 316). In Laderman's view, American support for the bombing of North Vietnam shows that Americans have the same respect for power as the Vietnamese. Using force against a foreign country is, however, quite different from using force within one's own. Americans, unlike the Vietnamese, have long abhorred the use of force against political oppositionists within their own country. Laderman adds that Vietnamese concerns about prestige and face were similar to U.S. concerns about credibility. There are some important similarities, but also important differences. Certain events that caused a devastating loss of face in Vietnam, such as public protests against the government, would not have had the same impact in the United States (46, 62–63, 216, 230–232). In denouncing my portrayal of an authoritarian culture, Laderman brings up Diem's discussion of democracy in the October 1955 referendum. As I explain in the book, Diem paid lip service to democracy and took some superficially democratic actions merely to please the United States and the small South Vietnamese intellectual class (75).

Laderman goes on to claim that my assessment of Vietnamese mass culture "echoes much too closely the racist suppositions of American policymakers in earlier decades." Laderman's unsubstantiated insinuation of racism is a poor and irresponsible substitute for dispassionate analysis. I never raise the issue of race in discussing Vietnamese political culture, nor do I say that authoritarian cultures have historically been peculiar to Asia or other non-Western regions—most Western countries have had authoritarian cultures at some point in their past. Most Vietnamese agree with my interpretation of Vietnamese political culture, which is one reason why my books are very popular among Vietnamese-Americans.

Laderman approvingly cites Gareth Porter's dispute of my claim that the Malayan communist insurgency never stopped. But numerous accounts show that Commonwealth forces continued counterinsurgency operations against Malayan communist guerrillas after the "Emergency" was officially declared over in July 1960.[1] Porter was also wrong when he alleged that one of my sources, Chin Peng's memoirs, stated that the Malayan insurgency ended in 1960. In actuality, Chin Peng stated that although the Malayan Communist Party had demobilized many guerrillas after July 1960, its guerrilla strength did not fall below 300 prior to the 1961 decision to accelerate the armed struggle.[2]

The claims of Edwin Moïse concerning the Tonkin Gulf that Laderman cites largely concern minute details of no significance to the big picture, such as Moïse's criticism that I referred to some North Vietnamese naval bases as torpedo boat bases—Moïse acknowledged that torpedo boats were present at the bases at the time in question, but claimed that they should not have been called torpedo boat bases because the torpedo boats were only there temporarily and had a permanent base elsewhere. Here, I will include only the segments of serious historical import. Moïse wrote: "On August 4, on a dark night in poor weather, the *Maddox* and another US destroyer, *Turner Joy*, believed themselves to be under attack by North Vietnamese torpedo boats. Moyar acknowledges that in retrospect the evidence does not support the reality of this attack, but he gives a misleading impression that the men on the destroyers had better reason to believe themselves under attack, at the time, than they actually had." My response:

> Moïse fails to explain how my description produces a misleading impression. The facts I cite—such as the reports from the *Turner Joy*'s crew of enemy gunfire and an enemy searchlight—are mentioned in Moïse's book. I mention these facts simply in explaining why the destroyer commanders, Admiral Sharp, and the Joint Chiefs became convinced that an attack had occurred. Moïse acknowledges in his book that, in the first two days following the August 4 incident, "There was considerable information coming from the Turner Joy that suggested a real attack." (Edwin Moïse, *Tonkin Gulf and the Escalation of the Vietnam War*, p. 144) He further states, "Captain Herrick and Commander Ogier both state at the time they wrote their replies to the JCS on August 7, the review they had made of the sighting reports had left them convinced that the attack had been real." (Ibid.)[3]

Laderman disputes my assertions that the Vietnamese communists killed tens of thousands of people by the end of 1946, and killed more in 1945 and 1946 than all other Vietnamese groups combined. In his description of Shawn McHale's writings, Laderman neglects a key phrase of McHale's upon which I base my assertions: "tens of thousands of Vietnamese were killed."[4] The available sources on this subject, which I summarized on pages 17 to 19, make it clear that the communists were the principal killers during 1945 and 1946. According to David Marr, the communists killed several thousand "alleged enemies of the revolution" in late August and September 1945 alone.[5] François Guillemot notes that "revolutionary purification" took between 4,000 and 8,000 lives in Quang Ngai and that the communists massacred significant numbers of Hoa Hao and Cao Dai believers.[6] And in 1946, the communists killed large numbers of people in overrunning several provinces held by the Vietnam Nationalist Party (19).

Next on Laderman's list is my citation of a former communist land reform cadre who said that the communist land reform campaigns killed 32,000 people. According to Laderman, I do not give any explanation as to why this person should be trusted, but the fact that this person had been a land reform cadre, which I stated in the text, is a very good reason. Laderman goes on to complain that I did not mention the fact that this individual was questioned by someone who was not an experienced interrogator, or that the questioner thought that only "most" of the rallier's answers were truthful, or that the rallier did not explain who compiled the figures in question, or that David Hunt had doubts about the testimony of ralliers, or that ralliers were frequently tortured, etc. If Laderman really believes that such considerations should be spelled out for every source in a book, he has no understanding of the limitations inherent in a publisher's word count. Had this document been challenged in the years after Arthur Dommen first cited it in his 2001 book, then perhaps its validity would have been worthy of elaboration in a footnote, but between 2001 and now, no one has challenged the document, or Dommen's manner of citation, which is very similar to mine.[7]

Some of the issues Laderman raises about this document do not merit significant attention from historians. David Hunt's objections, for example, do not carry much weight given that he wrote an entire article in *Radical America* that was based on the statements of ralliers.[8] Other issues Laderman cited, however, do deserve the scrutiny of historians, and I did scrutinize them before I chose to include this source in the book. The historians should consider what topics the rallier might have been inclined to lie about. Having read hundreds of similar rallier debriefings, I have a good feel for the likely topics. For reasons of self-protection, the individual might have been inclined to lie about his personal involvement in atrocities against South Vietnamese personnel, or about the participation of his family members in insurgent activities. He might have spoken more positively about the South Vietnamese government or the Americans than he really felt, in order to ingratiate himself with them. Many other defectors displayed such tendencies. But there was no compelling reason for him to fabricate a story about the number of land reform deaths. Ralliers rarely commented on such large issues, and I have seen no evidence that the South Vietnamese or Americans tried to pressure them into making false statements on such subjects. In addition, a variety of elements of his testimony support his claim to have been a land reform cadre, and the figure of 32,000 seems reasonable based upon what else is known on the land reform program.

Laderman proceeds to state that he is not persuaded by my dismissal of Edwin Moïse's estimate of deaths in the communist land reform campaigns. Rather than address the substance of my critique, Laderman merely contends that Moïse is more reliable because he spent seven pages making his case while I rebutted it in a single sentence. I remain convinced that one sentence suffices to call Moïse's calculations into doubt, for it takes but one sentence to state that his data came from a perennially untrustworthy and partisan source, the Hanoi government.

Laderman invokes William Turley and Alexander Kendrick to argue that the South Vietnamese government killed "as many as 75,000 persons" in the 1950s. He neglects to mention that Kendrick's book *The Wound Within* was Turley's only source, and that *The Wound Within* itself does not state its source for the 75,000 figure. I would be suspicious of anything contained in *The Wound Within*, considering that it contains no footnotes and it espouses some of the most egregious fictions concocted by the anti-war movement, such as that the Hue Massacre was a myth and that My Lai was "a typical incident in the war."⁹ In *Triumph Forsaken*, by contrast, I cite a communist complaint that the anti-communist campaigns took 4,971 lives through January 1959, which may well be an overstatement given the communists' track record on such matters (65).

Laderman alleges that I wrote *Triumph Forsaken* to promote a "militaristic foreign policy." It would have helped if he had clarified what precisely he meant. In the academic world, "militarism" is often used carelessly to mean something along the lines of "the glorification of warfare and the wanton use of force to impose a country's will on others," as exemplified by the militarists of Germany and Japan during World War II. I do not know of any influential Americans today who advocate that type of militarism. The term militarism does have other meanings: according to my American Heritage dictionary, it can mean "The glorification of the ideals of a professional military class"; "predominance of the military in the administration or policy of the state"; or "A policy in which military preparedness is of primary importance to the state." All three of those definitions have their virtues and vices. Most societies glorify at least some of the ideals of the professional military class, such as persistence and self-sacrifice. The American military has played a predominant role in administering Iraq and Afghanistan, even under the Obama administration. And military preparedness often deters aggressors or leaves countries in a better position when war breaks out, as Franklin Roosevelt's preparations for war before Pearl Harbor demonstrate. A country can cause great harm if it goes too far in these directions; as with most things political, moderation is preferable to extremism.

With his references to "militarism," Laderman may be accusing me, as others have already done, of supporting a foreign policy that involves frequent recourse to military force in service of the interests of the nation and/or large corporations and/or conservative white males. Let me first point out that *Triumph Forsaken* was written as a history, not as a vehicle towards promoting a specific present-day foreign policy agenda. The words "Iraq" and "Afghanistan" and "George W. Bush" do not appear in the book, which cannot be said of some recent orthodox histories like that of John Prados. As far as foreign policy is concerned, the idea that American conservatives simply wish to use force at every possible moment is a fantasy that could be believed by intelligent people like Professor

Laderman only if they had no real exposure to American conservatives. It is true that the Right tends to be more skeptical than the Left about the utility of nonviolent means of coercion and persuasion, and to attach more value to military preparedness and threats to use force. But most American conservatives of recent memory have not sought war eagerly, viewing it instead as a perilous last resort, and the Right has often been more cautious about war than the Left. The biggest American wars of the twentieth century all commenced on the watch of liberal Democratic Presidents. Although George W. Bush's plunge into Iraq was popular with neoconservatives, many other conservatives objected to using force to remake foreign civilizations, especially when they involved no obvious benefits for the United States.

A depressingly large number of university professors have presumed that I wrote *Triumph Forsaken* for the purpose of justifying the Iraq War. None of them actually asked whether I wrote it for that reason, or what I thought about the Iraq War, or when I began writing the book—I actually started it in 1999, long before George W. Bush had ever thought of going to war with Iraq. For professors who viewed all wars waged by the United States as reprehensible, it may have been easy to presume that anyone who supported one such war believed them all to be laudatory, but ordinary logic does not support that presumption. Those who denied the existence of objective truth and used it as an excuse to make history a slave to present-day political causes were liable to ascribe the same presentism to others. I wrote *Triumph Forsaken* because I believed that there was objective truth to be found. Based on what I already knew, I did believe that the objective truth had implications for the present, particularly in terms of the role of the United States in the world and the treatment of those who fought in the war, but did not put those implications before the facts. In the course of writing the book, I changed my mind on some key points, including the strength of French colonialism, American complicity in Diem's removal, and the validity of the domino theory, some of which altered my views on the present-day implications. After spending seven years on the book, I am more convinced than ever that objective truth exists and that historians should strive to learn and represent it to the best of their abilities. While each person views the past through different eyes, we will all see, if we look hard enough, that Ho Chi Minh consistently held the Chinese communists in high regard, that South Vietnamese military performance increased dramatically during 1962 and 1963, and that South Vietnam's neighbors dreaded a North Vietnamese victory in 1965.

Robert F. Turner uses years of service in Vietnam to shed light upon the controversies at hand. His discussions with Vietnamese observers during the war lend further support to the interpretation that American ambassador Henry Cabot Lodge committed a catastrophic error in sponsoring the overthrow of Ngo Dinh Diem. Turner examines the use of the term "revisionist" for scholars who share my general views on the war, a term that is obviously confusing for the uninitiated, since earlier "revisionists" like Gabriel Kolko and William Appleman Williams were leftists who disdained America's anti-communist foreign policies. But the usage of the term in the context of Vietnam War historiography is probably too deeply entrenched to be altered at this point.

Turner correctly notes that Eisenhower's statement about Ho Chi Minh receiving 80 percent of the vote has been quoted of context. I would add that I think that Eisenhower was wrong—Ho Chi Minh would not have received 80 percent of the votes even against Bao Dai, unless he had controlled 80 percent of the polling stations. The rural Vietnamese who comprised the large majority of the population were largely ignorant of national politics. Had they been asked to vote (something that would have struck them as very odd), they would have voted for whomever the polling authority recommended. Such is, indeed, what happened in both North Vietnam and South Vietnam from 1954 onwards. The American aversion to all-Vietnam elections in 1956 was based on the belief that the communists would get the overwhelming majority of North Vietnamese to vote communist by this means and thus would win by virtue of the North's superiority to the South in population size. Another indication of the relative popularity of Ho Chi Minh and his Southern opponents was the magnitude of relocation after the Franco-Viet Minh War. Some 120,000 people moved from the South to the North after the armistice, whereas one million left the North for the South, and a large number of others wanted to make the southbound trip but were stopped by the North Vietnamese authorities. Of the Vietnamese who voted with their feet, only 11 percent voted for Ho Chi Minh.

As Turner notes, the foreign journalists who worked with Pham Xuan An have now conceded that he was a North Vietnamese spy but continue to maintain that he served only as a collector of information, not a disseminator of misinformation. Their proof? Pham Xuan An told them so. For reporters who were so skeptical of everything uttered by American officials, they have been remarkably uncritical in believing the statements of a man who lied about his identity for much of his life.[10] The truth is that Pham Xuan An did disseminate false information to the American press, and with devastating effect. Long ago, before Pham Xuan An's duplicity came to light, David Halberstam said that Pham Xuan An had been his best source on the South Vietnamese officer corps during 1963, a period when Halberstam was writing inaccurate reports of military discontent with Diem (214–215). Pham Xuan An's spreading of misinformation about disgruntled officers played a major role in souring the United States government on Diem, since many American officials trusted the *New York Times* and Ambassador Lodge consulted Halberstam in Saigon repeatedly.

Jessica Chapman, near the beginning of her review, states, "the literature on the Vietnam Wars is vastly more complex and nuanced than [Moyar's] liberal orthodox/conservative revisionist dichotomy implies." I should begin by noting that this dichotomy is not a creation of mine. David Anderson, Marc Jason Gilbert, Stephen Vlastos, and many other well-known scholars have accepted and analyzed this dichotomy. In *Triumph Forsaken*, moreover, I note that not every book fits into one category or the other (xii). But all of the major works that address the war's biggest questions—such as the merits of U.S. intervention and the viability of alternative American strategies—clearly can be placed within either the orthodox or revisionist groupings.

In her essay, Chapman states, "I believe the historical profession welcomes solidly researched, well-argued work of any ideological persuasion." This assertion is only partially correct. It accurately characterizes a significant portion of diplomatic and military historians—the fact that many scholars are discussing *Triumph Forsaken* seriously is evidence. But other diplomatic and military historians, such as David Anderson and Robert Buzzanco, have not been welcoming to books on Vietnam that diverge sharply from their views, as I discuss in the book's preface. The character of some of the essays in this book, including Chapman's, suggests that their authors do not welcome *Triumph Forsaken*. In addition, academic historians in most other fields have refused to give fair consideration to research, such as mine, that directly challenges their ideological beliefs.[11]

According to Chapman, "Moyar contributes little of substance to what he has termed the revisionist perspective." The essay by James McAllister, which calls *Triumph Forsaken* "an original work of scholarship that can rightfully claim to be the most consequential revisionist book ever produced on the Vietnam War," does much to undermine Chapman's assertion, by enumerating some of the major original points in the book. Later, Chapman states, "rather than bringing up new veins of argument, [Moyar] revived a number of old debates that most scholars were all too happy to replace years ago with more sophisticated lines of inquiry." She appears to believe that old debates are off limits. Chapman does not mention the military history in the book, which, as McAllister notes, provides a significant portion of the book's original conclusions. As I pointed out in a recent journal article,[12] military history can be far more complex than is often believed. Some of the other sophisticated lines of inquiry in *Triumph Forsaken* that Chapman missed are the nature of conflict in Vietnamese history, Vietnamese political culture, the impact of the militant Buddhist movement, North Vietnamese strategy, American intelligence, and international opinion about Vietnam.

Chapman asserts, "Moyar's sources consist mainly of heavily mined US archives." Most of the US archives I used have, indeed, been used widely, since they are known to contain the most extensive collections of documents on the war. I was nevertheless able to obtain a great deal of new information from those archives by looking in new places or looking at old documents in new ways. Chapman next states, "Despite his claim to have rooted his work in Vietnamese sources, he does not appear to read Vietnamese, and makes only limited use of Vietnamese materials in translation." The suggestion that the book does not rely extensively on Vietnamese sources can be disproven by scanning the endnotes, in which can be found over 200 citations of Vietnamese-language sources. Many of those sources have never been cited before. I am not aware of any general history of the war that contains so many references to Vietnamese-language sources. Chapman also appears to fault me for not having spent time in archives in Vietnam. She is correct in noting that she, Edward Miller, Philip Catton, and Matthew Masur have done research in Vietnamese archives for extended periods of time. They have produced noteworthy works from this research, as I mention in *Triumph Forsaken*. What she fails to say is that most of the information presently available to foreign researchers in Vietnam is not relevant to the big questions of the Vietnam War, a fact reflected in the absence of any statement from Chapman about specific information from Vietnamese sources that would contradict my interpretations. As my endnotes attest, the works of Miller, Catton, and Masur (Chapman had not published any of her research by the time I finished *Triumph Forsaken*) contain only a handful of sources from Vietnamese archives that illuminate the big picture in ways that other sources do not.

Chapman criticizes me for relying on translations of Vietnamese sources rather than the originals. I do not see how reading voluminous translations from a world-class translator, Merle Pribbenow, is less effective than reading Vietnamese sources when one's own Vietnamese, like that of Chapman and most other scholars, is inferior to that of Pribbenow. A substantial number of other scholars of the Vietnam War, including some who read Vietnamese, have employed Mr. Pribbenow's translations because of their reliability, although I am not aware that any of them has been criticized for it as I have. No one has offered any evidence that the numerous translations Mr. Pribbenow provided were inaccurate in any way.

One might expect a historian with Chapman's interests to welcome the introduction of so many new Vietnamese sources, particularly since my Vietnamese sources offer many new insights into the thoughts and actions of the war's Vietnamese participants, which in turn help us evaluate American policy and strategy much more effectively. Most previous historians who have covered policy and strategy during the war have not used any such sources—for example, David Anderson, Larry Berman, Robert Buzzanco, George Herring, Michael Hunt, Seth Jacobs, Howard Jones, David Kaiser, Jeffrey Kimball, Fredrik Logevall (who was Chapman's Ph.D. advisor), Andrew Preston, and Robert Schulzinger. These historians have seldom been denounced for the absence of Vietnamese sources. They have received coveted book prizes and fellowships, and some have been rewarded with jobs at top universities. Why does Chapman instead try to find a way to hold the use of Vietnamese sources in *Triumph Forsaken* against me? It stems, I suspect, from the fact that my Vietnamese sources refute much of what the aforementioned individuals have written.

Chapman alleges that I am guilty of "fragmentary and often questionable use of evidence," and charges that there is "a disturbing lack of critical analysis throughout the book." Those are serious charges, not to be made lightly. Yet Chapman provides little evidence to support them. She provides only five specific supporting points, and all are incorrect.

Chapman states the first of the five points as follows: "I would certainly welcome clarification from Moyar on why Vietnam was of such vital strategic importance to the United States in 1954." In *Triumph Forsaken*, I do not state that Vietnam was of vital strategic importance in 1954. I note that Eisenhower did not consider Vietnam to be strategically vital in 1954 (27–28). Eisenhower had changed his views on the subject by 1961 (125), and Kennedy concluded later in 1961 that Vietnam was strategically vital (137–142), a conclusion that had considerable merit in my estimation.

Second, Chapman accuses me of inconsistency for accepting Ho Chi Minh's supplications to the Chinese as evidence of pro-Chinese sentiments while not accepting his entreaties to the United States as evidence of pro-American sentiments. I did not, as Chapman insinuates, rely primarily on Ho Chi Minh's overtures to China and the United States in analyzing his true sentiments. Rather, I studied Ho Chi Minh's actions, beliefs, and circumstances in depth to assess how he viewed the two powers. On many occasions, Ho Chi Minh professed that to have been inspired by Lenin, and his ideological writings and his actions as a national leader all show the influence of Lenin's ideology, including Lenin's internationalism (8–10, 14). Ho repeatedly advocated temporary alliances with non-communists against other non-communists followed by destruction of the surviving non-communists (10, 14, 104). He never advocated destruction of other communists (save for Trotskyites), whether foreign or domestic, and on numerous occasions he urged his followers to remember that they were not just fighting for their own country but for their fellow communists across the world (11, 83, 359). Ho lived in China for many years, serving in both the Comintern and the Chinese Communist Army (9–11, 14–15). He never lived in the United States and never served in the U.S. government or army. During the Franco-Viet Minh War, Ho let Chinese leaders dictate strategy and revolutionary policy (22–23), and during that war and the war against the Americans, he invited Chinese troops onto Vietnamese soil (27, 362–363). In the Sino-Soviet dispute, Ho usually stayed closer to the Chinese position while trying to get the two powers to patch up their differences in the spirit of international communist solidarity (60–61, 102, 138).

Third, Chapman contends that I depict "total unity" between the Chinese and North Vietnamese prior to 1963, and in this context asserts that I overlooked the works of Sophie Quinn-Judge, Ilya Gaiduk, Qiang Zhai, and Chen Jian. Chapman does not state specifically what pre-1963 problems between the Chinese and North Vietnamese I missed, but in the previous chapter, I listed five major disagreements covered in *Triumph Forsaken*. Concerning the contention that I overlooked Judge, Gaiduk, Zhai, and Jian, a quick look at the endnotes will show that I refer repeatedly to all four of these historians, frequently with respect to relations among the communist countries.

Fourth, Chapman asserts, "Ho Chi Minh was at once a communist and a nationalist, a duality which has long been recognized to pose no contradiction." That contention is also addressed in the preceding chapter.

Fifth, Chapman contends that I did not produce compelling evidence that Diem was an effective leader. I find it hard to understand how she arrived at this conclusion, because the book is packed with information about Diem's effectiveness. The early chapters relate that Diem consolidated control over a badly fractured country and defeated the underground communists. The middle chapters show how Diem, after initial problems in countering the insurgency, led a very effective counterinsurgency effort in 1962 and 1963. I provided an enormous amount of new information on the war in 1962 and 1963, much of it from communist sources, showing how the South Vietnamese were winning the war. Chapman does nothing to challenge the validity of any of this information.

Later on, Chapman invokes Philip Catton's study as evidence that the Strategic Hamlet program was a failure. As mentioned previously, however, Catton's critique in this volume does not even dispute my characterization of the Strategic Hamlet program. In his own book, Catton focuses on one province, whereas I present evidence covering the entire country in *Triumph Forsaken*. I show that American advisors, the American press, the South Vietnamese government, and, most important, the Vietnamese communists were in general agreement about the program's achievements.

No one has even attempted to explain away communist reports on the successes of the Strategic Hamlet program such as this high-level assessment in the late summer of 1963: "The enemy has been able to grab control of population and land from us, and he has drawn away for his own use our sources of resources and manpower. We have not yet been able to stop them. On the contrary, from an overall perspective, the enemy is still pushing his program forward into our areas." In addition, I discredited the idea that the Americans discovered, after Diem's death, that progress reports had been based on wild exaggerations (206–211, 246–249, 256–258, 281–287).

Chapman likens Vietnam after the Franco-Viet Minh War to the American South after the Civil War, and equates Ngo Dinh Diem's opposition (and mine) to giving the Vietnamese democracy to Southern white opposition to giving the freed slaves democracy. In addition, she contends that in Vietnam and every other non-Western European country during the Cold War, the United States made the blanket assumption that non-Western European races were inferior and therefore needed authoritarian government, based upon racist theories and the wrongheaded observations of Westerners rather than any direct understanding of local facts. She states, "Arguing that Vietnamese people by dint of their traditions required dictatorial leadership is at best a reassertion of the white man's burden used to justify European colonialism and the United States' related doctrine of Manifest Destiny."

I will first address the contention that America's Cold War foreign policy generally favored authoritarian rule based on beliefs about the inferiority of non-white peoples. Theories of inherent racial differences were influential in the America of the late nineteenth and early twentieth centuries, but were much less influential after World War II, and their influence declined further over the course of the Cold War. The United States did far more to promote democracy during the Cold War, even in its early years, than would have been the case had it favored authoritarian rule across the non-Western world. It facilitated the establishment of representative government in Japan and the Philippines. American presidents from Truman onwards provided large amounts of aid to support existing democratic governments or to help establish democracy in places from India to Turkey to Venezuela to Zimbabwe, often to the chagrin of N.A.T.O. allies that were trying to hold on to privileged positions in long-time colonies. In some instances, the countries developed into stable democracies; in others, democracy paved the way for the rise of autocrats, some of them dangerously anti-American like Kwame Nkrumah and Mohammed Mosaddeq.

During the Cold War, the United States did, of course, support plenty of dictators, and seldom tried to compel them to democratize, although it did try to pressure some of them to liberalize, including Ngo Dinh Diem. Oftentimes, the toleration of dictators was based simply on concerns that efforts to promote democracy would drive independent-minded rulers away from the United States. In other instances, American policymakers were worried that democracy would create disorderly conditions that could allow local communists to seize power, which usually reflected a belief that the population was not ready for democracy.

That brings us to Chapman's claim that doubts about the viability of democracy in Vietnam or other non-Western countries are necessarily racist. Chapman's accusation provides an excellent opportunity to address the trend, which has spread from race–class–gender social and cultural historians to diplomatic historians, of attributing the actions of America's white males to oppressive inclinations. According to the logic of Chapman and like-minded historians, past uses of white supremacist ideology to justify authoritarian rule, as in the Jim Crow South, show that the justification of authoritarian rule has always been based upon white presuppositions of the inferiority of other races. But if one looks back through the history of Europe, one will find plenty of examples of whites saying that other whites would be better off under authoritarian rule than democracy. Jean-Jacques Rousseau opposed democracy for the French, and Friedrich Nietzsche opposed it for the Germans. By the way, both of them were correct in the short term—democratization led to the horrors of the French Revolution and Nazism, respectively—and one could argue that those catastrophes could have been avoided by a more gradual transition from authoritarianism to representative government, as occurred for instance in Canada and Taiwan.

The second flaw in the automatic coupling of racism with views on authoritarian government is that all of Vietnam's most influential political figures throughout history have favored autocracy over democracy. These individuals were neither pawns of white racism nor blind followers of French or American treatises on Vietnamese politics. Rather, they were politically astute thinkers who grounded their political philosophies in their experiences in Vietnam.

In discussing Vietnamese politics, Chapman is curiously silent on the communist regime in the North. If authoritarian government were not productive, as she intimates, then how was Ho Chi Minh—who was even more dictatorial and harsh than Diem—able to maintain political stability and undertake a massive and effective mobilization of North Vietnam for a war in South Vietnam? Why has an authoritarian regime been able to survive in Vietnam to this day? The answer, of course, is that autocracy was and is well suited to Vietnamese political culture.

Chapman states that "Moyar's reliance on Ngo Dinh Diem's own judgment about the futility of democracy in Vietnam as evidence that democratic reforms had no appeal to Vietnamese people is bizarre." I brought up Diem's views on democracy in order to explain his own thoughts on the subject, as part of an effort to understand what guided his actions. Those views provided additional evidence that authoritarianism was embraced by intelligent, politically attuned Vietnamese and not just by Westerners. If one were writing a history of the American War of Independence, one would certainly want to understand what George Washington thought about democracy, both to help explain his actions and to illuminate the thinking of a savvy observer.

Chapman then goes on to say that my reading of Vietnamese culture "rests exclusively upon contemporary British and American commentary as well as some of Ngo Dinh Diem's own utterances." A close inspection of my sources, however, would reveal that much of the evidence comes from Vietnamese villagers and the Viet Cong, which are the most reliable sources available because they are first-hand.[13] I came upon these sources, and derived from them most of my views on Vietnamese political culture, while writing *Phoenix and the Birds of Prey*. At that time, I was seeking an answer to a fundamental question that surprisingly few people had investigated in a serious fashion—why had the Viet Cong been able to gain so much support from the population? In that book, I cited only those sources from which I quoted directly; not until the *Phoenix* book had been published did I fully appreciate that my works would be held to different standards and consequently began piling more information into footnotes. Even so, there are plenty of good examples to be found in that book as well as in *Triumph Forsaken*.

Before delving into some of these examples, I should clarify my conclusions about Vietnamese culture, because they are more nuanced than Chapman alleges. She claims that I consider the Vietnamese peasants to have been automatons who acted purely on instinct, not on any understanding of their own interests, and therefore "the success or failure of both Ho Chi Minh's and Ngo Dinh Diem's governments rested strictly on their ability to control the population." From my research, I determined that the most important considerations for Vietnamese peasants in choosing sides were strength and leadership. The two overlapped, for military strength depended heavily on the talent of the leaders of the armed forces. Leadership was also critical, because the peasants were swayed by charisma, skillful propaganda, asceticism, and benevolent treatment. I do believe that the influence of both strength and leadership on individual behavior had an irrational component. The same came be said in any country—few would deny, for instance, that Americans have an instinctive respect for displays of power like a formation of low-flying jet aircraft, or that they admire certain qualities in leaders that are not purely rational, such as height, voice, and good looks. But there was also a major element of rationality. Supporting the strong was better than supporting the weak because the strong were more likely to prevail in the end and would not look kindly on those who had supported their enemies. Supporting good leaders provided a better chance of living under the rule of someone who would provide services and avoid abuses of power. As a result of the frequency of conflict in Vietnam and the wide variations in leadership quality, these tendencies became ingrained in Vietnamese peasant culture, more so than in some other cultures. I also contend that the Viet Cong's land reform gained peasant support, although not as much as leadership and strength did—the peasants were not going to accept the political program of a movement that kept suffering military defeats, was unable to maintain regular contact with the people, or committed abuses of power inconsistent with the avowed political program (92–95).

To illustrate the validity of my sources on political culture, I will begin with a couple of quotes on political culture cited in *Triumph Forsaken* that originated with interviews conducted by Rand and Simulmatics, two corporations that interviewed large numbers of villagers and former insurgents. A Viet Cong officer observed:

> The common people usually pay attention to facts. The Vietnamese Communists promise to give a good future to the people by advocating the liberation of the country, but the people only believe in immediate facts, in something they can enjoy right now. If you give the people what they want right now, that is, tranquility and wealth, you will win in the countryside and, consequently, win the war. (93)

A Viet Cong sympathizer from Binh Dinh province, when asked why the Viet Cong had gained supporters, explained the importance of well-led Viet Cong personnel. The Viet Cong did chores for the elderly and showed respect for the people, he said, whereas the government's forces were not respectful. "For this reason," he concluded, "the villagers will aid the Viet Cong, tell them when ARVN is coming, and help them hide" (95–96).

Other useful Vietnamese sources have appeared in the many memoirs written by Americans who participated in the village war. The more observant Americans and those who spoke Vietnamese paid close attention to these sources, many of whom were more likely to speak truthfully to foreigners than to government officials who might punish them for speaking well of the Viet Cong or who might actually be Viet Cong spies. Stuart Herrington, who served as an advisor in Hau Nghia province, recounted that a former village Party leader candidly admitted that military strength accounted for much of the Viet Cong's support. When the government appeared to be on the ropes militarily in 1965, he told Herrington, the Viet Cong could obtain every villager's cooperation without threatening or kill anyone "because the people were nearly certain that the future lay with the Communists" (365).

Some of the best sources I found on Vietnamese political culture were contained in detailed studies by Westerners that I have been accused of disregarding (Chapter 3). In Jeffrey Race's *War Comes to Long An*, a high-ranking communist official emphasized the peasants' lack of interest in ideology, contravening Chapman's assertion that Vietnamese anti-colonialists had infused the peasants with ideas gleaned from Western political thought. The official said:

> The peasants in the rural areas have a very limited outlook "They live close to the land and are concerned with nothing else ... Thus they do not have the time or concern for large matters like the future of communism—such matters are of no concern to them. In the same way, they do not concern themselves with the government land-reform plan—how it will expropriate in a certain way, or how it will make small landowners of them. To the peasants, there is no point in thinking about these matters. Their concern is to see that their immediate interests are protected, and that they are treated reasonably and fairly.[14]

Another former high-ranking V.C. official quoted by Race provided compelling evidence that the use of force and the quality of leadership were crucial to the outcome of the struggle. By assassinating government leaders through the "extermination of traitors" campaign, the official said, the Communist Party eliminated the individuals most capable of providing counterinsurgency leadership, and at the same time increased the willingness of peasants to support the insurgents. He stated:

> The principal purpose of the "extermination of traitors" movement was to protect the very existence of the Party. Without exterminating the government's hard-core elements, the Party apparatus could not have survived. A second purpose was to aid in the development of the Party by creating fear in the enemy ranks and by creating faith among the masses in the skilled leadership of the revolution. Extermination activities had an enormous psychological impact, because the masses saw that the government hard-core elements were being eliminated.

The best type of target for assassination would be an "honest hamlet chief who has done much for the people" and "who is intent on destroying the communist apparatus in his area" (79–80).

Race cites a captured document as evidence of the importance of the Viet Cong's village-level Party leadership, the chi bo. The document reads as follows:

> The chi bo is the bridge between the Party and the masses, the eyes and ears of the Party among the masses, the brain of the masses, the source of Party plans and policies for the masses, and the leadership organization in the struggle of the masses. Without the chi bo, Party plans and policies could not be transformed into the strength of the mass struggle. Thus the revolution could not possibly succeed.[15]

On several occasions in his book, Race concludes that leadership was the crucial difference between the two competing sides. The communist leadership was better than the government leadership, he contends, because it attracted better people, thanks to its promises of upward mobility, promotion of the interests of the masses, and its openness to larger segments of the population.[16] In *Triumph Forsaken*, I concur that the Viet Cong had better leadership until 1962, but I also argue that the government's leadership improved dramatically in 1962, which indicates that promises of social mobility, claims of helping the masses, and broader recruitment of leaders were less important than Race would have it. I have seen little evidence that social mobility or concern about the whole society's welfare were very important in attracting young men to the Viet Cong; peasants showed much more concern for good governance and the welfare of their families. Furthermore, the government's exclusion of poor and poorly educated peasants from the leadership ranks was offset by the Viet Cong's exclusion of wealthy and well-educated Vietnamese, many of whom were easier to turn into leaders by virtue of their social status, experience, and education.

James Trullinger, in his study of a village in central Vietnam, concludes that support for the insurgent and counterinsurgent leaders depended heavily on their *uy tin*, which he described as a traditional concept combining "prestige, charisma, *chutzpa*, and *raison d'être*." I, and others, refer to it simply as "prestige." Trullinger asserted that the villagers "far preferred men of *uy tin* as leaders," and quoted a variety of Vietnamese in support of this assertion. One commented, "Why do we follow a political party or a government? We do it because we think it is best for us, but we also do it because the leaders are good. Leaders are very important in Vietnam." Another remarked, "The Vietnamese people always look for good leaders, because we feel that a government with good leaders must be a good one. We also feel that a government with bad leaders is a bad government. I do not mean only the leaders in Saigon. I mean leaders in the provinces, in the army, and even in the villages. Without good leaders a government cannot succeed."[17]

Trullinger also demonstrated the importance of strength in determining peasant allegiances. When the local balance of power "clearly shifted in favor of one side," he observed, "there were corresponding shifts among the uncommitted—and sometimes among the committed, too. Many began to support the side which appeared stronger, sometimes abandoning support for the seemingly weaker side."[18]

First-hand witnesses quoted in David Elliott's history of Dinh Tuong province also support my interpretation of peasant behavior. One communist leader attributed the Viet Cong's successes in gaining support to "the Front's ability to seize control over a lot of villages," and "the Front's skillful propaganda." In addition, former insurgents cited as crucial the fact that Viet Cong cadres "acted nicely" toward the people and were not "very cruel" as the representatives of Diem's administration were. Support for the Viet Cong increased when they scored military victories, Elliott also remarked. When South Vietnamese forces in one area killed or drove out all of the guerrillas, one interviewee said, "the people became discouraged and demoralized because such a short time ago the Front appeared to be so strong, but now it seemed that the Front just couldn't oppose the GVN."[19]

Chapman asserts, "Moyar provides no evidence to support the rather odd claim that Ngo Dinh Diem's ability to suppress opposition somehow proved that popular support for his government existed." Those who have followed the counterinsurgency debates of the past decade will have heard ad nauseam the contention that counterinsurgents cannot suppress insurgents without the support of substantial segments of the population. This theory is generally true, excepting the small number of cases in which counterinsurgents employ drastic measures like population relocation. It therefore follows that counterinsurgents that suppress powerful insurgent groups without such drastic measures most probably enjoy the support of substantial segments of the population. Like most counterinsurgent powers, the South Vietnamese government needed supporters within the population to inform them of the identity and location of the insurgents. In addition, most of South Vietnam's successes in thwarting the insurgents involved local militias, and recruitment of effective local militias required the existence of local supporters.

Chapman suggests that the political turbulence in South Vietnam could have been the result of the unleashing of dissatisfaction that Diem's policies had created. But the post-Diem opposition did not have widespread support and was not the result of widespread grievances. Even many Buddhist groups that had protested in 1963 abstained from the protests of 1964 and 1965 because they thought the demonstrators had gone too far and were influenced by communists. As North Vietnamese sources have revealed, much of the urban opposition during 1964 and 1965 was in fact guided by communist agents. Tri Quang also remained a central figure in that period, and if he was not a communist, then he was intent on wrecking the South Vietnamese government in the belief that he could step in and deal with the communists himself when the Saigon government was on its knees. Tri Quang himself does seem to have been motivated during this period by resentments towards the Diem regime, as indicated by his frequent attacks on the Can Lao and other "Diemists," but few other non-communists evidenced similar feelings (296, 316, 366).

After drawing a comparison between the tumultuous events of post-Diem South Vietnam and developments in the former Warsaw Pact countries in the early 1990s, Chapman suggests that the toleration and conciliation that worked in Eastern Europe would also have worked in Vietnam, or at least would have worked better than dictatorial suppression of dissent. But in the early 1990s, those former communist-bloc countries did not have to contend with hundreds of thousands of hostile soldiers and secret agents who were trying to kill people of differing viewpoints and impose a harsh dictatorial government on the country, as was the case in Vietnam in the 1960s. Those countries, moreover, were not Confucian countries and therefore their political factions did not have the same need to protect their prestige by squashing their rivals. As events in Vietnam showed time and again, failure to suppress hostile demonstrators created a loss in face for the government of such severity that key individuals would abandon support for the government and side with coup leaders.

Chapman cites Matthew Masur's work as evidence that Diem was less successful in shaping the culture to support his regime than in shaping the institutions. There is certainly some truth to this argument. The urban intellectuals never became very fond of Diem, and culture was a leading cause of their discontent. But the urban intellectuals of North Vietnam did not like Ho Chi Minh, either. Both Diem and Ho had more success in creating supportive cultures among the peasantry, by portraying themselves as dignified national leaders who were building on tradition. I do not think it was possible for Diem or Ho to attain broad support among the cultural elites, because those elites favored a degree of liberalization that would have undermined governmental stability and prevented fulfillment of both men's grand ambitions. What they did each need was a small group of dedicated, capable, and experienced leaders, and both eventually assembled a sort of group—Ho Chi Minh in the early 1950s, Diem a decade later.

Andrew Birtle has produced the first serious comparison of *Triumph Forsaken*'s interpretations of military affairs with the documentary record. He had a head start, because he had already conducted extensive research on the subject and, in 2006, published a book on counterinsurgency that covered Vietnam in depth.[20] In fact, he and I came to many of the same conclusions independently in the years leading up to 2006. In his essay, Birtle cites some of the same sources I used, as well as a considerable number of other sources that I had not seen before. As he notes, they bring him to agreement with *Triumph Forsaken* on most, but not all, counts.

In his critique of the "wrong war" thesis, Birtle makes some of the points I made when refuting that thesis in *Triumph Forsaken*, and he also raises some interesting new points. Among the most interesting arises from the citation of a C.O.S.V.N. report of September 1964, which stated, "the equipment of an enemy infantry platoon is less than that of our infantry platoons." This assertion, which I believe is accurate, reinforces much other evidence that the North Vietnamese were already geared up for full-blown conventional warfare in 1964, having infiltrated great numbers of weapons from North Vietnam in preparation for large, high-intensity battles. Birtle observes incisively that the insurgents were themselves organized along conventional lines, additional evidence that regulars are not inherently handicapped in the conduct of irregular warfare. In addition, Birtle points out, the ineffectiveness of the early South Vietnamese Army at regular as well as irregular warfare further undermines the claims that conventional organization and training rendered the South Vietnamese Army ineffective at counterinsurgency. The problems thus lie elsewhere.

Based on my study of Vietnam and other counterinsurgencies, I have concluded that unit effectiveness in counterinsurgency and the ability to switch from conventional warfare to counterinsurgency is primarily a function of individual leadership, not organization or training or doctrine. After writing *Triumph Forsaken*, and before completing its sequel, I wrote a book on counterinsurgency leadership that showed leadership to be the most important variable in a diverse series of counterinsurgencies stretching from the American Civil War to the present wars in Iraq and Afghanistan.[21] One can also find the same dynamics by going back thousands of years. Alexander the Great and his lieutenants were able to use their regular armies to crush potent guerrillas, and without any formal doctrine, because they excelled at adaptation.[22]

As Birtle notes, he and I arrived separately at the conclusion that most analysis of South Vietnamese security force development has wrongly neglected efforts to build militia and police forces. The emphasis of Ngo Dinh Diem and General Samuel Williams on those forces demonstrates that those men understood the guerrilla threat far better than is widely believed. Birtle also provides new information on the American advisory effort of the early 1960s showing that American advisors appreciated the peculiar requirements of counterinsurgency warfare. While acknowledging that not all American advice was good, Birtle emphasizes that the South

Vietnamese often disregarded or distorted valuable American advice. Much of the Vietnamese resistance to American advice, he relates, resulted from "institutional malaise and personal insecurity, incompetence, or indifference," as well as "sensitivity to foreign interference born from national pride, the politicization of the officer corps, and a military culture that discouraged field duty, aggressiveness, and initiative." I generally agree with this assessment, although I would put more emphasis on South Vietnamese conviction that American advisors lacked knowledge of the enemy and the Vietnamese people. I also think that the damage caused by South Vietnamese disregard for American advice varied widely from case to case during the war's early years. In some instances, American advisors understood guerrilla warfare and military organization better than their South Vietnamese counterparts and had much to offer; in others, the South Vietnamese commanders understood such matters better, in addition to understanding the Vietnamese people better. As the war went on, South Vietnamese commanders stayed and American advisors rotated every year, and therefore the South Vietnamese increasingly possessed more knowledge and understanding than their advisors and hence were less inclined to listen to them.

That the effectiveness of advisors was constrained by spotty South Vietnamese receptivity is an important point that I did not address fully in *Triumph Forsaken*, and in hindsight I probably should have addressed it in more depth, as I did in the earlier *Phoenix and the Birds of Prey*. It reinforces the important interpretation that the improvements of 1962 and 1963 had more to do with South Vietnamese leadership improvements than with the influx of American advisors. The limited influence of advisors ensured that South Vietnamese leadership quality remained paramount throughout the war. This feature of the war also provides a cautionary story for those today who believe that American advisors in Afghanistan can make up for all the shortcomings of Afghan commanders.

Birtle concurs in my view that during 1962 and 1963, South Vietnamese security forces improved dramatically in proficiency, increased their control over the populace, manned large numbers of viable strategic hamlets, and inflicted heavy casualties on the Viet Cong. He also agrees that the war effort was robust until Diem's demise and that it began to disintegrate immediately thereafter, and in the process draws upon telling rice production statistics of which I had previously been unaware. In addition, we both believe that the Viet Cong were too weak to capitalize initially on Diem's overthrow in some areas.

Birtle does argue that I gloss over ongoing South Vietnamese military problems in 1962 and 1963. South Vietnamese successes, he said, were "spotty, incremental, and easily reversible." My depiction of the war during this period, however, makes repeated reference to significant military problems. *Triumph Forsaken* states that the Civil Guard and South Vietnamese Army often suffered setbacks when they tried to relieve strategic hamlets and as a consequence often discontinued relief efforts (159). I note that General Paul D. Harkins brought up numerous major defects in South Vietnam's forces during conversations with Diem, and I conclude that Diem did not heed all of Harkins's recommendations for improvements (165–168). I recount the serious defeat suffered by South Vietnamese Rangers on October 5, 1962 (174). With an entire chapter devoted to the Battle of Ap Bac in January 1963, I state that the South Vietnamese commanders committed momentous errors during the battle, while also contending that they took blame for problems not of their own making (186–205). I note that the Strategic Hamlet program was not as successful in the Mekong Delta as elsewhere, and that it suffered major setbacks in two Delta provinces (207, 247–249). Lastly, I recount the South Vietnamese failure at Bai Ai in October 1963 (257). I disagree that the gains of 1962 and 1963 were easily reversible. As Birtle acknowledges, the communists were unable in much of the countryside to reverse the gains of the Diem period until 1965, despite a near-vacuum of South Vietnamese leadership from November 1963 to June 1965 (283–284, 328, 356–357, 392–393).

Birtle goes on to contend that the war was stalemated in 1962 and 1963, and therefore the United States forfeited stalemate rather than triumph when it backed Diem's overthrow. For the benefit of the reader, I should first revisit how I defined the term "triumph" in the book. It was not decisive military victory. As mentioned in my response to Edward Miller, *Triumph Forsaken* states explicitly that the North Vietnamese could have continued to wage war indefinitely as long as its infiltration routes through Laos and Cambodia remained open. As noted in my response to James Dingeman, the book also states that the Viet Cong were able to replace all of their many thousands of losses in 1963 through infiltration of personnel through North Vietnam. One point I did not mention in the book was that the Diem government, had it survived beyond 1963, might eventually have mounted robust operations of its own into Laos to choke off the infiltration; it was already conducting some operations in Laos in 1963, and South Vietnamese ground forces did ultimately launch an offensive into the Laotian panhandle without American forces, in 1971, although they did not stay long and halted the infiltration only temporarily. On the other hand, the White House might have pressured him into staying out of Laos, just as it kept the U.S. military out of Laos from 1964 on.

North Vietnam's ability to continue the infiltration could be used to support the interpretation of the war as a stalemate, but I think that the word "triumph" is more appropriate for 1962 and 1963, for several reasons.

First, as Birtle and a wide range of primary sources confirm, the South Vietnamese were increasing their control over the population and inflicting large numbers of casualties on the Viet Cong during this period. Second, as I show in detail in *Triumph Forsaken*, the South Vietnamese were winning the bulk of the battles with the Viet Cong, which could not be said of earlier years. Third, the South Vietnamese were able to achieve this progress despite the heavy influx of infiltrators from North Vietnam, an influx that many observers had believed would be more than the Saigon government could handle. Last and perhaps most important, South Vietnam was able to thrive under these conditions without American combat forces. A comparison with the present war in Afghanistan is instructive in this regard. If today's Afghan government suddenly were to become capable of holding the insurgents at bay without N.A.T.O. combat forces, the countries of N.A.T.O. would hail it as a tremendous victory. Many Americans are, in fact, defining success as an Afghanistan that can survive and control most of its population without foreign combat troops. If such an Afghanistan were to come to pass, N.A.T.O. forces would no longer incur the casualties that have been the main source of popular discontent in N.A.T.O. countries. The governments and peoples of N.A.T.O. would be more than happy to provide money to Afghanistan if their own combat troops were not required, which was likewise true of America with respect to Vietnam in the 1960s. Such an outcome in Afghanistan, it should be added, would be a considerably less impressive success than what Diem attained, because the Viet Cong forces were much more numerous, better equipped, and better led than the Afghan insurgents.

Birtle contends that evidence of South Vietnamese weaknesses during 1964 and 1965 in areas like tactics, morale, initiative, flexibility, night operations, and leadership undermine my arguments about the improvement of South Vietnamese forces in Diem's final years. The South Vietnamese forces did suffer badly in all of these areas in 1964 and 1965, as I state in *Triumph Forsaken* (294, 301, 303, 328, 365–366, 373–375, 394). Most of the blame for those defects could have been pinned on Diem, had the same officers commanded South Vietnam's forces in 1964 and 1965 as in the first ten months of 1963. But in reality, a large fraction of the best officers who fought under Diem were purged after the coup or the subsequent changes in government and replaced with officers lacking talent or experience or both (281–282, 296, 303, 318–319, 327, 364–366, 375). These purges were a leading cause of the dramatic deterioration of the war effort after Diem's overthrow, a deterioration that Birtle acknowledges to have transpired.

Birtle contends that because of North Vietnam's "determination to prosecute the war almost regardless of cost," the North Vietnamese would have escalated the war eventually if Diem had remained in power. I believe, as stated in *Triumph Forsaken*, that North Vietnam might never have essayed a large conventional invasion had Diem survived, because one of the principal reasons why they invaded in late 1964 would not have existed—political disintegration in Saigon. Furthermore, it is quite possible that another key reason for the decision for a massive invasion—Lyndon Johnson's squandering of America's deterrent power—would not have existed, either, for the whole sequence of events in 1964 could have been very different. U.S. involvement in covert action against North Vietnam, which led to the momentous Tonkin Gulf incidents, would have been considerably lower had the South Vietnamese not been in such disarray in 1964. I go on to state that North Vietnam might still have invaded at a later time, and that a South Vietnam that had not been debilitated by the 1963 coup might have been able to hold on without American combat forces, something the South Vietnamese achieved in the 1972 Easter Offensive after many years of rebuilding the South Vietnamese Army (286).

Notes

1. For instance, Peter Dennis and Jeffrey Gray, *Emergency and Confrontation: Australian Military Operations in Malaya & Borneo 1950–1966* (St. Leonards, NSW: Allen & Unwin, 1996); Christopher Pugsley, *From Emergency to Confrontation: The New Zealand Armed Forces in Malaya and Borneo, 1949–1966* (South Melbourne, Vic.: Oxford University Press, 2003).
2. Chin Peng, *My Side of History* (Singapore: Media Masters, 2003), 435.
3. After this text came the following: "For a good summation of the relevant information, see the 071101Z message at http://www.history.navy.mil/docs/vietnam/tonkin-1.htm#turnerjoy1. See also CTG 72.1 to CINCPACFLT, August 4, 1964, NA II, RG 59, Central Files, 1964–1966, box 2944; Telcon, August 4, 1964, LBJL, NSF, VNCF, box 228; FRUS, 1964–1968, vol. 1, 276; Gibbons, *The U.S. Government and the Vietnam War*, vol. 2, 296; Marolda and Fitzgerald, *The United States Navy and the Vietnam Conflict*, vol. 2, 432–433." The full exchange can be viewed at http://h-net.msu.edu/cgi-bin/logbrowse.pl?trx=vx&list=h-diplo&month=0707&week=b&msg=His1A0U%2bm1eSs3cy0auayw&user=&pw=
4. Shawn McHale, *Print and Power: Confucianism, Communism, and Buddhism in the Making of Modern Vietnam* (Honolulu, 2004), 36.
5. David Marr, *Vietnam 1945: The Quest for Power* (Berkeley: University of California Press, 1995), 519.
6. François Guillemot, "Au coeur de la fracture vietnamienne: L'élimination de l'opposition nationaliste et anticolonialiste dans le Nord du Vietnam (1945–1946)," in Christopher E. Goscha and Benoît De Tréglodé, eds., *Naissance d'un État-Parti: Le Viêt Nam depuis 1945* (Paris: Les Indes Savantes, 2003), 207–208.
7. Arthur J. Dommen, *The Indochinese Experience of the French and the Americans: Nationalism and Communism in Cambodia, Laos, and Vietnam* (Bloomington: Indiana University Press, 2001), 340.
8. David Hunt, "Villagers at War: The National Liberation Front In My Tho Province, 1965–1967," *Radical America*, vol. 8, no.1–2 (January–April 1974), 3–183.
9. Alexander Kendrick, *The Wound Within* (Boston: Little, Brown, 1974), 249, 256.
10. The claim that Pham Xuan An did not provide bogus information reared its head

again in two biographies published after the release of *Triumph Forsaken*. See Larry Berman, *Perfect Spy: The Incredible Double Life of Pham Xuan An, Time Magazine Reporter and Vietnamese Communist Agent* (New York: Smithsonian Books, 2007); Thomas A. Bass, *The Spy Who Loved Us: The Vietnam War and Pham Xuan An's Dangerous Game* (New York: Public Affairs, 2009).

11. Evidence can be found in the *New York Sun* of April 30, 2007, the *Dallas Observer* of May 24, and the *Cincinnati Enquirer* of June 7 and June 19.
12. "The Current State of Military History," *The Historical Journal*, vol. 50, no. 1, March 2007, 225–240.
13. Ironically, first-hand sources on this subject are much scarcer on the South Vietnamese government side because the Americans did not collect and preserve the observations of governmental personnel in the way they did with Vietnamese villagers, prisoners, and defectors, and captured communist documents.
14. *War Comes to Long An: Revolutionary Conflict in a Vietnamese Province* (Berkeley: University of California Press, 1972), 98.
15. Ibid., 161–162.
16. Ibid., 150, 167–171.
17. Trullinger, *Village At War: An Account of Conflict in Vietnam* (Stanford: Stanford University Press, 1994), 27.
18. Ibid., 110.
19. David Elliott, *The Vietnamese War: Revolution and Social Change in the Mekong Delta, 1930–1975* (Armonk, New York: M.E. Sharpe, 2003), vol. 1, 355, 408. See also the discussion of Elliott's book in the next chapter. In the latter part of the *Phoenix* book, which focuses on the period from 1967–1972, I cited much additional evidence supporting my interpretation of peasant attitudes and behavior, which will be incorporated into volume two of *Triumph Forsaken*: Mark Moyar, *Phoenix and the Birds of Prey: Counterinsurgency and Counterterrorism in Vietnam*, new edn. (Lincoln: University of Nebraska Press, 2007), 298–318.
20. Andrew J. Birtle, *U.S. Army Counterinsurgency and Contingency Operations Doctrine, 1942–1976* (Washington, D.C.: U.S. Army Center of Military History, 2006).
21. Mark Moyar, *A Question of Command: Counterinsurgency from the Civil War to Iraq* (New Haven: Yale University Press, 2009).
22. N.G.L. Hammond, *The Genius of Alexander the Great* (Chapel Hill: University of North Carolina Press, 1997); Peter Green, *Alexander of Macedon: A Historical Biography* (Berkeley: University of California Press, 1991); J.F.C. Fuller, *The Generalship of Alexander the Great* (New Brunswick: Rutgers University Press, 1960).

Section III

Orthodoxy and Revisionism

CHAPTER 13
Orthodoxy and Revisionism
The Domino Theory as a Case Study

DAVID L. ANDERSON

Mark Moyar has offered a bold and extensively documented defense of what historiographers of the Vietnam War have termed the "revisionist thesis." Indeed, the closing sentence of his volume is one of the most succinct statements of this thesis I have seen: it characterizes the conflict as "a wise war fought under foolish restraints." The majority of historians of the Vietnam War, usually termed "orthodox" because they represent the mainstream, would not choose the adjective "wise" to describe the origins and course of the American intervention into the politics and society of Vietnam. Indeed, they would consider such a characterization of the American experience in Vietnam as dangerous to the process of understanding the role of the United States in world affairs. I count myself among the orthodox.

In his preface, Moyar challenges my characterization of the revisionist historians as analysts who demonstrate "uncritical acceptance" of the Cold War consensus, which lay at the foundation of the containment strategy from the time of the Truman administration through that of Richard Nixon (although Nixon compromised with the communist Vietnamese in the end). Moyar contends that revisionists like himself also demonstrate the kind of "reasoned analysis" that I attribute to most orthodox historians.[1] Moyar's own reasoned analysis begins with the premise that South Vietnam was a place of vital strategic interest to the United States because the domino theory was, in his view, correct. He cites as evidence that the domino concept was accepted by the "elites" of Southeast Asia (382).

He also presents data that he thinks show that the Republic of Vietnam (R.V.N.) was making tremendous progress under Diem, whom the American press dubbed "the miracle man of South East Asia" in 1957, and he terms the U.S.-abetted coup against Diem in 1963 a foreign policy disaster for the United States. With Diem dead, President Johnson ultimately had no other strategic choice than to attempt to sustain the R.V.N. Moreover, Moyar claims that the war could have been taken directly into North Vietnam without risk of retaliation from China, Hanoi's backer, but that Johnson foolishly limited the U.S. effort. That decision compounded the mistake of withdrawing backing from Diem, and the result was a "forsaken triumph."

Moyar has amassed a great deal of evidence to support his thesis. It is not possible to analyze all of that evidence in a brief commentary, but its meaning and significance is open to question. For example, Moyar argues that the Strategic Hamlet system was working until Diem's death. His contention is based in part upon interviews he did with Rufus Phillips, the chief U.S. advisor to the Strategic Hamlet program. Phillips was a brave and patriotic official, as was his former boss at the Saigon Military Mission, Major General Edward Lansdale. I spoke briefly with Phillips, whom Moyar identifies as a protégé of Lansdale, at the Society for Historians of American Foreign Relations conference in Austin and was struck by his openness, but I have never had the pleasure of interviewing him. I did interview Lansdale at some length at his home in Virginia. Personally, I found Lansdale to be a marvelous storyteller, but a less-than-reliable historical source. Phillips may be a better source than Lansdale, but there is considerable testimony from other observers about the flaws in the Strategic Hamlet program.[2]

Moyar suggests that many of the scholars who have written about Vietnam are wrong, but it is difficult to comprehend how so many scholars could be so wrong on so many details about the war—Diem's successes, strategic hamlets, the Buddhists, China's intentions, and more. Moyar concludes, for example, that the Buddhist revolt in 1963 was almost certainly communist-led and communist-inspired. Yet Robert Topmiller's research, based upon hundreds of interviews in Vietnam, indicates that although the Buddhist peace activists in 1963 were not "typical" Buddhists, there is no evidence that they were communists. In fact, he contends that they were about as far removed politically and theologically from the communists as it was possible to be.[3] Moyar is also fairly confident that if Washington had invaded North Vietnam in 1964, the Chinese would not have responded, because they were too afraid of American power to risk war with the United States. What might have happened cannot be known definitively, but a number of Chinese authors, such as Yinhong Shi, Xiangen Wang, and others, have demonstrated the high strategic value Beijing placed on

Hanoi's ability to withstand U.S. pressure.[4] It is doubtful that Johnson or any U.S. president would have rolled the iron dice and invaded the north with so much uncertainty about what the United States might face.

Even without checking his footnotes, I find Moyar's reaffirmation of the domino theory troubling. William Duiker, one of the most respected American scholars of Vietnamese communism, has noted how Cold War thinking about Indochina gained momentum over time. Duiker cites Patrick Hatcher's argument in *The Suicide of an Elite* that the United States moved away from George Kennan's prudent application of containment in the 1950s to maximizing the stakes in Vietnam during the Kennedy–Johnson administrations. It was not wrong to include Southeast Asia in the containment strategy, but it was wrong to make South Vietnam the keystone in the arch, as Kennedy termed it. Washington reaped what it sowed. The "never again" school or the "go all out" school—of which Moyar is one of the most recent adherents—is wrong, Duiker contends. The United States can help others, but the key to effective foreign policy is for the United States to keep the means and ends in balance. That balance was never achieved in Vietnam. Vietnam was never a vital interest for the United States, never worth going all out for. But at what point did the United States go too far? When did Washington get on the slippery slope? Was it under Truman, Eisenhower, Kennedy, or Johnson? Vietnam was not of crucial importance to the United States, and there was no prospect for victory at reasonable cost; hence there was no rationale for the introduction of U.S. combat troops.

Neither Eisenhower nor Kennedy ever set clear limits for U.S. intervention, and thus Saigon never assumed responsibility for itself. Without that responsibility, there were no conditions for successful containment. It was all right to give Diem aid as long as he appeared to make reasonable use of it, but it was an error to tie U.S. credibility to Diem's long-term survival. Vietnam was not a noble effort (to paraphrase Ronald Reagan). It was commendable to try to stop communism. That is what I thought I was doing when I served in Vietnam in the U.S. Army, but American policy was marred by ignorance, shortsightedness, hubris, and self-righteousness. It is important for a great power not to lose a sense of proportion in foreign affairs. The Vietnam War was a civil war with regional implications, not a struggle for the global balance of power.[5]

In a January 1962 memorandum to Robert McNamara on "The Strategic Importance of the Southeast Asia Mainland," the Joint Chiefs of Staff described the "communist insurgency or aggression" in Southeast Asia as:

> ... part of a major campaign to extend communist control beyond the periphery of the Sino-Soviet Bloc and overseas to both island and

continental areas in the Free World, through a most natural and comparatively soft outlet, the Southeast Asian Peninsula. It is, in fact, a planned phase in the communist timetable for world domination.[6]

In February 1965, Connecticut Senator Thomas J. Dodd compared the danger that Hanoi posed to the United States to that of Nazi Germany. In both cases, the United States faced "an incorrigible aggressor, fanatically committed to the destruction of the free world." "If we fail to draw the line in Viet-Nam," Dodd warned, "we will find ourselves compelled to draw a defense line as far back as Seattle."[7] This vision of falling dominoes made no allowance for the power of nationalism or the historic abilities of individual states to resist domination by ambitious neighbors. Exactly who was it that, after it had conquered South Vietnam, was going to spread its power across Asia and the Pacific to threaten the European nations and the United States at their own borders? Would defeating Hanoi bring peace and stability to Asia? Inspired and empowered by Vietnamese nationalism, Hanoi had the capacity to be victorious in Vietnam and to unite the country, but it had neither the power nor the intent to expand or conquer other territories, including Seattle. The domino theory does not stand up to reasoned analysis.

Notes

1. David L. Anderson, "One Vietnam War Should Be Enough and Other Reflections on Diplomatic History and the Making of Foreign Policy," *Diplomatic History* 30 (January 2006): 3–4.
2. See, for example, Phillips's own report of Prime Minister Nguyen Ngoc Tho's complaints in U.S. Department of State, *Foreign Relations of the United States, 1961–1963*, vol. 4, *Vietnam August–December 1963* (Washington, D.C., 1991), 596–599.
3. Robert Topmiller, *The Lotus Unleashed: The Buddhist Peace Movement in South Vietnam, 1964–1966* (Lexington, KY, 2002).
4. Yinhong Shi, *Meiguo zai Yuenan de ganshe he zhanzheng, 1954–1968* [American intervention and war in Vietnam, 1954–1968] (Beijing, 1993), and Xiangen Wang, *Zhongguo mimi da fabing: Yuan Yue kang Mei shilu* [China secretly dispatched many troops: The real record of supporting Vietnam to resist America] (Jinan, 1992).
5. William J. Duiker, *U.S. Containment Policy and the Conflict in Indochina* (Stanford, CA, 1994), 380–383.
6. U.S. Department of Defense, *The Pentagon Papers: The Defense Department History of United States Decisionmaking on Vietnam*, The Senator Gravel edn. (Boston, 1971), 2: 664.
7. Thomas J. Dodd, speech in the Senate, February 23, 1965, *Congressional Record*, 89th Cong., 1st sess., Part 3: 3350.

CHAPTER 14
Caricature for Caricature?
The Vietnamese Context in Triumph Forsaken

MARK ATWOOD LAWRENCE

Mark Moyar has few kind words for the vast majority of his fellow historians of the Vietnam War. Most of them, Moyar contends in his aggressively revisionist *Triumph Forsaken*, have too readily embraced deeply mistaken ideas about the war and perpetuated the wrongheaded view that the United States erred badly when it chose to fight in Indochina. Moyar promises at the outset of his book to demolish this unfortunate groupthink by drawing on a broad array of newly available sources to craft a fresh narrative rooted in "historical accuracy" rather than obeisance to dominant assumptions.[1] In at least one respect, however, Moyar has more than he might like to admit in common with the broad community of historians of the Vietnam War. Like so many of his predecessors—including David Anderson, Fredrik Logevall, David Kaiser, and other "orthodox" scholars whose work he singles out for special criticism—Moyar focuses overwhelmingly on decision-making by top political leaders, diplomats, and military officers. For all of its revisionist claims, *Triumph Forsaken* is rather conventional diplomatic and military history.

Unsurprisingly, Moyar is most convincing when advancing arguments that spring most directly from the policymaking records that comprise the bulk of his evidence.[2] To be sure, he stands on shaky ground in his attempt to demonstrate that the Saigon government was on its way to military success when the United States torpedoed it by overthrowing Ngo Dinh Diem in November 1963—a crucial point dissected in other chapters of this collection. No matter where one comes down on that core issue, however, Moyar deserves credit for using diplomatic and military records to bear out three points that merit the careful attention of all scholars of the Vietnam War. First, Moyar exploits newly available North Vietnamese sources to show that communist forces, far from the unstoppable juggernaut sometimes described in orthodox scholarship, faced grave setbacks at various points and managed to avoid battlefield defeats by surprisingly thin margins.[3] Second, Moyar highlights American sources indicating the remarkable persistence with which U.S. military officers pushed for a limited ground invasion of North Vietnam or Laos, a strategy too often dismissed by commentators on the war as merely a fringe and reckless idea.[4]

Finally, and perhaps most originally, Moyar mines diplomatic records to demonstrate that the Philippine, Thai, Australian, and other Asian and Pacific governments allied to the United States sincerely believed their own security would be gravely threatened by a communist takeover of South Vietnam. In this way, *Triumph Forsaken* shows that American leaders were not unreasonable to fear a domino effect playing out across Southeast Asia and perhaps beyond.[5] Showing that other governments feared the consequences of defeat does not, of course, mean that American leaders could not sensibly have come to different conclusions on the subject or that escalation in Vietnam was the only option to bolster U.S. allies in the region. But Moyar's evidence calls into question the view, common in recent orthodox scholarship, that few important governments around the world backed U.S. policy toward Vietnam in the early and mid-1960s.[6]

Moyar is far less persuasive when his claims diverge from the kinds of sources upon which the core of the book is built. The mismatch between assertion and evidence is especially notable in the book's first chapter, where Moyar presents a disturbingly one-dimensional overview of Vietnamese history down to 1954. But this problem recurs throughout the book when Moyar leaves the realm of diplomatic and military decision-making and attempts to describe the relationship between ordinary Vietnamese and the various contenders for power in their country. At first glance, this shortcoming may seem no big deal. How, one might ask, can we fault Moyar for falling short in these areas, which concern him in only small sections of his 416-page tome, when he has delved so exhaustively into others and offered various insightful contributions? But a close reading of *Triumph Forsaken* reveals Moyar's questionable treatment of the broad Vietnamese context to be a major, even fatal, flaw.

Moyar's central point—that Ngo Dinh Diem was both Vietnam's preeminent nationalist and a "very wise and effective"[7] leader who was on his way to victory over communist insurgents when he was overthrown—rests fundamentally, after all, on judgments about Vietnamese history and about the character and political inclinations of the people of South Vietnam. To make the case that Diem was the quintessential embodiment of Vietnamese nationalism, Moyar attempts to tear down Ho Chi Minh's claim to that role and, more generally, to show that the anti-communists in Saigon, rather than the communists in Hanoi, were heirs to the noblest traditions running through Vietnamese history. To demonstrate that Diem was a far more popular leader than scholars have usually allowed, Moyar tries to paint a picture of a South Vietnamese populace easily impressed by displays of authority and generally content with Diem's paternalistic style. *Triumph Forsaken* succeeds in neither of these efforts. The problem lies above all in the categorical nature of Moyar's claims. Undoubtedly, he performs a useful service by urging readers to question old orthodoxies depicting Diem as a craven puppet of the United States and the South Vietnamese people as uniformly sympathetic to the communist-led revolution. But Moyar misses his opportunity to bring nuance to these issues. Instead, he merely substitutes new caricatures—ones that too often seem inspired by a deeply conservative agenda rather than a deep reading of the available evidence—for old ones. The sad cost may be that historians unimpressed by the main lines of Moyar's argumentation may ignore the valuable insights that the book offers along the way.

Contenders for Power

Readers surveying Moyar's table of contents may be tempted to breeze quickly through his first chapter, entitled "Heritage." Covering the long flow of Vietnamese history, the chapter may seem to provide mere background, perhaps necessary to lay the context for the sections that follow, but inconsequential to the book's overall argumentation. In fact, the chapter is one of the most crucial to Moyar's central claims about the Vietnam War. It is in these thirty-one pages that the author most directly attacks what he rightly views as one of the cornerstones of the orthodox interpretation. In choosing to back Ngo Dinh Diem in 1954, runs the orthodox argument, the United States aligned itself with a weak and hopelessly self-absorbed mystic who was so far out of tune with his people as to stand no chance of rivaling Ho Chi Minh for the mantle of Vietnamese nationalism. Washington officials thus confronted an impossible challenge as they struggled over the following years to build a viable South Vietnamese state that commanded the support of its own people. Moyar aims to demolish this argument by demonstrating that Ho Chi Minh was hardly a paragon of nationalist virtue and that, in fact, Diem was the more plausible contender to lead a genuinely independent Vietnamese state.

Moyar makes some valid points. As he suggests, Ho Chi Minh and his

Viet Minh movement relied on violence, intrigue, and deception to a degree often unappreciated by commentators who describe a benevolent and wise "Uncle Ho" heroically leading his people toward freedom from foreign oppression. Moyar is surely correct as well in pointing out Ho's close and often enthusiastic collaboration with the Soviet Union and communist China, a pattern of behavior that calls into question the large body of commentary emphasizing Ho's wariness of reliance on the communist powers and the possibility that he might have become an "Asian Tito" if the United States had tolerated him as ruler of a unified Vietnam. And Moyar is on safe ground in observing that Ngo Dinh Diem, far from an American stooge, enjoyed considerable legitimacy as a principled nationalist. Indeed, there is nothing terribly surprising about any of these observations, all of which dovetail with a growing body of scholarship seeking, like *Triumph Forsaken*, to reappraise the Vietnam War on the basis of newly available documentation. Scholars such as Philip E. Catton, William J. Duiker, Seth Jacobs, Chen Jian, Edward Miller, Sophie Quinn-Judge, and Qiang Zhai have, in various ways, made similar points before.[8]

What is surprising is the unapologetic boldness and simplicity with which Moyar advances his views on these subjects. Whereas the other scholars have challenged old understandings of Ho Chi Minh and Ngo Dinh Diem in order to develop a more refined, complex understanding of the Vietnam conflict, Moyar aims only to discard the orthodox view and replace it with its 180-degree opposite. Regarding Ho Chi Minh, for instance, *Triumph Forsaken* shows no sympathy for Duiker's effort in his masterly 2003 biography to paint Ho as a monumentally complex figure who seamlessly blended communism and nationalism.[9] In Moyar's telling, Ho emerges as a single-minded zealot who "firmly adhered" to Lenin's teachings after about 1920 and proved willing thereafter to practice almost any deception, form partnerships with the most despicable allies, and commit outrageous barbarities in order to impose a communist dictatorship over all of Vietnam.[10] Most shockingly, the book lingers over gruesome instances in which the Viet Minh, under Ho's leadership, buried one adversary alive, killed others by throwing them in a river to "drown slowly," and even "bludgeoned" yet another to death before carving up the corpse and scatting the bits to prevent the burial site from becoming a shrine for his followers.[11]

The sum total of such detail unquestionably leaves an impression, but it does not, in the end, convincingly demolish the possibility that Ho Chi Minh could have been both a brutal opportunist and, in part at least, a legitimate nationalist. The problem lies not so much in what Moyar reveals about Ho and the Viet Minh as in what he withholds. Remarkably, *Triumph Forsaken* makes no mention of Ho's well-documented nationalist activity before 1920, above all his moderate 1919 appeal to President Woodrow Wilson and other world leaders to grant Vietnam and other colonial territories a measure of self-determination. Without mention of that episode, one cannot properly weigh the possibility that Ho and his collaborators should be understood as disillusioned nationalists who turned to communism only after being rebuffed by the liberal West. This tale of disappointment and radicalization has, it is true, become something of a cliché in orthodox treatments of the origins of the Vietnam War. Yet to ignore this series of events exposes Moyar to the charge of cherry-picking evidence in order to sustain a view of Ho as a craven ideologue.

Other erasures raise similar concerns. Moyar passes over the Franco-Viet Minh war in a few pages, saying nothing of the fluidity of Viet Minh ideology as the movement struggled desperately to find foreign support.[12] Nor is the reader made aware of the numerous French, British, and American officials who regarded Ho Chi Minh as the embodiment of Vietnamese nationalism and despaired of their chance of crafting an alternative, anti-communist leadership for precisely that reason.[13] Just as Moyar's contention that the war was going well for Saigon in 1962 and 1963 suffers from the fact that most participants believed precisely the opposite, his claim that Ho was merely a ruthless communist is undercut by the fact that observers at the time saw him in a much more complicated light.

Moyar's depiction of Ngo Dinh Diem invites a similar critique. *Triumph Forsaken* rightly calls attention to Diem's impressive credentials as a nationalist and his strenuous efforts after 1954 to avoid becoming a mere puppet of the Americans. Yet Moyar strains credulity in his efforts to portray Diem as a self-denying, benevolent, and sagacious leader—we are told that he spent parts of his early life reading "countless" books and "building friendships" with other non-communist nationalists—who eschewed violence and possessed an appreciation rare among Vietnamese elites for the rural existence lived by most of his compatriots.[14] But the biggest problem, as in the depiction of Ho, is not so much what Moyar includes as what he omits. Diem's Catholicism, an attribute that, in most analyses, distanced Diem from the vast majority of his people, gets conspicuously scant discussion in Moyar's analysis of Diem's plausibility as a nationalist leader. Nor does the book, despite the excruciating detail with which it recounts Viet Minh depradations, go into the harsh details of Diem's "Denounce the Communist" campaign, Saigon's program to root out and neutralize communist activists among the South Vietnamese population. Moyar allows only that "some detainees" were tortured in their initial interrogations, while insisting that the body count exacted by Saigon authorities was far lower than that resulting from Viet Minh crackdowns of its enemies.[15] Although the latter point may be valid, the crucial question is whether the campaign, along with still more draconian repression carried out under Diem's infamous Decree 10/59, had the counterproductive effect of weakening the government's legitimacy in the eyes of its people. David W.P. Elliott's meticulous 2003 study of ordinary Vietnamese attitudes in one province of the Mekong Delta suggests that the answer is a resounding "yes."[16]

The Social Context

Triumph Forsaken skirts the matter of how ordinary Vietnamese perceived Ngo Dinh Diem's policies by asserting essentially that the question is irrelevant. Making breathtaking leaps into the realm of historical anthropology, Moyar contends throughout his book that the bulk of the Vietnamese population had been conditioned by cultural and historical factors to leave matters of policy in the hands of elites. "From the beginning of their history," Moyar writes, "the Vietnamese people had always been very inclined to support whichever political faction appeared strongest, in part because theirs was a culture that revered authority, in part because the enemies of a Vietnamese victor so often suffered nasty punishments."[17] In evaluating leaders, that is, ordinary people responded to displays of power and charisma rather than ideas or agendas. Moyar hits on this theme only occasionally, but it is central to his core argument. While orthodox historians have usually contended that the communists triumphed because they possessed a political program (especially a redistributive vision centered on land reform) that held strong appeal to the rural masses, Moyar attributes their success merely to superior leadership, the result of the experience and discipline gained in the long struggle against France.[18] This line of interpretation leaves open the possibility that skilled leadership on the South Vietnamese side—such as the leadership that Moyar claims Ngo Dinh Diem was ably providing when Washington erred by overthrowing him—could have produced a different outcome in the struggle to preserve an independent, non-communist state.

Moyar deserves credit for going where many Americans fear to tread by suggesting that foreign societies may be driven by something other than a desire for democracy and beneficent public policy. Political incorrectness notwithstanding, the point should be taken seriously, and it is worth noting that Moyar has a strange bedfellow ally in prominent left-leaning author Frances FitzGerald, who made a similar claim in her 1972 classic *Fire in the Lake*. The Vietnamese, FitzGerald argues, were prone to throwing their support en masse behind leaders whom they believed to possess the "will of heaven," the outward manifestation of divine favor.[19] The problem is that, on close inspection, Moyar's claim about Vietnamese political tendencies does not hold up especially well.

One reason for skepticism is the stridency with which proponents of imposing Western-oriented political solutions on Vietnam made similar arguments as far back as the 1940s. Over and over again, officials with little knowledge of Vietnamese history or culture drew on old orientalist notions of the Vietnamese as politically apathetic and unsophisticated as a key part of their effort to prop up pro-Western regimes designed to siphon support way from Ho Chi Minh's Democratic Republic of Vietnam—first Bao Dai's State of Vietnam and then the Diem Republic of Vietnam. Since the Vietnamese lacked any rational or deeply held sense of their own interests, the argument went, they could be induced to support an anti-communist government if the West created an aura of power and invincibility around it. Léon Pignon, the French high commissioner in Indochina, put the case succinctly in a 1950 meeting with a visiting delegation of U.S. officials charged with determining whether to throw American support behind the French-sponsored Bao Dai government. "The oriental," Pignon told his guests, made decisions about political leaders not on the basis of "political theories" but of a superstitious sense of who represented "the will of God."[20] Americans eager to support Bao Dai embraced the same logic. "The true measure of our success [in Southeast Asia]," asserted a Policy Planning Staff study in 1949, "will not be in what we do but how we do it. In this oriental setting, the gesture and the show are as important as the substantial deed."[21] American thinking had changed little by 1962, when one U.S. official expressed confidence in the ultimate success of the nation-building effort in South Vietnam because of the fundamental docility of the population. "His adaptability makes him extremely susceptible to the 'demonstration effect,'" the American wrote of the average Vietnamese male.[22] All the United States had to do, in other words, was to make a show of power and ingenuity.

Washington's failure to diminish the Vietnamese revolution through the provision of spectacular amounts of military and economic aid raises serious doubts about the validity of this theory. Still more damaging is the fact that, according to the best available evidence, popular support for the National Liberation Front (or Viet Cong) remained robust even in the period when Moyar suggests the Saigon government held the upper hand in the fighting. Admittedly, most of this evidence is anecdotal and comes from a small number of studies of local communities scattered around South Vietnam. One of the major tasks for scholars of the Vietnam War is to deepen our understanding of popular attitudes toward the rival political organizations.

Nevertheless, the overwhelming preponderance of existing evidence points to the conclusion that support for the N.L.F. increased sharply as a result of Diem's repressive policies undertaken in the late 1950s and remained strong thereafter, not least in 1962 and 1963 when, according to Moyar, Diem regained the initiative in war. James W. Trullinger's study of My Thuy Phuong village, for example, suggests that about 75 percent of the population backed the N.L.F. in 1962 and 1963, while only about 5 percent supported the government and 20 percent remained undecided.[23] Jeffrey Race's study of Long An province points in the same direction, indicating steady growth in revolutionary enthusiasm from 1959 through the mid-1960s. Race's statistical tables show that the government's success in collecting taxes—a useful way to measure Saigon's ability to exert power—declined each year in this period, while revolutionary military forces consistently expanded.[24] On the all-important question of motives, Mark Philip Bradley's 2009 *Vietnam at War* ably summarizes studies by Trullinger, Race, Elliott, and other scholars of Vietnam by noting that individual South Vietnamese supported the revolution for a variety of reasons. For some, Bradley observes, the N.L.F. seemed better able than the government to provide "a minimal level of well-being and safety for their families." Others were drawn by N.L.F. land redistribution policies that they rightly judged far more advantageous than the government's halting efforts in this domain, while still others appreciated N.L.F. tax policies that took account of an individual's ability to pay.[25] In short, following the logic of Bradley's summation, South Vietnamese supporters of the N.L.F. were driven by specific goals and grievances, not merely a sense of which side was likely to prevail.

This conclusion does not, it is true, rule out the possibility that ordinary Vietnamese were deceived into supporting the revolution in the false expectation of receiving material benefits. Perhaps the superior charisma of N.L.F. cadres, precisely as Moyar suggests, led ordinary South Vietnamese to act against their own interests. But on this point as well, there are good reasons for skepticism. For one thing, it is impossible to verify or disprove the impact of charisma, an intangible quality almost by definition. For another, Moyar seems to draw an unrealistically sharp distinction between the attitudes of ordinary people and the ideas propounded by political elites. Surely widely held ideas about politics are shaped to a considerable degree in any society by the efforts of would-be leaders to connect everyday grievances to a concrete political program. Surely, too, those efforts are successful only when there is a reasonable match between the elites' claims and lived experience. Finally, Moyar's analysis does not satisfactorily explain why the reader should not view the Saigon regime's failure to rival the persuasiveness of communist cadres as evidence of something more profound than the fact that the Democratic Republic of Vietnam had a head start in training effective administrators and proselytizers, while French colonizers prevented anti-communist Vietnamese from developing a similar capability. It may be, in short, that Ngo Dinh Diem's government simply suffered from a fundamental and irreparable lack of political legitimacy that rendered any effort to rival the work of revolutionary propagandists an impossibly uphill struggle.

Conclusion

Triumph Forsaken provides a fresh and salutary dose of evidence that orthodox commentators on the Vietnam War have gone too far over the years in painting Ho Chi Minh and his supporters as beneficent nationalists. Thanks to Moyar and several other recent scholars of the war, we now understand the crucial role of intimidation, cynicism, and outright violence in the successes of the Viet Minh, the Democratic Republic of Vietnam, and the National Liberation Front. We also know more reliably than ever before the degree to which communists dominated the Vietnamese revolution and the coziness of their relationships with the Soviet Union and China. Yet to acknowledge these facts does not necessarily invalidate the cornerstone tenets of the orthodox school of thought contending that the United States faced an impossible political problem in Vietnam and that no alternative military strategies would have made a major difference. The political landscape in South Vietnam may have been different from what liberal-left commentators claimed for many years without having been *decisively* different. One of the most accomplished historians of the Vietnam War, Gary R. Hess, makes this point eloquently in his incisive 2009 analysis of orthodox–revisionist debate, *Vietnam: Explaining America's Lost War*. Hess allows that revisionist arguments about the "confusing and complex world" of South Vietnamese politics "deserves fuller consideration," but he affirms that, on balance, the best available evidence continues to affirm at least the broad contours of the orthodox position.[26]

One need not rely on a historian's judgment, however, for an authoritatively nuanced reading of the political and social realities that lay beneath the Vietnam War. As the American role in Vietnam deepened in the years leading up to 1963, Indian leader Jawaharlal Nehru, a highly sophisticated observer of Asian politics (although he fails to appear at all in *Triumph Forsaken*), frequently expressed a complex view of the Vietnamese political situation in conversations with U.S. and other Western officials. Nehru, a staunch anti-communist, had little difficulty discerning Ho Chi Minh's communist loyalties and withheld any hint of active support for the Democratic Republic of Vietnam. Yet Nehru also understood that Ho, despite his communist identity, for better or worse embodied Vietnamese nationalism far more than any rival, and he warned Americans of the grave political difficulties they faced in trying to prop up rival leaders, first Bao Dai and then Diem. The revolutionary movement in Vietnam was unquestionably "Communist at the top," Nehru told an American diplomat in 1961, hastening to add, however, that it was not "altogether communist" and clearly benefited from its record of successful resistance to the French. Diem, by contrast, suffered form major "handicaps": the fact that he had lived outside Vietnam during the war against France, his Catholic religion, and his excessive reliance on family members."[27] Nehru's analysis stands up almost forty years later as a fair description of the basic political realities that so frustrated U.S. policymakers and ultimately led them to conclude that they could save South Vietnam only by Americanizing the conflict.

Notes

1. Mark Moyar, *Triumph Forsaken: The Vietnam War, 1954–1965* (New York: Cambridge University Press, 2006), xi.
2. Moyar, xi.
3. Published works pre-dating *Triumph Forsaken* also pointed toward this conclusion. See especially David W.P. Elliott, *The Vietnamese War: Revolution and Social Change in the Mekong Delta, 1930–1975*, 2 vols. (Armonk, NY: M.E. Sharpe, 2003) and Military History Institute of Vietnam, *Victory in Vietnam: The Official History of the People's Army of Vietnam, 1954–1975*, trans. Merle L. Pribbenow (Lawrence, KS: University of Kansas Press, 2002).
4. Moyar's obvious preference for this solution parallels the position of Walt Rostow, President Johnson's national security advisor. See Walt W. Rostow, *Concept and Controversy: Sixty Years of Taking Ideas to Market* (Austin, TX: University of Texas Press, 2003), chapter 10.
5. See especially Moyar, 375–391.
6. Moyar's focus on Asian and Pacific perspectives is a useful complement to Fredrik Logevall's influential *Choosing War*, which examines mostly the perspectives of N.A.T.O. governments in arguing that Washington faced little pressure from its allies to escalate. See Logevall, *Choosing War: The Lost Chance for Peace and the Escalation of War in Vietnam* (Berkeley: University of California Press, 1999).
7. Moyar, xiv.
8. On the "Uncle Ho" image, see Duiker, *Ho Chi Minh: A Life* (New York: Hyperion, 2000), and Quinn-Judge, *Ho Chi Minh: The Missing Years, 1919–1941* (Berkeley: University of California Press, 2003). On Ho's relationship with the communist powers, see Chen Jian, *Mao's China and the Cold War* (Chapel Hill: University of North Carolina Press, 2001), esp. chapters 5 and 8, and Qiang Zhai, *China and the Vietnam Wars, 1950–1975* (Chapel Hill: University of North Carolina Press, 2000). On Diem, see Catton, *Diem's Final Failure: Prelude to America's War in Vietanm* (Lawrence: University of Kansas Press, 2003); Jacobs, *America's Miracle Man in Vietnam: Ngo Dinh Diem, Religion, Race, and the U.S. Intervention in Southeast Asia* (Durham, NC: Duke University Press, 2005); Jacobs, *Cold War Mandarin: Ngo Dinh Diem and the Origins of America's War in Vietnam, 1950–1963* (Lanham, MD: Rowman and Littlefield, 2006); and Miller, "Vision, Power, and Agency: The Ascent of Ngo Dinh Diem, 1945–1954," in Mark Philip Bradley and Marilyn B. Young, eds., *Making Sense of the Vietnam Wars: Local, National, and Transnational Perspectives* (New York: Oxford University Press, 2008): 135–170.

9. See also Mark Philip Bradley, *Imagining Vietnam and America: The Making of Postcolonial Vietnam, 1919–1950* (Chapel Hill: University of North Carolina Press, 2000).
10. Moyar, 9.
11. Moyar, 17, 18, 21.
12. See Christoph Giebel, *Imagined Ancestries of Vietnamese Communism: Ton Duc Thang and the Politics of History and Memory* (Seattle: University of Washington Press, 2004).
13. See Mark Atwood Lawrence, *Assuming the Burden: Europe and the American Commitment to War in Vietnam* (Berkeley: University of California Press, 2005), esp. chapter 5.
14. Moyar, 12–13.
15. Moyar, 65.
16. Elliott, 101–105.
17. Moyar, 16.
18. Moyar makes this point especially forcefully on pp. 92–96.
19. Frances FitzGerald, *Fire in the Lake: The Vietnamese and the Americans in Vietnam* (Boston: Little, Brown, 1972), 32–42. It is perhaps no coincidence that the arch-orthodox historian (FitzGerald) and the arch-revisionist (Moyar) essentially agree on this point. Both wish to emphasize the cultural and psychological distance that prevented Americans from properly understanding Vietnamese society. However, the two authors spin this observation in different directions. For Moyar, Diem possessed a keen knowledge of his own people and ran afoul of the United States when his correct approach to governing them failed to live up to Western expectations of democratic behavior. For FitzGerald, Diem was an American creation who exuded the same cultural obtuseness that characterized the U.S. approach to Vietnam.
20. Memo by Philip Jessup, Memorandum of Conversation with High Commissioner Pignon and Associates, Jan. 25, 1950, Record Group (RG) 59, Central Decimal Files, 751G.00, National Archives and Records Administration, College Park, Maryland (N.A.R.A.).
21. Policy Planning Staff study, "Suggested Course of Action in East and South Asia," July 7, 1949, RG 59, Lot 64D563, box 26, N.A.R.A.
22. Quoted in James M. Carter, *Inventing Vietnam: The United States and State Building, 1954–1968* (Cambridge: Cambridge University Press, 2008), 132.
23. James W. Trullinger, *Village at War: An Account of Conflict in Vietnam* (Stanford, CA: Stanford University Press, 1980), 91.
24. Jeffrey Race, *War Comes to Long An: Revolutionary Conflict in a Vietnamese Province* (Berkeley: University of California Press, 1972), esp. 284–285.
25. Mark Philip Bradley, *Vietnam at War* (Oxford: Oxford University Press, 2009), 96.
26. Gary R. Hess, *Vietnam: Explaining America's Lost War* (Malden, MA: Blackwell, 2009), 210.
27. Ernest K. Lindley to Dean Rusk, "Meeting with Prime Minister Nehru," Nov. 9, 1961, RG 59, Records of the Policy Planning Council, Subject Files, 1954–1962, box 141, N.A.R.A.

CHAPTER 15

Familiar Territory

Mark Moyar's Call to Revisionism and the Counterfactual

MICHAEL LIND

As a contribution to the debate about the Vietnam War, Mark Moyar's *Triumph Forsaken* is impressive in many respects. Too much of the scholarship about the Vietnam War has been a continuation in the academy of the campus-based anti-Vietnam War movement. Too many scholars have sought to portray the conflict as an inexplicable atrocity committed by the United States, rather than as one of several major proxy wars that took place during the Cold War, including the Korean War and the first Afghan War. By drawing on archival material from the communist bloc and by treating the Vietnam War in its context as part of the Cold War, Moyar lives up to the new, higher standard that must be met by contemporary historians of the Vietnam War.

Despite the wealth of new information he adduces in its support, Moyar's basic argument is neither original nor persuasive. If the anti-war Left since the 1970s has interpreted the Vietnam War as a senseless mistake or a horrible crime, the consensus on the political Right, and among many in the U.S. military, has been that the Vietnam War was an easily winnable war forfeited by the U.S. because President Lyndon Johnson and civilian defense intellectuals foolishly tied the hands of General Westmoreland and other soldiers. The late Colonel Harry Summers provided the first sustained defense of this thesis in his work *On Strategy: A Critical Analysis of the Vietnam War*, published in 1982. *Triumph Forsaken*, as the very title indicates, is a new restatement of this old theme.

According to Moyar, the Vietnam War "was not to be a foolish war fought under wise constraints, but a wise war fought under foolish constraints." The culprits responsible for the "foolish constraints" are the villains of conventional American conservative political demonology: "What would doom Johnson was neither the illness of the patient nor a faulty diagnosis but a poor choice of remedy. His refusal to order some very feasible actions in Laos and North Vietnam; the result of misplaced fears and faulty intelligence and unwarranted confidence in brainy civilians"—note the slur—"forfeited opportunities to deny the Communists the great strategic advantages that they were to enjoy for the next ten years."[1] Like Summers a generation ago, Moyar argues that if only the civilian liberals of the Kennedy and Johnson administrations had not been so pusillanimous, then the U.S. could have prevented the communist conquest of South Vietnam by cutting off the Ho Chi Minh Trail, invading North Vietnam, or both.

The Johnson administration's self-imposed constraints on how the U.S. waged war in Vietnam reflected fear that China would intervene, as it had done in the Korean War. Like Summers, Moyar argues that this fear was unjustified and that China would not have entered the war, even if the U.S., using decisive and overwhelming force, had invaded North Vietnam. As a number of reviewers of *Triumph Forsaken* have observed, this argument is unconvincing.

Moyar himself notes that, in February and March of 1965, "China's stance on Vietnam shifted, because the risks associated with greater involvement were decreasing while the risks associated with less involvement were increasing." As a result of this shift toward increased intervention, China steeply increased arms deliveries to North Vietnam. In addition, "Mao agreed to provide seven divisions of Chinese troops for road construction and other projects, and he offered to provide any additional support that the North Vietnamese needed. Demonstrating his ambitions for lands beyond Indochina, Mao added, "Because we will fight large-scale battles in the future, it will be good if we also build roads to Thailand."[2]

To square Mao's bellicose statements and actions in 1965 with the claim that the Johnson administration was foolish to worry about Chinese intervention, Moyar argues that earlier there had been a window of opportunity during which Mao would not have intervened, even if the U.S. had invaded and occupied North Vietnam. Moyar's evidence for this assertion is weak. He puts great emphasis on, among other things, a statement on January 9, 1965, by Mao to the journalist Edgar Snow that "China's armies will not go beyond their borders to fight. That is clear enough. Only if the United States attacked China would we fight." According to Moyar, this statement of Mao to one pro-communist Western journalist "should have eliminated any doubt that [Mao] was foreswearing an attack on U.S. forces in any part of Vietnam. Fortune was on Hanoi's side again, for Johnson did not capitalize on the opportunity here presented to march into North Vietnam without risking Chinese intervention."[3] Moyar's thesis, however, is not supported by the scholarship based on Chinese archives of Qiang Zhai, Chen Jian, and Xiaoming Zhang, which suggests that there was always a strong chance that China would have responded to a U.S. invasion of North Vietnam by escalating its own involvement in the conflict.[4]

Even if Mao and the Chinese leadership initially had sought to avoid direct participation in the war, under the pressure of events they might well have changed their minds. We now know that the Chinese leadership was initially reluctant to intervene in the Korean War and did so, with disastrous effects for the U.S.-led effort, only under pressure from Stalin and the prospect of the reunification of the entire Korean peninsula under non-communist rule. Whatever he might have done earlier, it is difficult to imagine that Mao, then at the height of his domestic and geopolitical radicalism, would have acquiesced to a U.S. occupation of North Vietnam right up to China's borders.

Indeed, new evidence from Vietnamese communist sources underlines the fact that, as the war went on, Mao grew more bellicose in his attitude toward the U.S. than the North Vietnamese themselves. According to Ang Cheng Guan in *The Vietnam War from the Other Side: The Vietnamese Communists' Perspective*, Mao, who told the North Vietnamese in October 1964 that they should wage a protracted guerrilla war, was by 1967 suggesting "a strategy of annihilation."[5] Mao was so enraged by Hanoi's decision to engage in peace talks with the U.S. that he refused to meet with the North Vietnamese envoy to Paris, who had made a stopover in Beijing.[6]

Moyar writes: "Repeating a most unfortunate mistake, the Johnson administration kept announcing that it did not intend to conquer North Vietnam or attack China."[7] This raises an obvious question: if the U.S. should have threatened to end the Vietnam War by attacking China, should it also have threatened to attack the Soviet Union, North Vietnam's other major patron and supplier? In the 1960s, only the lunatic fringe Right in the U.S. fantasized about ending the Vietnam war by "going to the source" in China or the Soviet Union.

To be sure, Moyar thinks that China would have been cowed by a U.S. threat, so that a Sino-American war would have been unnecessary. But any American bluff that was credible enough to intimidate Mao would have had to seem credible as well to the U.S. public and other nations. Had the Johnson administration threatened to bomb China, the result would have been alarm in the U.S. and confirmation to those abroad who portrayed the U.S. as a reckless, aggressive empire.

If Moyar and Summers are wrong to minimize the possibility of

Chinese intervention and a Sino-American war comparable to the Korean War, then their case for a quick military fix to the conflict by cutting off the Ho Chi Minh Trail and/or invading and occupying North Vietnam collapses. Quite apart from the China factor, Moyar's counterfactuals are insufficiently sketched out. If communist insurgents had fought U.S. troops occupying North Vietnam, what reason is there to believe that the U.S. would have been more successful in pacifying the North at a reasonable cost in American lives than it was in pacifying the South?

What would have followed a U.S. invasion of North Vietnam? Would the purpose of a U.S. invasion of North Vietnam have been to unify the country under a noncommunist regime? If not, it is difficult to imagine American public support for turning North Vietnam back over to the very enemy who had just been defeated. If, on the other hand, the U.S. had successfully restored the status quo ante, would tens or hundreds of thousands of U.S. troops be stationed in Laos and/or North Vietnam today? Despite numerous clashes, North Korea has not sought to conquer South Korea a second time. But what if North Vietnam, following a defeat by the U.S., had attacked the South again, by conventional if not unconventional means? Would the U.S. public have supported several successive Vietnam wars, at enormous cost? Counterfactuals are a legitimate tool of historical analysis, if used properly. But all of the options must be considered in detail and weighed realistically. Moyar's claim that the U.S. missed an opportunity "to march into North Vietnam" and end the conflict quickly is far too casual.[8]

Having fought a total war in Iraq that annihilated the regime with overwhelming conventional force, the U.S. now finds itself unable to defeat insurgents and facing the prospect of an inglorious retreat, accompanied by the collapse of public support and military morale. The timing could not be less auspicious, therefore, for Moyar's resurrection of the Summers thesis about Vietnam. If insurgents succeed in driving the U.S. out of Iraq, then the U.S. will have forfeited two wars, Vietnam and Iraq, because the U.S. military failed to help its allies carry out pacification campaigns at a cost in U.S. military casualties that was low enough to maintain support for the war on the part of the American public. In the aftermath of Iraq, present-day strategists as well as historians are likely to find more of interest in critiques of U.S. failures in counterinsurgency warfare in Vietnam than in claims that there were straightforward but foolishly ignored conventional military fixes to the crisis in Indochina a generation ago.[9]

Notes

1. Mark Moyar, *Triumph Forsaken: The Vietnam War, 1954–1965* (Cambridge: Cambridge University Press, 2006), 416.
2. Ibid., 363.

3. Ibid., 360–361.
4. Qiang Zhai, *China and the Vietnam War; 1950–1975* (University of North Carolina Press, 2000); Chen Jian, *Mao's China and the Cold War* (University of North Carolina Press, 2001); Xiaoming Zhang, "The Vietnam War 1964–1969: A Chinese Perspective," *Journal of Military History* 60 (1996): 731–762.
5. Ang Chen Guan, *Vietnam War from the Other Side* (New York: RoutledgeCurzon, 2002), 82–83, 123.
6. Ibid., 133.
7. Mark Moyar, *Triumph Forsaken: The Vietnam War, 1954–1965* (Cambridge: Cambridge University Press, 2006), 361.
8. Ibid., 360–361.
9. Andrew F. Krepinevich, Jr., *The Army and Vietnam* (Johns Hopkins University Press, 1986); Guenter Lewy, *America in Vietnam* (Oxford University Press, 1978); Lewis Sorley, *A Better War, the Unexamined and Final Tragedy of America's Last Years in Vietnam* (Harcourt Brace, 1999).

CHAPTER 16

Throwing Down the Gauntlet
Triumph Forsaken *and the Revisionist Challenge*

JAMES McALLISTER

Historical scholarship on the Vietnam War, as opposed to the war itself, has largely been a peaceful and cooperative enterprise. The predominant puzzle for virtually all historians of the war has been to figure out how American policymakers, from Franklin Roosevelt to Lyndon Johnson, became involved in a senseless conflict that could and should have been avoided. Within that basic framework, of course, historians have argued endlessly about the role of various individuals, bureaucracies, and potential missed opportunities for an earlier American withdrawal or a negotiated settlement to the war. More recently, some historians have published important books and articles that are far more sensitive to the role of international actors, cultural forces, and Vietnamese perspectives on the war. Nevertheless, the basic paradigm for historians has scarcely changed over the course of the last three decades. Unlike historical scholarship on the origins and course of the Cold War, in which you could easily find historians on opposing sides of the fundamental questions of the conflict from the 1960s to the present, scholarship on the Vietnam War has always been marked by a great deal of consensus.

Mark Moyar's goal in his bold and ambitious book is nothing less than to shatter this enduring consensus about the Vietnam War. In an analogy sure to displease both the author and his critics, the purpose of *Triumph Forsaken* is to spark a revolution in the area of Vietnam War scholarship equivalent to the one sparked by William Appleman Williams in *The Tragedy of American Diplomacy*. Moyar's revisionism is certainly not as sophisticated as that of a Williams, or A.J.P. Taylor on the origins of the Second World War, but his ambition is the same. Many historians will be tempted to lump Moyar's book in with previous revisionist books by Guenter Lewy, Lewis Sorley, Norman Podhoretz, Harry Summers, Michael Lind, General Westmoreland, and William Colby. This temptation should be resisted, however, because none of the figures previously associated with revisionism ever produced a work of diplomatic and military history as comprehensive and wide-ranging as *Triumph Forsaken*. While many historians can and undoubtedly will vehemently disagree with all or most of the arguments Moyar advances, it is important to recognize that this is an original work of scholarship that can rightfully claim to be the most consequential revisionist book ever produced on the Vietnam War.

Indeed, while historians will undoubtedly focus their attention on Moyar's disagreements with so-called "orthodox" accounts of the Vietnam War, his disagreements with previous revisionists are no less fundamental. It is instructive to compare the central arguments of *Triumph Forsaken* with the main conclusions of Guenter Lewy's book *America in Vietnam* (1978) and Michael Lind's *Vietnam The Necessary War* (1999). Both Lind and Lewy are highly critical of the military strategy pursued by General William Westmoreland and strong advocates of the so-called pacification/counterinsurgency approach to the conflict. In Lewy's view, the United States "never really learned to fight a counterinsurgency war and used force in largely traditional ways, and the South Vietnamese copied our mistakes." Lewy also rejects the idea that the war could have been won by changing the location of the battlefield: "Military action in Laos and Cambodia at an early stage of the war, seeking permanently to block the Ho Chi Minh trail, would have made the North Vietnamese supply effort more difficult, but basically an expansion of the conflict would not have achieved the American task. Certainly, an invasion of North Vietnam would only have magnified the difficulties faced."[1]

It is precisely this perspective on the military aspects of the Vietnam War that Moyar rejects throughout *Triumph Forsaken*. In contrast to revisionist and orthodox scholars alike, Moyar enthusiastically endorses the general military strategy and tactics advocated by Lieutenant General "Hanging Sam" Williams, Paul Harkins, and General Westmoreland from the late 1950s to the summer of 1965. In his view, and in marked contrast to the historical consensus, Williams was correct in organizing the South Vietnamese army primarily on the model of the United States during the 1950s, and in emphasizing the primary need for the South Vietnamese to stop a conventional invasion rather than develop the ability to deal with counterinsurgency warfare.[2] Whether the target is scholars like Andrew Krepinivich or practitioners like John Paul Vann, *Triumph Forsaken* consistently argues against the idea that the Vietnam War could or should have been fought largely according to the principles of counterinsurgency warfare or that "winning hearts and minds" was a truly important or relevant objective for either side. Advocates of a counterinsurgency strategy are generally viewed by Moyar as people who are ignorant of the realities of the war in general, or the realities of the Vietnam War in particular. Unlike Lewy and countless other historians, Moyar rejects the idea that the possibility of direct Chinese intervention, which he thinks was highly unlikely before March 1965, constituted sufficient reason to refrain from either cutting off the Ho Chi Minh Trail or even invading North Vietnam. In his view, both of these options would have been better ones for Lyndon Johnson than "fighting a defensive war within South Vietnam's borders in order to avoid the dreadful international consequences of abandoning the country."[3]

Unlike Colonel Harry Summers Jr., who long ago suggested in his book *On Strategy* that Johnson might have been able to invade North Vietnam without provoking Chinese intervention, Moyar is making his argument primarily as a historian rather than as a military strategist. Does he, in fact, make a compelling and persuasive case to support the idea that China would not have intervened in the event of an American invasion of North Vietnam before March 1965? Unfortunately, the answer is "no", and his whole treatment of the issue raises some real questions about Moyar's tendency to base very important arguments on weak or ambiguous evidence. Over the last ten years, scholars such as Chen Jian, Qiang Zhai, James Hershberg, and Xiaoming Zhang, among others, have produced an impressive body of scholarship on the question of what China might have done in the event of an American invasion of North Vietnam.[4] Moyar himself cites these authors in his footnotes, as well as some of the documentation that has been published by the *Cold War International History Project*. But all of these authors, all of whom have far more expertise and experience with documents from the Chinese side, would not come anywhere close to endorsing his emphatic argument that China would not have intervened in the event of an American invasion of North Vietnam. While no scholar can ever be certain what Mao would have done in the event of an American invasion, both Qiang Zhai and Xiaoming Zhang have explicitly considered and rejected the Summers/Moyar thesis that threats of Chinese intervention were simply a bluff. In *Mao's China and the Cold War*, Chen Jian shows that Mao and other Chinese leaders repeatedly indicated between 1962 and August 1964 that an American invasion of North Vietnam would be met by Chinese ground forces. "If the United States attacks the North," Mao argued in August 1964, "they will have to remember that the Chinese also have legs, and legs are used for walking."[5]

If the Chinese were clear about their determination to respond up to August 1964, and Moyar essentially agrees with the argument that China's commitment to intervene in the event of an invasion of North Vietnam was solidified by March 1965, the evidence for his case has to fall within this six-month period. The only truly compelling piece of evidence that Moyar presents from this period to support his argument is a conversation between Mao and Pham Van Dong from October 1964 in which Mao seems to suggest that North Vietnam should be prepared to fight a long guerrilla struggle on its own in the event of an American invasion. This conversation is certainly interesting and invites legitimate speculation as to its larger meaning, although the very same document also makes clear that Mao did not believe that the Johnson administration had either the intention or the capabilities to invade North Vietnam anytime in the immediate future. I do not think that Moyar is being at all intellectually dishonest in making his argument about the possible consequences of an American invasion of North Vietnam, but I do believe that this example shows that he sometimes tends to hang very important and substantial arguments on an inadequate and very slim body of evidence. Even more frustrating is the fact that, in the end, it is not at all clear where Moyar himself stands on the entire question of whether the Johnson administration should have invaded North Vietnam in late 1964. After stating the case for an invasion of North Vietnam in very positive terms, Moyar concludes his discussion by acknowledging that: "President Johnson had sound reasons for refusing to invade North Vietnam prior to March 1965, the month in which China returned to expressing a willingness to fight in North Vietnam."[6] If Moyar's argument is that Johnson was ultimately right to reject the idea of an invasion of North Vietnam, then his position is essentially no different from that held by most historians today and the one held by American analysts at the time.

It would certainly be a mistake to suggest that *Triumph Forsaken* is exclusively concerned with issues of military strategy. Military issues are a very important part of the book and some of the most compelling passages in the book provide vivid and graphic depictions of the fighting on the ground between the South Vietnamese Army and the communist insurgency. But Moyar's central argument is that America could have easily avoided the massive military commitment it later wound up making by not overthrowing President Ngo Dinh Diem in November 1963. In his view, the overthrow of Diem was "by far the worst American mistake of the Vietnam War."[7] Moyar is far from the first scholar to make positive arguments about Ngo Dinh Diem, or to suggest that the overthrow of Diem in November 1963 was a tragic error, but one will not find a more elaborate and passionate defense of the Diem regime in all of the existing scholarship on the Vietnam War. In his view, Diem was a wise and effective leader who understood the nature of Vietnamese political culture in a way that his many American critics did not, and that his decisions and methods of governance were appropriate given this context. If American policymakers had refrained from trying to impose Western standards and mistaken concepts on Diem, Moyar firmly believes that South Vietnam ultimately would have been able to win its struggle against the North largely on its own. In his view, the Buddhist crisis of 1963 provided an opening for Diem's State Department opponents and journalists such as David Halberstam and Neil Sheehan to make the case for removing Diem from power. If America had simply ignored the mischievous and unfounded protests of the Buddhists, reined in Ambassador Henry Cabot Lodge, and concentrated their attention on the military successes and the tremendous progress of the Strategic Hamlet program in 1963, Moyar suggests that the South Vietnamese might have been able to prevail without the introduction of any American ground forces.

Assessing all of the various strands that compose Moyar's argument about the Diem regime and his assessment of the war's status in 1962–1963 is beyond the scope of this review. I strongly suspect that even scholars who are generally sympathetic to the idea of Diem revisionism will argue that he goes too far in his defense of various aspects of the Diem regime. Historians of the Vietnam War certainly do not have to accept Moyar's argument that Diem was a better leader and a more independent nationalist than Ho Chi Minh, but *Triumph Forsaken* does suggest that historians would be better served viewing Diem more as an independent actor with his own goals and less as a simple American puppet.

Moyar does advance an interesting and unique interpretation of South Vietnamese politics after the fall of Diem. Most historians suggest that the chronic instability and dismal performance of the South Vietnamese government after November 1963 was more or less inevitable. Some scholars emphasize that the generals inherited a situation in the countryside that was badly deteriorating long before Diem was overthrown, while other scholars would agree with William Bundy that the quality of the post-Diem leadership was "the bottom of the barrel, absolutely the bottom of the barrel." However, Moyar rejects both of these interpretations of the post-Diem era. Drawing on a wide variety of sources, Moyar vigorously argues that the deterioration of the security situation in South Vietnam did not begin until after Diem's overthrow. In addition, while Moyar certainly does believe that Diem was a far better leader than all of those who followed him, he rejects the contention that the quality of leadership was so inherently poor that South Vietnam was destined to fall into a combination of anarchy and ineffectiveness. In his view, at the very least, both

Nguyen Khanh and Nguyen Van Thieu were capable anti-communist leaders. The key question that Moyar seeks to answer is why the South Vietnamese government performed so poorly after November 1963, despite the fact that the elements of effective leadership were still present even after the overthrow of Diem.

Moyar's answer is that the militant Buddhists, primarily inspired by the leadership of Thich Tri Quang, made it nearly impossible for the South Vietnamese government to function. Any account of the post-Diem era is bound to emphasize the important role played by the Buddhists, but Moyar is the first historian to suggest that the American journalist Marguerite Higgins was correct in arguing that Tri Quang was a communist agent. While Moyar briefly concedes that Tri Quang might not have been controlled by Hanoi, he writes that the "sum of the evidence strongly suggests that Tri Quang was a communist operative."[8] Unfortunately, the argument and the evidence presented about Tri Quang's communist affiliation in *Triumph Forsaken* is ultimately no more compelling than the evidence put forward by Higgins in her book *Our Vietnamese Nightmare* (1965). Analysts from the C.I.A. and the Saigon Embassy thoroughly examined the question of Tri Quang and his alleged communist connections on three occasions between August 1964 and January 1965, and each time they concluded that the evidence simply did not support such conclusions. As the C.I.A. concluded in August 1964, "The 'reports' claiming that he is a communist fall into the categories of hearsay, gossip, and accusations without any supporting evidence."[9] Even after the events of December and January 1965, when American officials were in complete despair over the seeming ability of Tri Quang and the Buddhists to throw the Saigon government into complete chaos, all of the leading American analysts of the Buddhist movement still concluded that there was little reason to accept the thesis of communist control or inspiration.

Moyar's new evidence on Tri Quang amounts to little more than some documents that suggest Hanoi tried and was sometimes successful in infiltrating Buddhist organizations—efforts that were well known to all at the time and in no way an indication of communist influence or agency at the top leadership level. Tri Quang was a demagogue and cared little about democracy, but he was also very anti-communist and privately supportive of aggressive American military actions against the North, much like the ones Moyar favors in *Triumph Forsaken*. The communists, both during and after the war, certainly saw him as an irreconcilable enemy rather than as a partner. As one captured V.C. document from late 1966 stated, "It is necessary to make our cadre, monks, nuns, and believers realize that Thich Tri Quang is nothing but a deck of cards played by the US imperialists' political organizations."[10] In short, the "sum of the evidence" strongly suggests that Tri Quang was not a communist operative. As in the case of a hypothetical American invasion of North Vietnam, Moyar first puts his energies and passion into making a very controversial argument, but in the end, he also acknowledges that it is quite possible that Tri Quang may have had his own independent reasons for the course of action he pursued.

Historians of the Vietnam War are unlikely to welcome Moyar's revisionism with any great enthusiasm. Judging by the early reaction to the book, *Triumph Forsaken* is likely to be highly praised by conservatives and rudely dismissed by academic historians. Both sides will attribute their reaction to the strong pull of ideology on the other. Personally, I wish that Moyar had written a book that could transcend the revisionist–orthodox divide in the way that Melvyn Leffler's *A Preponderance of Power* seemed to defuse similar controversies over the origins and course of the early Cold War. Nevertheless, mainstream diplomatic historians should not dismiss this book as merely an ideologically driven justification for America's Vietnam policy. If Moyar were merely attempting to appeal to a constituency that already accepts his basic view of the war, he would not have immersed himself in all of the secondary literature on the war, conducted serious archival research, read numerous unpublished dissertations, or tried to integrate various communist sources on the war. While the author could and should have left out some sweeping dismissals of the work of some honest and able historians from the footnotes, *Triumph Forsaken* is a work of scholarship that should be taken seriously. At the very least, Moyar has produced the first "revisionist" account of the Vietnam War by a diplomatic historian, and this is quite an achievement for a young scholar. For all of my own disagreements with many different aspects of *Triumph Forsaken*, including several not brought up in this review, I believe that historians should engage this work like they would any other book on Vietnam. Diplomatic historians should readily accept the challenge to defend a fundamental consensus over the war that has so far stood the test of time.

Notes

1. Guenter Lewy, *America in Vietnam* (New York: Oxford University Press, 1978), 438. It should be noted that Lewy himself has recently praised Moyar's book as an excellent contribution to the literature on the war: see Guenter Lewy, "The War That Could Have Been Won," *New York Sun*, November 24, 2006. Nevertheless, the differences between *America in Vietnam* and *Triumph Forsaken* on many crucial issues could not be greater. It is also worth noting the contrasting perspectives on American military strategy found in *Triumph Forsaken* and Lewis Sorley's *A Better War: The Unexamined Victories and Final Tragedy of America's Last Years in Vietnam* (New York: Harcourt Brace, 1999), 1–16.
2. Mark Moyar, *Triumph Forsaken: The Vietnam War 1954–1965* (Cambridge: Cambridge University Press, 2006), 67–71.

3. Moyar, *Triumph Forsaken*, xxiii.
4. Chen Jian *Mao's China and the Cold War* (Chapel Hill: University of North Carolina Press, 2001), 205–221; Qiang Zhai, *China and the Vietnam Wars, 1950–1975* (Chapel Hill: University of North Carolina Press, 2000); Xiaoming Zhang, "The Vietnam War, 1964–1969: A Chinese Perspective," *The Journal of Military History*, vol. 60, no. 4 (October 1996), 731–762; James G. Hershberg and Chen Jian, "Reading and Warning the Likely Enemy: China's Signals to the United States about Vietnam in 1965," *The International History Review*, vol. 27, no. 1 (March 2005), 47–84.
5. Jian, 213.
6. Moyar, *Triumph Forsaken*, 322.
7. Ibid., xvii.
8. Ibid., 218.
9. See C.I.A., "An Analysis of Thich Tri Quang's Possible Communist Affiliations, Personality and Goals," L.B.J. library, N.S.F., V.N.C.F., box 7, vol. 16. For a full analysis of Thich Tri Quang's views and his relationships with American officials, see James McAllister, " 'Only Religions Count in Vietnam': Thich Tri Quang and the Vietnam War," *Modern Asian Studies*, vol. 41, no. 4 (2007), 1–31.
10. Saigon Embassy to State Department, "Captured Viet Cong Document on VC Policy Towards Buddhist Movement," February 21, 1967, NAII, POL 27 VIET S, box 2776.

CHAPTER 17
Ngo Dinh Diem and Vietnam War Revisionism in Mark Moyar's *Triumph Forsaken*[1]

EDWARD MILLER

"History does not repeat itself," the British statesman A.J. Balfour once observed. "Historians repeat each other." Whatever its general validity, Balfour's remark seems applicable to many of the historical writings about the Vietnam War. For decades, Anglophone scholarship on the war has been polarized between the "orthodox" and "revisionist" schools. Those in the former group maintain that the war was unwinnable and America's defeat inevitable. The denizens of the latter camp insist just as stridently that a U.S. victory was attainable—and indeed was very nearly achieved, before it was abandoned due to incompetence, perfidy, or some combination of the two.

The sound and the fury of the clashes between the proponents of orthodoxy and revisionism have sometimes obscured a simple but important historiographical fact: the debate between these two schools has been, at root, a debate about the United States and about Americans. The histories produced by members of both schools have focused equally and overwhelmingly on American sources, perspectives, and experiences. The key questions on which the two sides disagree invariably turn on the interpretation of American decisions, beliefs, and motives. To be sure, both orthodox and revisionist authors make reference to non-Americans, and such actors are sometimes acknowledged to have played key roles in the Vietnam War drama. But even when their roles are noted, these non-American characters are almost always rendered in flat and reductive ways. They are also described primarily or exclusively by reference to U.S. archival documents and other American sources. For all of their differences, therefore, the purveyors of orthodoxy and revisionism have a shared propensity for American-centered approaches.

In recent years, some scholars have taken steps to broaden the study of the Vietnam War in ways that pay relatively more attention to Vietnamese actors and Vietnamese sources. As several observers have noted, much of this new scholarship is not readily classified according to the established terms of the orthodox–revisionist debate.[2] The efforts to transcend the old binaries are particularly apparent in a recent wave of studies on Ngo Dinh Diem, the founding leader and first President of the Republic of Vietnam (South Vietnam). Until recently, almost all of those who wrote about Diem were preoccupied with the question of whether he was more deserving of praise or condemnation. As a result, Diem has long been sketched in simplistic and caricatured terms. The new scholarship on Diem, in contrast, has been much less polemical. Its authors have mostly rejected the old caricatures in favor of more nuanced—and more historical—interpretations of Diem's motives, ideas, and actions. Significantly, they have based these interpretations not only on research in American sources, but also on extensive research in Vietnamese materials. The latter includes the official internal records of the Diem government (held in the Vietnam National Archives II in Ho Chi Minh City), as well as speeches and other writings produced by Diem and the other top officials in his regime.[3]

These recent studies of Diem provide a useful interpretive backdrop against which to evaluate Mark Moyar's 2006 book, *Triumph Forsaken: The Vietnam War, 1954–1965*. By focusing in this chapter on Moyar's interpretation of Diem, I do not mean to slight those aspects of his work that deal with other topics. (Indeed, *Triumph Forsaken* is a bold and sprawling book that intervenes in a host of important questions in Vietnam War historiography, not all of which have to do with Diem and his regime.) Nevertheless, Moyar's claims about Diem are crucial to the validity of the larger argument he advances in the book. Thus, an assessment of his interpretation of Diem provides a way to think critically about *Triumph Forsaken* and its contributions to the study of the Vietnam War.

Moyar's interpretation of Diem is one of the most interesting and historiographically significant aspects of the book. Moyar claims to be making new kinds of arguments about Diem and also draws upon some previously unused sources—including several Vietnamese-language histories published recently in Vietnam. In the end, however, his analysis of Diem is disappointing and unpersuasive. Moyar's main objective in writing about Diem is not to offer a new interpretation of the Vietnamese leader; rather, it is to defend Diem from his critics. In this regard, *Triumph Forsaken* perpetuates the old debates much more than it promotes the new efforts to find more historically minded ways of studying Diem and his regime.

Moyar is a Vietnam War revisionist, but his revisionism is unusual both for its interpretive scope and for its pugnaciousness. In *Triumph Forsaken*, Moyar has merged two strands of revisionist interpretation that had previously been advanced separately. The first of these is derived from the work of Guenter Lewy and Michael Lind, both of whom have stridently insisted that the domino theory was valid and that the United States could and should have held the line in South Vietnam.[4] However, where Lewy and Lind located America's fatal strategic mistakes mostly in the post-1965 era, Moyar dates the first major U.S. error to 1963, when the Kennedy administration backed a South Vietnamese military coup, which resulted in Diem's ouster and assassination. In decrying Washington's abandonment of Diem, Moyar draws on a second vein of revisionism, one that runs through the writings of the C.I.A.'s William Colby, Ellen Hammer, and others. Even the title of *Triumph Forsaken* seems a deliberate echo of Colby's 1989 memoir *Lost Victory*.[5] Moyar describes Diem as "a very wise and effective leader",[6] and he fully agrees with Colby that the Republic of Vietnam president was on his way to victory over the Vietnamese communists in 1963. Moyar's positive representation of Diem is thus one of the main linchpins on which his overall argument turns. But is this admiring portrait a convincing one?

Like many other historians who have written about Diem (including myself), Moyar argues that the Vietnamese leader achieved a number of unexpected successes during the first years of his rule. However, Moyar disagrees with those scholars who maintain that Diem's tactics and strategies were counterproductive in the long run. For example, Moyar notes that R.V.N. security forces came close to wiping out the Communist Party's organizational apparatus in South Vietnam during the late 1950s—a fact that is now widely accepted. Yet he rejects the view that the harshly repressive measures used by Diem's police and military served to alienate the rural population from the Saigon government. Moyar acknowledges that the N.L.F. (Viet Cong) insurgency turned the tables on Diem in 1960 and 1961 and scored impressive battlefield gains against the Army of the Republic of Vietnam (A.R.V.N.). However, this two-year period was the only time during Diem's tenure that "he fared poorly in the struggle for the villages."[7] By 1962, Moyar asserts, Diem had righted the ship and reclaimed the initiative in the countryside, thanks in part to a massive new infusion of U.S. military aid.

Having portrayed Diem as hugely successful and wildly popular in South Vietnam, Moyar blames his downfall on ignorant U.S. journalists and officials who had mistakenly concluded that Diem was losing the war, and on malevolent South Vietnamese leaders who saw Diem as a threat to their personal ambitions. Moyar is especially critical of the monks who led the 1963 anti-Diem Buddhist protest movement. He depicts the bonze Tri Quang and other "militant Buddhists" as cynical liars who manufactured specious claims of religious persecution and who were covertly working for the communists.[8] He is also unsparing in his treatment of those Kennedy administration officials who pushed for Diem's overthrow—especially Ambassador Henry Cabot Lodge. Thus, in Moyar's telling, Diem was undone not by his own shortcomings, but by the treason of his allies and subjects.

Moyar's admiring depiction of Diem can be understood as a reaction against the simplistic caricatures that have long dominated historical writing about the R.V.N. president. Orthodox historians have typically depicted Diem either as an American puppet or as a hopelessly backwards exponent of "tradition," who was predestined to fail. Moyar is commendably skeptical of such interpretations. Unfortunately, however, he undermines his own attempt to provide a persuasive alternative view by frequently flying to the opposite interpretive extreme. This is especially apparent in his analysis of the military situation in South Vietnam, in his assessment of Diem's popularity, and in his questionable use of certain historical sources. The lionized portrayal of Diem that emerges in *Triumph Forsaken* is just as distorted as the negative caricatures that the book aims to refute.

Moyar's assessment of Diem's military efforts against the communist-led insurgency illustrates his propensity for turning keen historical insights into exaggerated and unsustainable conclusions. While other historians may have been too quick to dismiss the gains made by the South Vietnamese army between 1962 and 1963, Moyar himself is far too eager to minimize or dismiss evidence of communist military progress in this period. His downplaying of communist gains is especially apparent in his treatment of data showing an increased number of insurgent attacks in the Mekong Delta during the summer of 1963. Moyar suggests that these attacks were strategically insignificant because they were concentrated in just four provinces.[9] The geographically focused nature of these strikes is certainly an interesting finding. However, since the four provinces in question had a combined population of over 2.2 million people—comprising 40 percent of the population of the Delta and 18 percent of South Vietnam's total population—the communist advances there were more significant than Moyar lets on.[10] Moyar also neglects to mention that, because of tactical withdrawals by government forces, communist forces in some provinces were able to increase the amount of territory under their control without mounting numerous attacks.[11] Diem might not have been on the verge of losing the Vietnam War in 1963, but it does not follow from this that he was on the verge of winning.

In one case, Moyar's desire to depict Diem as militarily dominant leads him to transform an A.R.V.N. defeat into a victory. In the famous battle of Ap Bac in January 1963, Viet Cong fighters inflicted heavy casualties on a much larger A.R.V.N. force and shot down five U.S. helicopters. Although historians have long debated the reasons for the U.S.–R.V.N. defeat, none has questioned the fact of the defeat—none except Moyar, who describes the battle as "a defeat for the Viet Cong in a strategic sense." This breathtaking claim is based on rather unconventional military logic:

> At the beginning of 1963, the government's regular forces outnumbered the Viet Cong's regulars by approximately ten to one, yet the ratio of government to Viet Cong casualties at Ap Bac was no higher than two to one, so the Viet Cong lost a much higher [pro]portion of their total armed strength.[12]

Even if Moyar's staggeringly high estimate of the enemy casualty rate during the battle (a hundred or more casualties out of 300-odd total fighters) is correct, his argument here rests on a misunderstanding of N.L.F. strategic objectives. Communist commanders chose to fight at Ap Bac in order to demonstrate their ability to use a medium-sized military formation to maul a numerically and technologically superior enemy force. Ap Bac was therefore a tactical *and* a strategic victory for the insurgents.

Moyar also makes erroneous claims about Diem's nation-building programs. For example, he incorrectly portrays Diem as conducting a sustained campaign of land reform, and he asserts that this campaign "seriously interfered" with the communists' efforts to win peasant support.[13] Moyar derives this claim from the translated version of a 1962 N.L.F. document. But the relevant portion of the document actually refers to "the U.S.–Diem policy of land expropriation," not to land redistribution. Another passage in the document makes it clear that South Vietnamese officials were undertaking this expropriation not to establish more equitable patterns of land ownership, but to increase their own wealth and power at the expense of the insurgents.[14]

Moyar's assertions notwithstanding, Diem never made more than desultory attempts to carry out land reform in South Vietnam.[15] Diem was not indifferent to the plight of poor peasants; however, he preferred to pursue rural reconstruction by redistributing people rather than by redistributing land. Strangely, Moyar makes no reference to Diem's program of "Land Development" (*Dinh Dien*), which relocated nearly a quarter of a million poor peasants from crowded lowland areas to new settlements in the central highlands and elsewhere. Like the later Strategic Hamlet program, the Land Development Program also reflected Diem's communitarian convictions and the abstruse "Personalist" philosophy of development espoused by his brother Ngo Dinh Nhu. If Moyar wanted to make the case for the effectiveness of Diem's nation-building programs, he ought to have focused on the most important of those programs, not on land reform.

Moyar's already shaky analysis of the situation in the South Vietnamese countryside is further weakened by his invocation of an outdated and condescending understanding of the peasants who lived there. Moyar depicts Vietnamese farmers as caught in a sort of time warp: "The basic outlook of the peasant had changed little since the early centuries of Vietnamese history . . . He venerated the bones of his ancestors, served his parents dutifully, and hoped that his children would remain to till his land after he was gone." Such peasants, Moyar asserts, "looked at the power of the opposing forces when deciding which side held the mandate of heaven, and they almost invariably threw their support to the strongest."[16] By invoking this patronizing and orientalist notion of "power-minded villagers,"[17] Moyar seeks to explain away a key contradiction lurking within his argument: his claim that peasant support for Diem rose at precisely the same time that his rule became more authoritarian and the behavior of R.V.N. officials became more arbitrary and onerous. The ironic effect of this move is that Moyar ends up affirming the arguments of those anti-Diem authors who have emphasized his "traditional" qualities. "Diem governed in an authoritarian way because he considered Western-style democracy inappropriate for a country that was fractious and dominated by an authoritarian culture."[18]

Moyar's superficial understanding of Vietnamese political history and political culture is also revealed in his explanation of the origins of the 1963 Buddhist protest movement. Moyar believes that Vietnam was "a nation where Buddhist monks rarely engaged in political activities." He therefore concludes that the 1963 movement was an aberration, and that Tri Quang and the other leaders of the movement must have been communist operatives.[19] In fact, Moyar is mistaken: Vietnamese Buddhist monks have frequently engaged in political activities, and the 1963 movement is best understood as part of the long-running "revival" of Vietnamese Buddhism that began during the 1920s. This revival eventually became linked to a distinctive form of Buddhist nationalism and to the promotion of Buddhism as the key to Vietnam's national destiny.[20] Moyar does not cite any reliable evidence showing that Tri Quang or any other leader of the 1963 movement was a communist, because no such evidence exists. There is, however, extensive evidence that these monks had embraced the Buddhist revival and the nationalism associated with it. There is also substantial evidence that suggests that the brand of Buddhist nationalism they endorsed was incompatible with communism. For example, a 1951 Viet Minh secret intelligence report specifically identified Tri Quang and other reform-minded monks as "reactionaries" whose goals were antithetical to those of the party.[21] It seems that communist leaders were cognizant of the ideological differences that separated them from the Buddhist leadership, even if Moyar is not.

As the above examples suggest, there are many points in *Triumph Forsaken* at which Moyar's interpretation of particular documents is open to criticism. Yet these interpretive problems are not the most troubling aspect of Moyar's use of sources. In a few cases, Moyar does not merely misinterpret sources; he actually misrepresents their textual content. On pages 165–166, Moyar writes about a July 1962 meeting between Diem and General Paul Harkins, the top U.S. military advisor in South Vietnam. For Moyar, Harkins is an admirable figure because he was one of Diem's staunchest American supporters and because he advised Diem "with enough tact and confidence to keep Diem's ear and respect." However, in his zeal to show the warm rapport that he says existed between the two men, Moyar exercises what might be generously described as poetic license. He relates what purports to be a verbatim account of the dialog between Harkins and Diem, as indicated in his use of quotation marks to indicate what each said to the other. But the sole document that Moyar cites for this exchange is an American memorandum of the conversation, which does not contain anything that can be construed as a verbatim record of the meeting. Instead, the memcon is a detailed paraphrasing of the key points made by the participants. The resulting differences between Moyar's rendering and his source are striking. For example, Moyar relates part of the meeting as follows:

> Diem admitted to Harkins, "I am concerned over the number of senior officers who have reached the height of their potential and who lack the education and initiative required in higher grades."
>
> "Such men should be eliminated," said Harkins.
>
> "The situation was inherited from the French, who were too easy and made colonels and lieutenant colonels who had no real capability or training," Diem explained. "One of the difficulties in identifying incompetent officers lies in the fact that my generals do not want to recommend the separation of officers who are old friends." Despite the problems involved, Diem said, "I am considering the thought of elimination."

The relevant portion of the memorandum reads as follows:

> [Diem] then added that he was concerned over the number of senior officers who have reached the height of their potential and who lack the education and initiative required in higher grades. In response to General Harkins' remark that such men should be eliminated, the President commented that the situation had been inherited from the French, who were too easy and had made colonels and lieutenant colonels who had no real capability or training. He was considering the thought of elimination. General Harkin's [sic] suggested that there might be an examination given and that those who failed to qualify would be eliminated. President Diem commented that one of the difficulties in identifying incompetent officers lies in the fact that his Generals do not want to recommend separation of officers who are old friends.[22]

Moyar might argue that the text of the memorandum still supports his interpretive claim about Harkins's ability to "coach" and advise Diem. But such an argument does not excuse the fact that Moyar has reconstructed a historical event in a way that dramatically embellishes the available record of that event. That Moyar repeats this practice elsewhere in the book—for example, in his account of a 1963 meeting between Diem and Robert McNamara on page 254—raises worrisome questions about whether and how frequently he plays fast and loose with his sources.

Triumph Forsaken is a bold and ambitious book that reflects the author's determination to challenge some long-held beliefs about the Vietnam War. Especially in the case of Ngo Dinh Diem, such an overhaul of the conventional wisdom is long overdue. Unfortunately, however, Moyar drains the persuasive power out of many of his arguments by making key interpretive and factual mistakes. As a result, the representation of Diem that he offers is as simplistic and distorted as the ones he proposes to replace. In this regard, *Triumph Forsaken* misses an opportunity to refute— or at least to qualify—Arthur Balfour's observation about historians and their propensity to repeat each other. The debate between the proponents of Vietnam War orthodoxy and revisionism seems destined to go on, at least for a little while longer.

Notes

1. An earlier version of this essay appeared under the title "Revisionism with a Vengeance: A Review of Mark Moyar's *Triumph Forsaken: The Vietnam War, 1954–1965*" in the December 2007 edition of *Passport*. The author thanks the editors of *Passport* for permission to publish this essay here in revised form.
2. James McAllister, "The Vietnam War: Orthodoxy, Revisionism, or None of the Above?" *History: Reviews of New Books* 37, no. 3 (March 2009): 85–87.
3. Examples of recent scholarship on Diem based partly or primarily on research in

Vietnamese sources include: Philip Catton, *Diem's Final Failure: Prelude to America's War in Vietnam* (Lawrence: University of Kansas Press, 2002); Edward Miller, "Vision, power and agency: the Ascent of Ngô Đình Diệm, 1945–1954," *Journal of Southeast Asian Studies* 35, no. 3 (October 2004): 433–458; Jessica Chapman, "Staging Democracy: South Vietnam's 1955 Referendum to Depose Bao Dai," *Diplomatic History* 30, no. 4 (Sep. 2006): 671–703; Matthew Masur, "Exhibiting Signs of Resistance: South Vietnam's Struggle for Legitimacy, 1954–1960," *Diplomatic History* 33, no. 2 (April 2009): 293–313. Another important contribution that is based on research in French and U.S. sources is Kathryn Statler, *Replacing France: The Origins of American Intervention in Vietnam* (Lexington, KY: University Press of Kentucky, 2007), esp. chapters 4–8. For an overview of the South Vietnamese government collections held at Archives II in Ho Chi Minh City, see Matthew Masur and Edward Miller, "Saigon Revisited: Researching South Vietnam's Republican Era (1954–1975) at Archives and Libraries in Ho Chi Minh City," Cold War International History Project, October 2006, accessible online at http://www.wilsoncenter.org/topics/docs/Saigon-Masur_Miller.pdf

4. Guenter Lewy, *America in Vietnam* (New York: Oxford University Press, 1978); Michael Lind, *Vietnam, the Necessary War: A Reinterpretation of America's Most Disastrous Military Conflict* (New York: Free Press, 1999).
5. William Colby, *Lost Victory: A Firsthand Account of America's Sixteen-Year Involvement in Vietnam* (Chicago: Contemporary Books, 1989); Ellen Hammer, *A Death in November: America in Vietnam, 1963* (New York: E.P. Dutton, 1987).
6. Mark Moyar, *Triumph Forsaken: The Vietnam War 1954–1965* (Cambridge: Cambridge University Press, 2006), xiv.
7. Ibid., 124.
8. Ibid., 212–218.
9. Ibid., 247.
10. Provincial population statistics are available in C.I.A. Intelligence Memorandum, "Laos, Cambodia, Vietnam, Thailand: Zone of Conflict in Southeast Asia," March 14, 1961, Folder 78, Box 05, Central Intelligence Agency Collection, The Vietnam Archive, Texas Tech University, Lubbock, TX (hereafter Vietnam Archive).
11. For example, government forces conceded large parts of Binh Duong province to the communists during the summer and fall of 1963: see Catton, *Diem's Final Failure*, chapter 7, especially pp. 180–182.
12. Moyar, *Triumph Forsaken*, 194.
13. Ibid., 72–73.
14. See "Assessment of the Status of the Revolution in Vietnam," September 25, 1962, Folder 2, Box 1, Douglas Pike Collection, Vietnam Archive. The "seriously interfered" quote appears on p. 26; the other referenced passage is on p. 22.
15. Diem's government did expropriate some land, but less than half of it was ever redistributed to farmers, and less than 10 percent of peasant families in South Vietnam benefited from the program.
16. Moyar, *Triumph Forsaken*, 92–93.
17. Ibid., 153.
18. Ibid., xiv.
19. Ibid, 217–218.
20. Nguyên Thê Anh, "L'engagement politique du Bouddhisme au Sud Viêt-Nam dans les années 1960," in *Bouddhismes et Sociétés Asiatiques: Clergés, sociétés et pouvoirs*, eds. Alain Forest et al. (Paris, 1990), 111–124.
21. Translated document No. 8602/2-R, "Traduction d'un document V.M. récupéré à BA-TRINH (KE-SACH) le 21 Septembre 1951," October 11, 1951, Box 10 H 4202, Archives de la Service Historique de l'Armée de la Terre, Vincennes, France.
22. Memorandum for the Record, 31 July 1963, *Foreign Relations of the United States, 1961–1963*, vol. III, Vietnam 1962 (Washington, D.C.: G.P.O., 1990), 244.

CHAPTER 18
Section III Response

MARK MOYAR

When I originally agreed to participate in a roundtable discussion of *Triumph Forsaken* for *Passport*, a publication of the Society for the History of American Foreign Relations, I did so with the understanding that the composition of the group would be balanced. But the editor of *Passport* solicited commentaries only from individuals who had previously expressed disdain for my work or that of like-minded historians. One of the four who produced commentaries was on the record as saying that people who interpret the Vietnam War as I do argue only on emotion, not reason;[1] a second had launched a pointed attack on me at the conference at Williams College;[2] the third was so far to the Left that he had attacked historians for accepting thoroughly documented facts such as the communists' slaughter of thousands of civilians at Hue in 1968[3] or the anti-war movement's hostility to the Americans who served in Vietnam;[4] and the fourth had assailed many of my book's main arguments in a journal article the previous year.[5]

Three of those four commentators employed the same approach in the roundtable: they attacked the book on a few points, ignored the rest, and then issued sweeping condemnations. Two alleged, in addition, that the book contained little of historical significance. Of the four, three agreed to contribute to *Triumph Revisited*, and two of those are included in this section. The first is David Anderson, the only one who eschewed ad hominem attacks and blanket fulminations in the course of registering his disagreements. Anderson's essay in this volume, which is very close to his roundtable contribution, is a model of civil discourse. Most of the issues

Anderson discusses have been addressed elsewhere in *Triumph Revisited*, so I will not repeat my responses here. One crucial exception is an issue that most of the other commentators, surprisingly, ignored—the validity of the domino theory. Anderson contends that the domino theory was invalid because the Vietnamese communists were nationalists who did not have the intentions or capabilities to expand beyond Vietnam. But I believe that they had the intentions and, increasingly, the capabilities. Ho Chi Minh and his disciples fervently believed in Marxist–Leninist internationalism, and tried time and again to promote revolution beyond Vietnam's borders (8–11, 25, 83, 359, 425, note 51). By the early 1960s, they already had large numbers of troops in Laos, and later in the war they would have a large military and political presence in Cambodia. In the late 1970s, they ran into trouble in Cambodia and could not get beyond it, but their failure was a result of Hanoi's falling out with China, which was a by-product of the Vietnam War. During 1965, Hanoi and Beijing were working in unison to spread communism across Asia. Meeting in the spring of 1965, Ho Chi Minh and Mao discussed building roads to Thailand in order to fight future wars (362–363).

Had the United States not prevented North Vietnam from overrunning South Vietnam in 1965, other U.S. allies in the region, such as Thailand and Japan, almost certainly would have switched allegiance to China without direct Chinese or North Vietnamese military action. Others, like Malaysia, probably would have fallen victim to communist insurgency. Absent U.S. intervention in Vietnam, Indonesia's pro-Chinese government most likely would not have fallen to anti-communist military officers as it did in late 1965. The United States thus would have lost many of its military bases and trading partners, with profoundly damaging long-term implications (376–391).

I was pleased to see that Mark Lawrence was convinced by some of the book's main points—in particular those concerning the difficulties faced by the Vietnamese communist forces, the pressure by American military officers for ground action in Laos and North Vietnam, the support of Asian and Pacific governments for American intervention in Vietnam, the dark deeds of the Vietnamese communists, and Ho Chi Minh's close collaboration with China and the Soviet Union. I do, however, disagree with many of Lawrence's other comments. Lawrence contends that I overturn simplistic caricatures of the Vietnamese only to replace them with new ones, which, he says, "often seem inspired by a deeply conservative agenda rather than a deep reading of the available evidence." He appears to be saying, as Edward Miller appears to say later, that I first decided that American support for Diem and Vietnam was good and then I looked for ways of portraying the Vietnamese and Diem to prove that point. But if one looks at my first book, I portrayed the Vietnamese in much the same way but did not come out in favor of Diem—at that time, I had studied peasant culture extensively but had not discovered the gross fallacies in the conventional depictions of Diem.[6] As stated in the previous chapter, I changed my views on central questions of the war while researching *Triumph Forsaken* in accordance with the discovery of new facts.

Lawrence faults me for not mentioning Ho Chi Minh's nationalist activity before 1920, especially his unsuccessful appeal to President Woodrow Wilson in 1919 for Vietnamese self-determination. These events, Lawrence says, indicate that "Ho and his collaborators should be understood as disillusioned nationalists who turned to communism only after being rebuffed by the liberal West" instead of "a craven ideologue." I did not include the information in question because Ho had already begun participating in socialist political organizations before he sent the appeal to Wilson, and hence Wilson's rebuff was not a deciding factor in his attraction to socialism. As Ho's biographer William Duiker noted, it is possible that Ho had no hope at all that Wilson would provide a favorable response and that he "merely counted on the impact of the petition to popularize the cause of anticolonialism and radicalize the Vietnamese community in France."[7] Frustration with French colonialism certainly did make Ho Chi Minh more receptive to radicalism; had French colonialism been absent, Ho's political views might well have been different—not only because he would have had less cause to resent imperialism and capitalism, but also because he would not have gone to France, where he was exposed to the ideas of the radical Left. But acknowledging these realities does not mean that Ho's subsequent actions were justified, or that he posed no danger to the United States. Many Vietnamese nationalists who were disillusioned with the French, including Ngo Dinh Diem and Ngo Dinh Nhu, did not turn to radicalism, did not embrace the concept of violent global revolution, and did not come out in favor killing huge numbers of defenseless civilians as Ho Chi Minh did. The West might have been able to steer Ho off the path to radicalism through its actions during the early years of Ho's life, but Ho was a diehard communist by the 1940s, when Vietnam became a serious concern of the United States.

My treatment of the Franco-Viet Minh War comes under attack from Lawrence for "saying nothing of the fluidity of Viet Minh ideology as the movement struggled desperately to find foreign support." Yet I do mention that the Viet Minh professed to be a conglomeration of diverse nationalists, rather than a hierarchy led by doctrinaire communists. I also argue this portrayal was a deceitful attempt to gain support from the United States and other foreign powers; the Viet Minh organization was always controlled by people dedicated to communist ideology. Ho's ideology and that of his Communist Party did not change; he was merely resorting to the old communist trick of gaining the temporary assistance of one enemy to destroy another as a stepping stone towards destroying all of his enemies (1–25).

According to Lawrence, *Triumph Forsaken* suffers from omitting the belief of many French, British, and American officials that Ho Chi Minh embodied Vietnamese nationalism. I do not believe that this view was as prevalent as Lawrence maintains, although it certainly did exist. That such officials came to that conclusion is largely a reflection of their narrow range of information sources and their general ignorance of Vietnamese politics.

Lawrence criticizes my recounting of the Denounce the Communists campaign for not providing as much gory detail as my descriptions of Ho Chi Minh's wrongdoing. It is a legitimate point to raise, since such descriptions can influence perceptions. As Lawrence notes, I state that the South Vietnamese government engaged in torture and killed a significant number of communist prisoners, but do not go into the same level as detail as I do with some of the communist atrocities. Undoubtedly, the Diem government did commit some gruesome killings during the Denounce the communists campaign, and a more detailed description could be useful. The available sources, however, do not provide the details on the government side that we have on the communist side. In addition, the South Vietnamese government was more inclined than the Viet Cong to arrest people rather than kill them, and less inclined to commit the most horrific types of violence, because it did not share the Leninist ideology of the communists. Even accounts that are generally sympathetic towards the revolutionaries, like David Elliott's, show that Diem's crackdowns of the late 1950s were not nearly as bloody or cruel as the North Vietnamese land reform or the "Destruction of the Oppression" in 1960.[8]

Lawrence's criticisms of my depiction of South Vietnamese political culture largely mirror those of Chapman, which I addressed in the previous section. He makes several additional supporting points that deserve a response. According to Lawrence, David Elliott's study shows that the Denounce the Communists campaigns undermined "the government's legitimacy in the eyes of its people," contrary to what I argued in *Triumph Forsaken*. Elliott argues that the repression following Decree 10/59 of May 1959 "pushed tensions in the countryside to the breaking point," creating grassroots resentment that sparked the communist assassination campaign of 1960. Yet if the repression had created such a backlash, then one would have expected the communist counterattack and shifts in peasant attitudes to have commenced later in 1959, not in 1960. Other sections of Elliott's book, in fact, contradict the claim that the government's actions produced mass unrest. Elliott himself acknowledges that the peasants looked back fondly on the period up to 1960 as a time of peace and tranquility, not a time of seething discontent with the government. He also states that the Diem government's arrests during the campaigns of the late 1950s mainly created popular fear of aiding the Viet Cong, rather than popular anger against the government.[9]

Communist histories make clear that the reason the assassination campaign began in 1960 was that higher headquarters ordered it to begin at that time, not that popular opposition to the government surged at that time. Elliott downplays the importance of military factors in gaining popular support for the insurgents in 1960.[10] Yet, as Elliott concedes, the insurgency enjoyed a resurgence of popular support only after the armed struggle began in 1960, and many of his sources support the view that force played a crucial role. A district cadre recounted that only a few people wholeheartedly supported the insurgency, while "the majority of them followed it out of fear ... How could the people help being scared of the Front when in most of the villages where the Destruction of the Oppression campaign was carried out, there were always so many villagers who were either beheaded by machetes or stabbed by blunt bayonets?"[11] Sau Duong, the regional Communist Party leader, noted that killing "tyrants" had "brought out the revolutionary spirit in the masses."[12] In addition, Elliott shows that the assassination campaign drove off or killed South Vietnamese officials who had been able to obtain the assistance of the population, thereby weakening support for the government and reducing the government's ability to counter the insurgency's military and political actions.[13]

I do agree with Elliott that dissatisfaction with abusive government officials helped the communists gain supporters from 1960. As Elliott rightly notes, these same officials had been in power before any of the Denounce the Communists campaigns had begun.[14] It was thus a longstanding problem of bad governance; the fact that it had persisted until 1960 is another indicator that it was not the principal cause of the uprising, but rather was a facilitator for the principal cause, the armed revolt.

In Lawrence's view, the interpretation that force profoundly influenced peasant behavior is undermined by America's failure to weaken the Vietnamese revolution militarily or to reduce its popular support with huge amounts of military and economic aid, even during 1962 and 1963. The best available evidence on this score, he asserts, comes from a few studies of local communities, specifically the studies of James Trullinger, Jeffrey Race, and David Elliott. Lawrence contends that those three authors concluded that the Viet Cong received support for a large variety of reasons, of which force was not a dominant one.

These are important points, for the three studies mentioned by Lawrence are the studies most commonly used in assessing the causes of support for the insurgency. They are, indeed, fine historical studies: I read each of them cover to cover, and cited each in the footnotes to *Triumph Forsaken*. As previous sections have indicated, they support many of my arguments. With respect to the war in 1962 and 1963, however, they must not be used as representative cases, for they differed from most areas of the country. Trullinger's work covered a single village in Thua Thien province, and one that Trullinger states was "atypical of most Vietnamese villages in size, location, history, and so forth." This village had a history of unusually strong support for the Vietnamese communists dating back to the Franco-Viet Minh War. It was not, moreover, included in the Strategic Hamlet program because the program was established across the rest of the province.[15] Long An and Dinh Tuong provinces—covered by Race and Elliott, respectively—were the only two of South Vietnam's forty-four provinces where the Strategic Hamlet program endured major setbacks during the first ten months of 1963 (247–248). The South Vietnamese leadership in these two provinces was generally weaker than in other provinces because Diem generally put his least competent leaders in the Mekong Delta and because the provinces' proximity to Saigon inclined Diem to assign them leaders of certain loyalty and less certain merit in case of a coup attempt (202). Elliott himself acknowledged, "It cannot be stated that My Tho/Dinh Tuong is 'representative' of the larger situation in Vietnam during the 1930–75 period, nor is any other region or province."[16] And even in Long An and Dinh Tuong, the two worst provinces for the Strategic Hamlets, the government was causing serious problems for the insurgents until Diem was overthrown and the Strategic Hamlet program collapsed (285). As mentioned in the previous section, *Triumph Forsaken* cites a multitude of sources covering all areas of South Vietnam and shows that the Strategic Hamlet program and the rest of the war effort were generally running in the government's favor during Diem's last two years.

Lawrence contends that Diem's Catholicism "distanced Diem from the vast majority of his people." Catholicism distanced Diem from fanatical Buddhists like Tri Quang, but few other South Vietnamese ever said or showed that they thought less of him because of his religion. Diem's efforts to impose Christian morality, such as the laws against adultery, created some resentment among the urban population, but it is doubtful that the fractious Saigonese would have thought much differently about Diem had these laws not existed. Large numbers of non-Catholics supported Diem and served loyally in the highest positions in his government (216). The cabal that ousted Diem, which included men of all of South Vietnam's major religions, had deemed him the best leader for the country and ousted him only because of American pressure (229–262). Villagers and former Viet Cong who were interviewed about peasant political concerns focused on whether national leaders and local leaders were corrupt, disrespectful, or cruel, not whether they belonged to one religion or another.

Michael Lind contends that American intervention in North Vietnam likely would have led to a repetition of the Korean War—an approach of U.S. forces toward the Chinese border would have sparked Chinese intervention. But the United States would not have needed to move huge forces near China's border with North Vietnam. The October 5, 1964, conversation between Chinese and North Vietnamese leaders, referenced in the first section of this volume, states that the North Vietnamese intended to withdraw from the coast and fight from the mountains as they had fought against the French. The United States could have deployed its forces to the same general areas as the French, with large numbers in and around the populous areas, some mobile units in the hinterlands to combat enemy forces, and little military activity near the Chinese border for at least a year or two.

Lind doubts that a war in both Vietnams would have been any better than a war restricted to South Vietnam, but in fact it would have been much better. The communists would have lost control of most of their logistical infrastructure and most of the areas from which they recruited troops. Many of the one million anti-communist Vietnamese who had fled from the North to the South in 1954 would have helped create formidable anti-communist armed forces in the North. In a war encompassing all of Indochina, the French had nearly destroyed the communists with only 150,000 foreign troops, far fewer than the 550,000 troops the United States eventually put in South Vietnam (26). And Vo Nguyen Giap believed that the United States could have invaded North Vietnam successfully with just three ground divisions (321–322, 480–481).

In discussing my criticism of Lyndon Johnson for publicly foreswearing offensive warfare against North Vietnam and China, Lind underestimates the damaging effects of Johnson's rhetoric. By pledging that he had no intention of attacking North Vietnam and China, and by portraying himself as a man of peace by word and lack of deeds, Johnson dissipated the power of American deterrence, power that had held North Vietnam and China in check for a decade. Johnson should have followed the example of President Eisenhower, who, by keeping all options on the table and issuing subtle threats, had intimidated and deterred the communists without starting a war.

Lind is mistaken in suggesting that China was as likely to intervene if the United States invaded southern Laos (to cut the Ho Chi Minh Trail) as if it invaded North Vietnam. Whereas the Chinese sometimes discussed the possibility of sending their troops to North Vietnam in response to an American invasion of that country, they made no comparable remarks on Laos. The Ho Chi Minh Trail was nowhere near China's borders, so China's own security would not have been imperiled by the arrival of American ground forces in the Laotian panhandle. Nor would American intervention in Laos have threatened to destroy a key Chinese ally. The Chinese would have faced tremendous logistical difficulties fighting in the rugged terrain of Laos, for China lacked the massive air transportation and engineering capabilities of the United States. The North Vietnamese and Soviets clearly did not expect the Chinese to send forces to protect the Ho Chi Minh Trail, as they predicted that between three and five U.S. divisions would have been enough to shut down the infiltration routes (322–334, 360).

Lind contends that the United States lost the Vietnam War because its pacification efforts failed to defeat the insurgents. But, as is shown in my first book and also in Lewis Sorley's *A Better War*, pacification ultimately succeeded. South Vietnamese and American forces wiped out the Viet Cong insurgents by the early 1970s.[17] South Vietnam fell in 1975 because over half a million well-equipped North Vietnamese regulars attacked South Vietnamese forces that had been deprived of fuel, weapons, ammunition, and spare parts by American aid cuts.

I find James McAllister's comparison of *Triumph Forsaken* with other revisionist works to be incisive. It is tempting and easy to lump all of the revisionists together and then argue that *Triumph Forsaken* differs little from the rest, as a variety of other commentators have done. I do disagree with the contention of many revisionists that Westmoreland and other military leaders before Creighton Abrams were wrong to devote so many troops to chasing communist units in the hinterlands. A few others had advanced arguments similar to mine previously, but without getting very far into the details or the documentary record. One of the reasons that *Triumph Forsaken* covers the big battles from late 1964 to mid-1965 in depth is to show the power of the communists' conventional military capabilities and the perils of allocating insufficient conventional military forces to fight them. Since the publication of *Triumph Forsaken*, several other historians have published similar appraisals of Westmoreland's strategy and the weaknesses of focusing primarily on population security, including some that were written before the release of *Triumph Forsaken*.[18]

A number of McAllister's comments on the China question have been addressed in my previous responses. But in those responses, I did not cover his argument that I differ little from other historians on Johnson's refusal to invade North Vietnam in late 1964 and early 1965. As McAllister points out, I largely absolve Johnson for not invading North Vietnam during those months, but I do so for a very different reason than other historians—the failure of American intelligence to predict Hanoi's change in strategy (322). In addition, I differ from others in arguing that Johnson bears some responsibility for the Chinese decision in March 1965 to deploy Chinese troops to North Vietnam. The restraints he placed on the bombing of the North and his public denials of any intention to conquer North Vietnam or China gave the Chinese grounds to conclude that Chinese troops sent to North Vietnam would not get into a fight with American troops. So too did the manner in which he deployed the first U.S. troops to South Vietnam, although this behavior is more excusable because of the inadequacy of American intelligence. I am also the first to argue that even after the Chinese troops were deployed, they might still have retreated in the face of an American invasion rather than stayed and fought, for as the troops began arriving, the Chinese stated again on several occasions that they would fight the Americans only if they attacked China itself (413).

McAllister disputes my assertion that Tri Quang was likely to have been a communist agent. The evidence of Tri Quang's communist affiliation presented in *Triumph Forsaken*, he contends, is no more convincing than what Marguerite Higgins presented in her 1965 book *Our Vietnam Nightmare*. First, it must be said that Higgins presented some important, and wrongfully neglected, evidence. My research shows that Higgins' work was more accurate than that of David Halberstam or Neil Sheehan; the fact that she has largely been forgotten, while Halberstam and Sheehan have become iconic figures, reflects the biases of many who have written about Vietnam and the unfortunate fact that Higgins died in 1966. Higgins revealed, among other things, that Tri Quang's brother was a senior North Vietnamese official, and that Tri Quang had at one time belonged to the Viet Minh State Department, and C.I.A. documents from 1963 and 1964 confirm that Tri Quang acknowledged both of these facts to be true (458, note 59).

I also incorporated some evidence not used by Higgins. During the 1963 crisis, Tri Quang advocated collaboration with the communists, and in 1964 some of Tri Quang's followers turned against him and declared him to be a communist (218). In 1964 and 1965, Tri Quang frequently used false charges of wrongdoing to demand that the Saigon government remove some of the best anti-communist officers (317, 319, 364, 394). Tri Quang had ties to the People's Revolutionary Committees established in Annam in 1964, which were viewed by many as tools of the communists (317). Tran Van Huong, like Diem, believed Tri Quang to be an accomplice of the communists, and both Huong and Diem knew more about Vietnamese politics than any Americans (334). Furthermore, *Triumph Forsaken* is the first history to provide evidence from North Vietnamese sources of extensive communist participation in the Buddhist movement in 1963, evidence that none of the reviewers has disputed (217, 231).

Let us imagine that a present-day American critic of U.S. government policy toward Muslims was found to be the brother of a senior Al Qaeda official, that he admitted to having belonged to Al Qaeda in the past, and that he recently declared that all good Muslims should cooperate with Al Qaeda in toppling the Obama administration. Let us also assume that some of his closest associates later said that he still belonged to Al Qaeda, that he made absurd charges of discrimination against the best American anti-terrorism officials, that many of his American followers were actually Al Qaeda operatives, and that his actions led to a drastic weakening of American actions against Al Qaeda. Would one not have strong suspicions that such an individual was a member of Al Qaeda?

McAllister emphasizes that American analysts at the time believed that Tri Quang was not a communist. It is true that contemporary American intelligence analysts concluded that Tri Quang was not a communist agent, although the C.I.A. acknowledged that its assertions about Tri Quang's affiliation were very subjective and some American officials did believe that Tri Quang was working with the communists (317). C.I.A. analysts did not have access to all of the information we now possess, and I think they did not show very good judgment in this instance. They were far from infallible—as noted above, the C.I.A. was also spectacularly wrong about North Vietnamese intentions in late 1964 and early 1965. American intelligence analysts did not believe that Pham Xuan An was a communist agent, either. Identifying a secret agent is a difficult business and the inability to spot an agent at the time is not a very good indicator of that person's true loyalties.

According to McAllister, Tri Quang was "very anti-communist and privately supportive of aggressive American military actions against the North." McAllister is correct in noting that Tri Quang told the Americans on a variety of occasions that they should take aggressive actions against North Vietnam. I, like some observers at the time, suspect that such statements were insincere and were intended merely to increase his credibility with the Americans. It is very doubtful that Tri Quang, or the people for whom he may have been working, believed that his recommendations would influence America's policy toward North Vietnam. Tri Quang opposed anti-communism much more often than he expressed support for it. As mentioned above, he advocated collaboration with the communists in 1963, and he later made absurd demands for the removal of fiercely anti-communist officials. In August 1964, Tri Quang threatened to abandon the anti-communist struggle unless Diemist elements were purged from the government (316). In early 1965, he publicly called for negotiations between Hanoi and Washington, which was widely interpreted to mean that he wanted the United States to cave in, since negotiations at that point likely would have ended with nothing better than a neutral regime in the South that was highly vulnerable to communist predations (366). In the end, what is most important is not whether Tri Quang was taking orders from Hanoi, but whether he did tremendous harm to the South Vietnamese government, for the nature and impact of Tri Quang's meddling can corroborate or refute the arguments that Diem led a reasonably just and effective government and that his government and its successors were wrecked not by popular upheaval but by the conniving of a small minority. I spent much of the book showing that Tri Quang caused great harm to the South Vietnamese government, another critical aspect of the book that has not been questioned.

McAllister states, "The communists, both during and after the war, certainly saw [Tri Quang] as an irreconcilable enemy rather than as a partner," and backs this view with a communist document from late 1966 that denounced Tri Quang. This document is interesting and significant, but it does not prove that Tri Quang was not a communist. If Tri Quang had been working secretly for North Vietnam, most North Vietnamese officials, including the author of this document, would not have been informed of it. Extraordinarily tight security procedures would have been maintained with such a profoundly important agent. In addition, the date of the document in question comes well after the events I describe in *Triumph Forsaken*, and after the showdown between the Buddhists and the government in the spring of 1966, and it is possible that the communists parted ways with Tri Quang sometime between the end of *Triumph Forsaken* and late 1966. I have not yet studied the Buddhist troubles of 1966 in detail; as I work on volume two of *Triumph Forsaken*, I will explore this issue further. How the communists treated Tri Quang after the war is not entirely clear (458, note 63). But even if they were not kind to him, we could not conclude that he had never served the communists—the North Vietnamese maltreated numerous South Vietnamese communists after the fall of Saigon for abetting the enemy or various other reasons.

Edward Miller is correct in noting that the debate over the history of the Vietnam War has, too often, been a debate about Americans, in which the Vietnamese are merely stage props. That reality is one reason why I was able to break new ground in *Triumph Forsaken*—by devoting much more coverage to the opposing Vietnamese parties, I uncovered facts that are essential to understanding the war. I found that North and South Vietnamese actions were not fixed, but instead resulted from perceptions of the other parties and judgments derived therefrom—perceptions and judgments often as faulty as those of the United States. American actions influenced their behavior as much as their actions influenced American behavior. Thus, for instance, the fallout from the pagoda raids of August 1963 was not the inevitable next step of a government in a downward spiral, as it has often been portrayed, but rather the product of duplicitous political opposition and an ensuing debate within the government over the consequences of tolerating the Buddhist opposition, in which the domestic costs of losing face were weighed against the benefits of retaining American approval. It precipitated a debacle that began with an American decision to support a coup by generals who had advocated the raids and then misled the Americans about their complicity after the Americans became outraged. I discovered that the North Vietnamese decision in late 1964 to invade South Vietnam was not a foregone conclusion, but rather was the result of extensive deliberations that focused on American actions, perceived American intentions, conditions in South Vietnam, and international circumstances.

In an effort to portray me as one unpalatable extreme and the standard orthodoxy as the other unpalatable extreme (the "Goldilocks" method), Miller repeatedly misstates the content of *Triumph Forsaken*. As described by Miller, the book acknowledges communist advances in four Mekong Delta provinces during the summer of 1963, advances that Miller contends were more important than I let on because these provinces were heavily populated. What I actually state in *Triumph Forsaken* is that the communists concentrated their attacks in four provinces but caused major damage in only two (247–248). I subsequently observe that even in those two provinces, the communists did not inflict severe damage on the strategic hamlets until after Diem's assassination (285). Miller gives the impression that I believe that Diem "was on the verge of winning" in 1963. I actually argue the following: "Had Diem lived, the Viet Cong could have kept the war going as long as they continued to receive new manpower from North Vietnam and maintained sanctuaries in Cambodia and Laos, but it is highly doubtful that the war would have reached the point where the United States needed to introduce several hundred thousand of its own troops to avert defeat, as it would under Diem's successors." (286)

Miller takes me to task for not mentioning that the South Vietnamese government ceded large amounts of territory to the communists in 1963 in Binh Duong province—the province from which Philip Catton extrapolated in his book—and other provinces. But the Saigon government's abandonment of some territory in Binh Duong, which resulted from unusually intense enemy military activity and difficult terrain, ran contrary to trends in most provinces. Nationwide, the South Vietnamese government was increasing its control of both population and territory in the summer and fall of 1963 (248, 283–285). Within Binh Duong, withdrawal from certain areas did not prevent the Diem government from using the Strategic Hamlet program to expand its control over the province's population, which mattered more than territory. Although the Strategic Hamlet program encountered more difficulties in Binh Duong than in the other III Corps provinces, it was not in the same category as the worst Delta provinces (247–248, 284–285). A September 1963 U.S.O.M. report stated that, in Binh Duong, the South Vietnamese were succeeding militarily, and "substantial gains are being made in the strategic hamlet program." It noted that of 205 strategic hamlets planned for Binh Duong, 108 had been completed and fifty were under construction. The strategic hamlets contained 209,944 people of the province's total population of 302,655.[19] A Viet Cong report on Binh Duong in the late summer of 1963 confirms that the South Vietnamese government was militarily and politically aggressive and was able to recruit most of the province's youths into its service, while the Viet Cong were enduring heavy losses and could not obtain any popular support in the strategic hamlets.[20]

Miller contends that I use "rather unconventional military logic" in making the "breathtaking claim" that the Viet Cong succeeded tactically at Ap Bac and may have suffered fewer casualties than their enemies, but failed strategically because they lost a much larger fraction of their total armed forces. That logic is far from unconventional. Historians of the American Civil War commonly contend that although Union casualties outnumbered Confederate casualties in battles like Shiloh, Antietam, Murfreesboro, and Chancellorsville, these battles benefited the Union strategically because the smaller Confederate armed forces were losing a larger fraction of their total strength.[21] In most wars, the numerical strengths of the opposing forces are a very important or the most important factor. For the communists to achieve their final objective—the seizure of South Vietnam's cities—they had to mass great numbers of troops. They were not going to take Saigon or Da Nang with a few hundred guerrillas.

According to Miller, the communists' strategic objective at Ap Bac was to maul a numerically and technologically superior force. That is a tactical objective. Their strategic objective was to destroy large numbers of government forces, for they viewed the South Vietnamese armed forces as the principal impediment to final victory (70–71, 300–301, 339–340, 359), and also hoped that heavy casualties would encourage dissension within the Saigon government (146, 161). The South Vietnamese casualties at Ap Bac were by themselves too small in scale to constitute significant progress toward the realization of that objective. Ap Bac could have provided a strategic benefit for the Viet Cong had it served as the blueprint for many subsequent Viet Cong victories, but in the ensuing ten months, the Viet

Cong usually suffered defeat when they assembled in large numbers as they had at Ap Bac (208–211, 246–248, 256–257).

Miller claims that a communist acknowledgment of damage caused by "land expropriation" does not mean that Diem's land reform achieved substantial results. Miller's reasoning is not entirely clear, but he does say that a different passage in the document shows that the South Vietnamese undertook "land expropriation" not to provide more equitable land distribution, but to increase their own power. The passage he cites actually says nothing of the kind; it merely lists land expropriation as one of many governmental initiatives that should be opposed.[22] Lamenting the negative political consequences of expropriation while ignoring the positive consequences of its redistribution, as Miller appears to be doing, is akin to lamenting the political cost of taxation while ignoring the benefits of government spending. What hurt the insurgents was not the expropriation of the land, but the distribution of this land to farmers who had owned no land, for landowning farmers were poor targets for Viet Cong promises of land redistribution.

In Miller's estimation, Diem's land reform was "desultory." Before the start of Diem's land reform in 1956, nearly 80 percent of the peasants in the highly populous Mekong Delta owned no land. By 1960, only 44 percent of Delta peasants remained landless.[23] How Miller considers this achievement unimpressive is difficult to fathom. Would we consider it unimpressive if the number of Americans below the poverty line in a large and populous area went from 80 percent to 44 percent in four years?

Miller leads the reader to believe that I view Diem's land reform as an unalloyed success. In reality, I note that the program suffered from major problems, including an excessively high ownership limit and a lack of funding, and that it left a large number of peasants in the Mekong Delta without land (73). Miller then claims that I overlooked Diem's relocation of peasants to the highlands, but in fact I discuss how and why Diem relocated these peasants, as well as their subsequent influence on the war in the highlands (72, 392).

Miller's claim that Vietnam's Buddhist monks had frequently engaged in political activities is followed by no enumeration of such activities. According to Miller, I argue that "Tri Quang and the other leaders of the movement must have been communist operatives," but I actually argue that Hanoi's influence among top Buddhist leaders is not certain, although considerable evidence suggests that one of them, Tri Quang, was a communist (217–218). Miller goes so far as to say that there is no reliable evidence that any leaders of the 1963 Buddhist movement were communists. Although no such proof has appeared with respect to higher-level leaders, the Hanoi government has acknowledged that it had agents in the Buddhist movement who organized some of the antigovernmental activity, so those agents must have held leadership positions of some type (217, 231). In addition, as mentioned in my response to James McAllister, a large amount of evidence on Tri Quang cannot be easily dismissed as Miller suggests.

Miller then asserts that I "misrepresented" the "textual content" of sources, which "dramatically embellishes the available record" and "raises worrisome questions about whether and how frequently he plays fast and loose with his sources." Miller seems to be asserting that I seriously misrepresented the meaning of sources, but when he gets down to specifics, it turns out that he is discussing something of much less significance, which begs the question of why he used such ominous and inflammatory language. What he is discussing is merely the use of meeting notes as verbatim transcripts—a matter of style rather than content, upon which reasonable people sometimes disagree. Other historians have employed this same method without incurring invective. Richard Reeves, for example, used it extensively in his highly acclaimed *President Kennedy*, which won best non-fiction book of the year accolades from *Time Magazine* and P.E.N.

In Miller's opinion, I invoke "an outdated and condescending understanding of the peasants." He offers no explanation to back up this accusation, although presumably he takes exception to some of the same interpretations as previous contributors. His next bold denunciation, that I possess a "superficial understanding of Vietnamese political history and political culture," also goes unsubstantiated. That a respected scholar feels free to take such cheap shots at a purveyor of unfashionable thinking is but one more negative consequence of the one-party state at our colleges and universities.

Notes

1. David L. Anderson, "One Vietnam War Should Be Enough and Other Reflections on Diplomatic History and the Making of Foreign Policy," *Diplomatic History*, vol. 30, no. 1 (January 2006), 1–21.
2. David Kaiser at the conference entitled "New Vietnam War Revisionism: Implications and Lessons," Williams College, March 2–3, 2007. Kaiser chose not to include his *Passport* contribution in this book. For that exchange, and my exchange with the *Passport* editor about the choice of reviewers, see the December 2007 issue of *Passport*.
3. Scott Laderman, " 'They Set About Revenging Themselves on the Population': The Hue Massacre in Travel Guide Books, and the Shaping of Historical Consciousness in Vietnam," available online at http://just.nicepeople.free.fr/The_Hue_Massacre.htm
4. Scott Laderman, "Recovering the Reality of 'Supporting Our Troops,' " *Minnesota Daily*, March 14, 2003.
5. Edward Miller, "War Stories: The Taylor–Buzzanco Debate and How We Think about the Vietnam War, *Journal of Vietnamese Studies*, vol. 1, No. 1–2 (2006), 453–484.
6. Moyar, *Phoenix and the Birds of Prey*, 3–5, 36–37, 292.

7. William J. Duiker, *Ho Chi Minh* (New York: Hyperion, 2000), 60.
8. On the 1960 violence, see Elliott, *The Vietnamese War*, vol. 1, 245–270.
9. Ibid., 163–188.
10. Ibid.
11. Ibid., 315.
12. Ibid., 251.
13. Ibid., 258–265.
14. Ibid., 166, 183–184.
15. Trullinger, *Village at War*, xii, 48–63, 73.
16. Elliott, *The Vietnamese War*, vol. 1, xxii.
17. Moyar, *Phoenix and the Birds of Prey*; Lewis Sorley, *A Better War: The Unexamined Victories and Final Tragedy of America's Last Years in Vietnam* (New York: Harcourt Brace, 1999).
18. Andrew J. Birtle, *U.S. Army Counterinsurgency and Contingency Operations Doctrine, 1942–1976* (Washington, D.C.: Center of Military History, 2007); Andrew J. Birtle, "PROVN, Westmoreland, and the Historians: A Reappraisal," *Journal of Military History*, vol. 72, no. 4 (October 2008), 1,213–1,247; Dale Andrade, "Why Westmoreland Was Right," *Vietnam*, vol. 21, no. 6 (April 2009), 26–32; Gian Gentile, "Let's Build an Army to Win All Wars," *Joint Force Quarterly*, 52 (January 2009), 27–33.
19. U.S.O.M. Rural Affairs, "Second Informal Appreciation of the Status of the Strategic Hamlet Program."
20. "Binh Duong Monthly Report," August 1963, Virtual Vietnam Archive, item 23119056001.
21. See, for instance, James M. McPherson, *Drawn with the Sword: Reflections on the American Civil War* (New York: Oxford University Press, 1996); Alan T. Nolan, *Lee Considered: General Robert E. Lee and Civil War History* (Chapel Hill: University of North Carolina Press, 1991).
22. VCD 257, September 1962, TTU, Pike Collection, Unit 1, box 1.
23. Carlyle A. Thayer, *War By Other Means: National Liberation and Revolution in Viet-Nam, 1954–60* (Sydney: Allen & Unwin, 1989), 119; Roy L. Prosterman, "Land Reform in Vietnam," *Current History*, December 1969, 327–332.

Conclusion

MICHAEL J. DOIDGE

In 1999, the satirical newspaper *The Onion* published a collection of mock headlines in a work titled *Our Dumb Century*, which contained several articles that addressed the U.S. war in Vietnam. One of the more provocative headlines read "U.S. Loses Vietnam War; Ford Urges All Americans to Salute Our Vietcong Rulers."[1] With a flair for biting satire and wit, the mock headline and its subsequent article took aim with pointed humor at U.S. war aims, the war's results, and finally the adage that "winners write history," jesting that the Viet Cong would write U.S. history. *The Onion*'s headline contained an even greater irony than its satirists knew: despite its ownership of the "loser" position, the United States has produced more scholarship dedicated to the study of the Vietnam experience than any other nation, to include Vietnam itself. Roles were reversed, the losers did write the history.

And the irony has not stopped there. Mark Moyar is the most visible proponent of a group of insurgent intellectuals representing the "revisionist" school of Vietnam War history, and he argues that *The Onion*'s fake headline was right: even though the losers *have* written the war's history, they did so from the winners' vantage point. According to Moyar, the reigning "orthodox school" of thought is so pervasive in popular and scholarly spheres that its ideological stamp dominates the U.S.'s collective thinking on its Vietnam experiences, and its adherents argue that U.S. involvement in Vietnam was "wrongheaded and unjust," a claim that directly parrots the North Vietnamese perspective.[2] Against this, Moyar and his revisionist defenders wage their struggle by hurling counterarguments against what they perceive to be an oppressive and conventional orthodoxy. What has resulted, in Moyar's view, is nothing less than a revolutionary struggle, with the revisionist's school's most vocal advocate fervently claiming that the orthodox school is not only wrong in its ideological foundations, but also duplicitous in its design.

In formulating his rebuttal, Moyar has accepted that "new historical books on the Vietnam War have been appearing at an impressive pace," but has conceded that "most of them come from what is known as the orthodox school." The revisionist school "sees the war as a noble but improperly executed enterprise," but has "published much less, primarily because it has few adherents in the academic world." In writing *Triumph Forsaken*, Moyar found that "initial research on the early years of the Vietnam War revealed that many of the existing strands were flawed and that many other necessary strands were missing altogether. Historical accuracy, therefore, demanded the rebuilding of existing strands and the creation of new strands."[3] Ultimately, these fresh sources and interpretations led Moyar to the conviction that Vietnam was "a wise war fought under foolish restraints."[4]

Yet, although armed with copious amounts of new historical research, Moyar argues that revisionists are forced to engage the orthodox school's prevailing wisdom in an attritional debate because revisionists remain mired at the edges of academic thought. According to Moyar, this stems from the staunch and often dismissive opposition revisionist arguments encounter in the face of the orthodoxy. He states:

> The orthodox–revisionist split has yet to become a full-fledged debate, because many orthodox historians have insisted that the fundamental issues of the Vietnam War are not open to debate. Most scholars consider it "axiomatic" that the United States was wrong to go to war in Vietnam. Some prominent orthodox scholars have gone so far as to claim that revisionists are not historians at all but merely ideologues, a claim that is indicative of a larger, very harmful trend at American universities whereby haughty derision and ostracism are used against those whose work calls into question the reigning ideological orthodoxy, stifling debate and leading to defects and gaps in scholarship of the sort found in the historical literature on the Vietnam War.[5]

Were Moyar's arguments presented for the sake of disagreement, it might have been possible for the academic community simply to address his arguments, take note of whatever relevant evidence he presents, and ignore him, thus relegating his work to one among many failed attempts to reorient Vietnam War historiography. And there can be no doubt—many historians would like to do just that. But Moyar's brand of revisionism has little interest in reinterpreting a single person, place, or event. His work is so vast in scope, so comprehensive in design, so copiously documented, and so aggressively stated that only a complete and total reorientation of historiographic thought can account for it. *Triumph Forsaken* acts simultaneously as a lightning rod and the elephant in the room, its strident arguments painted with such broad brush-strokes that even where scholars' specialties may only lightly touch upon Moyar's arguments, they must still account for what he states.

Beginning with a brief overview of Vietnamese history, the bulk of *Triumph Forsaken* covers the time period when the U.S. first engaged in South Vietnam and culminates with eighty-three pages of footnotes to support its conclusions. In order to address his argument, any potential critic of Moyar's interpretation—and there are many—must address the impressive source base that provides the power for Moyar's arguments. Although most of his critics are loath to admit it, works such as *Triumph Forsaken* improve the overall quality of the debate by ensuring that scholars check and recheck their sources and interpretations. As Edmund Burke once stated, "He that wrestles with us strengthens our nerves and sharpens our skills, our antagonist is our helper." In combining a rich source base with incisive arguments, Moyar has ensured that his critics must do the same in order to counter him. By challenging the orthodox viewpoint with his brand of aggressive scholarship, Moyar's work improves the quality of the orthodox–revisionist debate, and scholarship on the Vietnam War as a whole. For that he is to be commended.

In as much as Moyar's *Triumph Forsaken* has served to increase the level of scholarship, it is also evidence of the continual divide that has marked the orthodox–revisionist debate since its inception. A by-product of its polemical nature, the orthodox–revisionist debate was never burdened by objectivity. Many of the most prominent harangues between historians are reminiscent of Republican–Democrat politicking during an election year, complete with hyperbolic descriptions of doom and gloom should one subscribe to the other party's principles. Although many of the orthodox–revisionist arguments were originally formed in the 1960s and 1970s, they continue to make their presence felt even today, thus reinforcing the power the Vietnam War's past holds over contemporary circumstances. In 2004, rather than discuss the policies they would pursue in the coming years as president, for a better part of their presidential run Senator John Kerry and incumbent George W. Bush spent days justifying actions they took during the Vietnam War. Holding fast to the original polemics that eventually resulted in the U.S. departure from Vietnam, the ideological tenets that originally framed the orthodox and revisionist viewpoints have remained largely unchanged over time.

At the debates' extremes, the orthodox perspective speaks like a protestor's condemnation of U.S. intervention in Vietnam, while the revisionist perspective echoes the dogmatic determination of a Cold War warrior. Take, for example, Moyar's argument: he states that Diem was a wise and effective leader, that it was a mistake for the U.S. to get rid of Diem, that Vietnam was a noble cause worth defending, and that the domino theory was very much correct, the threat real. This argument could very well have been lifted directly from the policy papers of any number of members on President Kennedy's National Security Council. On the other hand, the orthodox viewpoint argues that the war was a foolish enterprise, and, to borrow from David Anderson, that acceptance of Moyar's characterization of the war is equivalent to militarizing the United States' role in world affairs. Such an understanding of the war was also equally liable to be found in the 1960s, albeit from a picket line rather than a policy paper. The Vietnam debate began amid an ideologically charged atmosphere that has endured long after the war's conclusion. The binary environment it has created defines current historiography, and coats the subsequent analysis and debate in a bipolar framework mimicking the Cold War ideals over which the war was originally fought.

That Vietnam scholarship must be drawn from a binary understanding of the war as either right or wrong is the one point on which the revisionist and orthodox schools agree wholeheartedly. In as much as Moyar bemoans the "ideologue" label that orthodox historians have placed upon revisionists, the fact is that he *is* an ideologue, as are many of his critics and defenders. Whether one subscribes to a belief that Vietnam was a "foolish and misguided effort" or a "wise war fought under foolish constraints," both are judgments that are binary in nature and, as result, each school of thought defines its nature as much by its separation from the other school as by its own principles. The resultant historiography permits no middle ground, and the vociferous nature of this debate continues to spill into the public realm, with predictably caustic results.[6]

It should therefore come as no surprise that where most academic historians are content to add greater depth or nuance to an existing debate, Moyar writes to supplant the history entirely. At the outset of *Triumph Forsaken*, Moyar states,

> U.S. intervention in Vietnam was not an act of strategic buffoonery, nor was it a sinister, warmongering plot that should forever stand as a terrible blemish on America's soul. Neither was it an act of hubris in which the United States pursued objectives far beyond its means.[7]

Moyar seeks nothing short of a historiographic revolution, one in which the U.S.'s collective understanding of the Vietnam War is shifted to rest in complete reversal from where it once lay. For Moyar, the Vietnam War is a battleground to be fought over for more than simply the search for an accurate interpretation of U.S. intervention in Southeast Asia; it is a battle fought over the soul, the heart, the character, and the legacy of America.

Long before the last U.S. soldiers left South Vietnam in April 1975, and before Mark Moyar was even born, the orthodox interpretation of the Vietnam War was already in power. Words and phrases like "My Lai," "Pinkville," "wasted," "Tet '68," "hearts and minds," "quagmire," "sweep and clear," and "body count," among others, burned themselves into the U.S.'s national identity, where they potently remain to this day. Evocative images like Malcome Browne's 1963 picture of a Buddhist monk protesting through self-immolation and Thai Khad Chuon's 1975 iconic photograph of a U.S. official punching a refugee in order to close the doors to an evacuating helicopter reinforce the public mindset of the war's wrongness and cruelty, even well beyond the expected wanton suffering that warfare causes. The entertainment industry has picked up on the public's general antipathy and has utilized it to create an entire market driven by the war's hopelessness. Spread through literature, movies, and video games, the media's use of the war's collective image continually reinforces the U.S.'s sense of lost innocence. Moreover, the effect of the Vietnam War on the U.S. national conscience is not limited to cultural expressions.

Since the war's conclusion, before the U.S. endorses any foreign policy action, its enactors must first contend with the ghosts of Vietnam. As with popular cultural expressions, here Mark Moyar finds a great deal to lament, as most of the Vietnam War's political meanings reinforce the orthodox interpretation. Such is the case with the Weinberger Doctrine in which, in 1984, Secretary of Defense Casper Weinberger embodied his definition of the spirit of the "lessons learned from Vietnam." Stated explicitly within his doctrine were provisions that the U.S. would not go to war unless vital U.S. interests were at stake, that the U.S. military had to have the people's and Congress's support before commitment, and that upon committing to military action, the U.S. would only do so with the intent to win. Seven years later, at the conclusion of a war fought under these premises, and what was largely hailed at the time to be the "anti-Vietnam," a triumphant George H.W. Bush declared: "By God, we've licked the Vietnam syndrome once and for all!" President Bush spoke prematurely: after the Gulf War, the specter of Vietnam would continuously creep into media reporting on U.S. military engagements worldwide, to include Somalia, Kosovo, and Bosnia during President Bill Clinton's tenure in office and during President Bush Sr.'s son President George Walker Bush's time in office with engagements in Iraq and Afghanistan.

It is in the U.S.'s latest wars in Iraq and Afghanistan that many Vietnam scholars appropriate Vietnam's meanings to the present environment, and here Moyar's work is representative. Having published several articles that address the current Iraq war, both *Triumph Forsaken* and Moyar's latest work, *A Question of Command: Counterinsurgency from the Civil War to Iraq*, in many ways examine the past in order to provide a roadmap for improved policy decision making in future conflicts.[8] Utilizing classroom examples at Quantico, in writing *A Question of Command*, Moyar argues that the current U.S. Army–Marine counterinsurgency manual has left out an important element—that is, "the role small unit leaders play in defeating insurgencies."[9]

Here again the historical community is split on the use of Vietnam for the purposes of policy guidance in modern-day world affairs. Many of Moyar's defenders agree with his sentiment that the Vietnam War does have applicable lessons for the future—and by extension that, in understanding the Vietnam War through the orthodox perspective, the U.S. has drawn many of the wrong lessons. In terms of his critics, most staunchly oppose Moyar's attempts to graft his interpretation of Vietnam as a worthwhile venture into contemporary U.S. military affairs, believing what will result are historical justifications for present-day robust military policies. These critics assert that Vietnam and Iraq's circumstances are vastly different, and that historical lessons are not directly transferable. Such criticisms are not new to Moyar nor are they new to the historical profession as a whole. One of the great and consummate criticisms within the historical profession is often leveled at scholars who step beyond the historical realm and into policy analysis by utilizing history as their guide. Although this divide between the orthodox and revisionist school is currently a minor one, it contains the potential to further exacerbate the orthodox–revisionist split and explode into its own full-fledged debate, subsuming historical explanations of the Vietnam War within contemporary foreign policy debates.

A current danger to fruitful development within the orthodox–revisionist debate rests on a judgmental and sometimes counterfactual landscape on which the debate is so often carried, a boundary that is largely artificial in design and accepted by both sides. To take one example, on the grounds that it is far too speculative to assume the Vietnam War had been won by the time of Diem's assassination, or lost because of it, Andrew Birtle's argument that human affairs are full of decisions that shift the balance of history is astute. Birtle states that a more appropriate title for Moyar's work would have been "Opportunity Lost", rather than 'Triumph Forsaken". Recent works within both schools are rife with "what if" judgments, their books operating on the assumption that key mistakes made impossible a "better" future, unraveling the war effort, and leading the U.S. and South Vietnam down a disastrous path. Often these works boldly proclaim their ideological framework with pejorative, nostalgic, or romanticized titles, reinforcing orthodox–revisionist disagreements, retarding fruitful intellectual disagreement, and discouraging the reader from critically analyzing the work's contents for new interpretive schemes.[10] In Moyar's work, this trend is especially noticable. Perhaps Moyar felt that, in order to shake the dominant orthodox school, a bold and counterfactual revisionist title was needed. Nevertheless, Moyar's work engages the reader on a counterfactual premise. He argues, "the most terrible mistake [the U.S. made] was the inciting of the November 1963 coup, for Ngo Dinh Diem's overthrow forfeited the tremendous gains of the preceding nine years and plunged the country into an extended period of instability and weakness."[11] To argue that the Diem assassination was a mistake is not unique, nor is it an unreasonable historical judgment to make, because most orthodox and revisionist historians agree on this very point. But to argue that eliminating Diem was equivalent to denying victory presents an impossible conclusion, and therefore an equally impossible point for critics to argue. Diem did *not* live, and the U.S. did *not* succeed in Vietnam. To presume anything else belongs to a future that never occurred, and thus cannot be known.

If the ultimate goal of U.S. intervention in Vietnam was to create a viable nation state with a capitalistic model, one possible productive line of revisionist inquiry could assume that the U.S., in fact, won the war after all. Although Vietnam still remains a one-party dictatorship, the heavy foreign investments during the French and U.S. war years into Vietnam's infrastructure laid the foundation for an emergent nation of small shopkeepers and of industrious capitalist growth. Contemporary Vietnam is among the top exporters of rice and coffee. With the U.S. lifting its trade embargo in 1994, economic opportunities have created a growing culture of abundance. Chronicling contemporary Vietnamese society, Hy V. Luong argued within *Post-war Vietnam: Dynamics of a Transforming Society*, "By the end of the 1990s, more than a few wealthy Hanoi residents owned three-star hotels in the city and four-star tourist resorts in other parts of Vietnam. Conspicuous consumption had also emerged in the form of private automobiles, among other things."[12]

David G. Marr, another of the work's contributors, came to similar conclusions in his argument. Examining the growth of Vietnamese televised advertising, he argued that "The expensively produced, artistically slick, technically advanced foreign TV ads for soft drinks, cosmetics, condoms, motorbikes, and CD players captivated viewers, especially adolescents and children."[13] Additionally, Vietnam is privy to a rapidly growing

Conclusion • 231

increase in tourism—especially among U.S. war veterans—in the past two decades. Perceiving their pasts as inextricably linked to Vietnam, they return there for a variety of personal reasons. Especially illuminating was the comment of one veteran, who returned to Vietnam in 2000 and upon seeing Saigon's bustling local businesses, remarked that the city was as communist as New York.

Placing the orthodox–revisionist split into a larger ideological context helps get at the heart of *why* the Vietnam War is unique among historical debates, and what it is about Vietnam that sets hearts afire and critical minds feverishly typing sharp rebuttals. The Vietnam War matters because the legacies of Vietnam and the United States matter. Those who have made it their life's profession to understand the war's importance are well aware that the historical period they so passionately devote themselves to is also under continual scrutiny and reinterpretation by the public at large. But it is on the national stage that stakes are at their highest, and where the Vietnam War serves as the main event for battles over mainstream culture, political memory, foreign policy, and military policy. The Vietnam War, as it was more than forty years ago, is still being fought to this day, excepting that its combatants must now content themselves to fight with words rather than ammunition.

Notes

1. Scott Dikkers, *The Onion Presents Our Dumb Century: 100 Years of Headlines from America's Finest News Source* (New York: Three Rivers Press, 1999), 123.
2. Mark Moyar, *Triumph Forsaken: The Vietnam War, 1954–1965* (Cambridge: Cambridge University Press, 2006), xi.
3. Ibid., xi.
4. Ibid., 416.
5. Ibid., xii.
6. Edward Miller, "War Stories: The Taylor–Buzzanco Debate and How We Think about the Vietnam War," *Journal of Vietnamese Studies* 1: 1–2. Robert Buzzanco, "Fear and (Self) Loathing in Lubbock, Texas, or How I Learned to Quit Worrying and Love Vietnam and Iraq," *Passport*, December 2005, 5–14.
7. Mark Moyar, *Triumph Forsaken: The Vietnam War, 1954–1965* (Cambridge: Cambridge University Press, 2006), xxii.
8. "Iraq, Five Years Later—still too soon to judge," *Christian Science Monitor*, March 20, 2008, Vol. 100, Iss. 80, 9; "An Iraq Solution, Vietnam Style," *New York Times* Opinion–Editorial, November 26, 2006; *A Question of Command: Counterinsurgency from the Civil War to Iraq* (New Haven: Yale University Press, 2009).
9. Mark Moyar, *Question of Command: Counterinsurgency from the Civil War to Iraq* (New Haven: Yale University Press, 2009), viii.
10. For example, an examination of the following titles reveals much about where they sit in the orthodox–revisionist debate: B.G. Burkett, *Stolen Valor: How the Vietnam Generation was Robbed of its Heroes and its History* (Dallas: Verity Press, 1998); H.R. McMaster, *Dereliction of Duty: Lyndon Johnson, Robert McNamara, The Joint Chiefs of Staff, and the Lies that Led to Vietnam* (New York: Harper Perennial, 1998); Lewis Sorley, *A Better War: The Unexamined Victories and Final Tragedy of*

America's Last Year in Vietnam (New York: Harcourt Brace, 1999); John Prados, *Vietnam: A History of the Unwinnable War, 1945–1975* (Lawrence: University Press of Kansas, 2009).
11. Mark Moyar, *Triumph Forsaken: The Vietnam War, 1954–1965* (Cambridge: Cambridge University Press, 2006), xxiii.
12. Hy V. Luong, ed. *Post-war Vietnam: Dynamics of a Transforming Society* (Lanham, Rowman and Littlefield, 2003), 81.
13. Ibid., 287.

Contributors

David L. Anderson is Professor of History in the Division of Social, Behavioral, and Global Studies at California State University, Monterey Bay. He is a past president of the Society for Historians of American Foreign Relations (S.H.A.F.R.). His books include: *Trapped by Success: The Eisenhower Administration and Vietnam* (Columbia University Press, 1991, Robert H. Ferrell Book Prize from S.H.A.F.R.); *Shadow on the White House: Presidents and the Vietnam War* (University Press of Kansas, 1993); *Facing My Lai: Moving Beyond the Massacre* (University Press of Kansas, 1998); *The Human Tradition in the Vietnam Era* (Scholarly Resources, 2000); *The Columbia Guide to the Vietnam War* (Columbia University Press, 2002, "Best of the Best" designation from the American Library Association and the American Association of University Presses and a *Choice* magazine "Outstanding Academic Title"); *The Vietnam War* (Palgrave Macmillan, 2005); and *The War That Never Ends: New Perspectives on the Vietnam War* (University Press of Kentucky, 2007). The Council for the Advancement and Support of Education named him the C.A.S.E. Professor of the Year for the state of Indiana in 1991. He has a B.A. degree in history from Rice University and M.A. and Ph.D. degrees in history from the University of Virginia. He is a U.S. Army veteran of the Vietnam War.

Andrew J. Birtle holds a Ph.D. in American Military History from Ohio State University. He is the Chief of the Military Operations Branch, U.S. Army Center of Military History, where he specializes in the history of the U.S. Army's experience in counterguerrilla warfare. He is the author of a two-volume history about U.S. Army Counterinsurgency and Contingency Operations Doctrine, as well as an article entitled "PROVN, Westmoreland and the Historians: A Reappraisal," that appeared in the October 2008 edition of the *Journal of Military Affairs*. He is currently writing a book about U.S. Army activities in Vietnam between 1961 and 1965.

Philip E. Catton is an Associate Professor of History at Stephen F. Austin State University, where he teaches both undergraduate and graduate classes on the Vietnam War. He is the author of *Diem's Final Failure: Prelude to America's War in Vietnam* (2002), as well as articles and essays that have appeared in the *International History Review*, *Historical Research* and the *OAH Magazine of History*.

Jessica Chapman is an Assistant Professor of History at Williams College. She received her Ph.D. from the University of California at Santa Barbara in 2006 under the supervision of Fredrik Logevall. She is currently revising her dissertation, "Debating the Will of Heaven: South Vietnamese Politics and Nationalism in International Perspective, 1953–1956," into a book manuscript. Her articles appear in *Diplomatic History*, the *Encyclopedia of the Cold War*, the *Encyclopedia of the Modern World*, and are forthcoming in the *Journal of Vietnamese Studies*.

James Dingeman was educated at Wesleyan and Columbia University. He worked as a researcher for C.B.S. during the *C.B.S. vs. Westmoreland* trial. He has worked on numerous media and research projects concerning the wars in Indochina since the late 1960s. He helped create the Arms Control Workshop at Columbia University in the 1970s and the New York Military Affairs Symposium. The Symposium has, from the start, held conferences and seminars on the Indochina war since 1984. Since the 1970s, he has focused on reporting and analyzing conflicts in the Third World, including the Arab–Israeli Conflict, wars in Africa, the Iran–Iraq War, and the Gulf War. Mr. Dingeman has been involved in television broadcasting since 2001 and is currently setting up a multifaceted website named "Noisy Reality," which will focus on history, culture, and politics.

Charles Hill teaches in international affairs and the humanities at Yale, where he is Brady–Johnson Distinguished Fellow in Grand Strategy. He is also Research Fellow at the Hoover Institution, Stanford University. He held the rank of Career Minister of the Foreign Service of the United States, having been assigned to posts in Europe, East and Southeast Asia, and the Middle East, and as an aide to Secretaries of State Kissinger, Haig, and Shultz. From 1970 to 1973, he served as executive aide to Ambassador Ellsworth Bunker and as Mission Coordinator at the American Embassy, Saigon, Vietnam. Following his foreign service career, he was special advisor on policy to United Nations Secretary-General Boutros Boutros-Ghali.

Scott Laderman, an Assistant Professor of History at the University of Minnesota, Duluth, received his Ph.D. in American Studies from the University of Minnesota, Twin Cities, in 2005. He is the author of *Tours of Vietnam: War, Travel Guides, and Memory* (Duke University Press, 2009), which is an examination of the intersections of history, tourism, and memory in postcolonial Vietnam. His research articles, covering topics as varied as Hollywood's conceptualization of Vietnam before 1965, nineteenth-century federal Indian policy, and a 2006 multimedia campaign to sell the Iraq war, have appeared in publications ranging from the *Pacific Historical Review* to the *American Indian Culture and Research Journal*. He is presently working with the historian Edwin Martini on an edited collection on the United States and Vietnam since 1975. His second monograph, which draws on extensive research in the United States and Australia, is tentatively entitled *A World Made Safe for Discovery: Surfing, Surf Culture, and U.S. Foreign Relations*.

Mark Atwood Lawrence is Associate Professor of History and Senior Fellow at the Robert S. Strauss Center for International Security and Law at the University of Texas at Austin. He received his B.A. from Stanford University in 1988 and his Ph.D. from Yale in 1999. After teaching as a lecturer in history at Yale, he joined the History Department at UT-Austin in 2000. Since then, he has published two books, *Assuming the Burden: Europe and the American Commitment to War in Vietnam* (University of California Press, 2005) and *The Vietnam War: A Concise International History* (Oxford University Press, 2008). Lawrence is also co-editor of *The First Indochina War: Colonial Conflict and Cold War Crisis* (Harvard University Press, 2007), a collection of essays about the 1946–1954 conflict. He is now at work on a study of U.S. policymaking toward the developing world in the 1960s and early 1970s.

Michael Lind is a Senior Research Fellow and Policy Director of New America's Economic Growth Program. He is the author, with Ted Halstead, of *The Radical Center: The Future of American Politics* (Doubleday, 2001). He is also the author of *Made in Texas: George W. Bush and the Southern Takeover of American Politics* (New America Books/Basic, 2003) and *What Lincoln Believed* (Doubleday, 2005). Mr. Lind has been an editor or staff writer for *The New Yorker, Harper's Magazine*, and *The New Republic*. From 1991 to 1994, he was executive editor of *The National Interest*. He has also been a guest lecturer at Harvard Law School. Mr. Lind has written for *The Atlantic Monthly, Prospect* (U.K.), *The New York Times Magazine, The Washington Post*, the *Los Angeles Times, The Financial Times*, and other leading publications, and has appeared on C-SPAN, National Public Radio, C.N.N.'s *Crossfire* and P.B.S.'s *NewsHour* with Jim Lehrer. Mr. Lind's first three books of political journalism and history, *The Next American Nation: The New Nationalism and the Fourth American Revolution* (Free Press, 1995), *Up From Conservatism: Why the Right Is Wrong for America* (Free Press, 1996), and *Vietnam: The Necessary War* (Free Press, 1999), were all selected as *New York Times* "Notable Books". He has also published several volumes of fiction and poetry, including *The Alamo* (Houghton Mifflin, 1997), which the *Los Angeles Times* named as one of the "Best Books" of the year, and a prize-winning children's book, *Bluebonnet Girl* (Henry Holt, 2004). His groundbreaking study of American grand strategy, *The American Way of Strategy: U.S. Foreign Policy and the American Way of Life* was published by Oxford University Press in October 2006.

James McAllister is Professor of Political Science and chair of the Leadership Studies program at Williams College. He is the author of *No Exit: America and the German Problem, 1943–1954* (Ithaca: Cornell University Press, 2002). His research on various aspects of the Vietnam War has been published in *Modern Asian Studies, Pacific Historical Review, Journal of Vietnamese Studies*, and *Small Wars and Insurgencies*. He is currently working on a book exploring the role of American ambassadors to Vietnam during the Lyndon Johnson administration.

Edward Miller is an Assistant Professor of History at Dartmouth College. He is currently writing a study of American relations with Ngo Dinh Diem's South Vietnam that is based on research in American, French, and Vietnamese archives. His work has appeared in the *Journal of Southeast Asian Studies*, the *Journal of Vietnamese Studies*, and on the website of the Cold War International History Project.

Mark Moyar is Professor of National Security Affairs at the Marine Corps University. His books include: *A Question of Command: Counterinsurgency from the Civil War to Iraq* (Yale University Press, 2009); *Triumph Forsaken: The Vietnam War, 1954–1965* (Cambridge University Press, 2006); and *Phoenix and the Birds of Prey: Counterinsurgency and Counterterrorism in Vietnam* (Naval Institute Press, 1997, and University of Nebraska Press, 2007). Dr. Moyar's writings have appeared in the *New York Times*, the

Washington Post, the *Wall Street Journal*, and many other publications. He received a B.A. summa cum laude from Harvard and a Ph.D. from Cambridge.

Dennis Showalter is Professor of History at Colorado College and Past President of the Society for Military History. Joint editor of *War in History*, he specializes in comparative military history and the military history of modern Germany. His recent monographs include *The Wars of Frederick the Great*, *Patton and Rommel: Men of War in the Twentieth Century* and *Hitler's Panzers*.

William Stueck grew up in Connecticut and received a B.S. from Springfield College, an M.A. from Queens College, and a Ph.D. in history from Brown University. Among his books are *The Korean War: An International History* (Princeton, 1995) and *Rethinking the Korean War: A New Diplomatic and Strategic History* (Princeton, 2002). He is currently Distinguished Research Professor of History at the University of Georgia.

Keith W. Taylor, Professor in the Department of Asian Studies at Cornell University, has authored several books and articles about Vietnamese history and literature. He served with the U.S. Army in Vietnam, has visited Vietnam many times since the mid-1980s, and lived in Hanoi for two years in the early 1990s.

Professor **Robert F. Turner** wrote his 450-page undergraduate honors thesis on the Vietnam War at Indiana University in 1966–1967 and was an active participant in more than a hundred debates, lectures, teach-ins, and other programs on the conflict. Upon graduation and commissioning through R.O.T.C. as an Army lieutenant, he turned down a law school deferment and volunteered for duty in Vietnam. After qualifying as an Expert Infantryman, he was assigned to work directly for Lieutenant General William P. Yarborough, who had commanded Special Forces under JFK. Following the 1969 death of Ho Chi Minh, Turner predicted Le Duan would emerge from the leadership struggle as "first among equals." When that came true, Turner was asked to accept assignment as the newly created "Assistant Special Projects Officer" in the North Vietnamese/Viet Cong Affairs Division of J.U.S.P.A.O., a branch of the U.S. Embassy in Saigon—where he served twice before leaving the Army as a Captain in 1971. He then became a Public Affairs Fellow at Stanford's Hoover Institution on War, Revolution, and Peace, where he wrote *Vietnamese Communism: Its Origins and Development*. In 1981, he co-founded the Center for National Security Law at the University of Virginia School of Law, from which he holds both academic and professional doctorates. Turner has taught undergraduate and postgraduate seminars on Vietnam at Virginia since 1990, and is co-editor of *The Real Lessons of the Vietnam War* and *To Oppose Any Foe*.

Qiang Zhai is Professor of History at Auburn University Montgomery. He received his doctoral degree from Ohio University, where he studied with John Lewis Gaddis. He is the author of *The Dragon, the Lion, and the Eagle: Chinese–British–American Relations, 1949–1958* (Kent State University Press, 1994) and *China and the Vietnam Wars, 1950–1975* (University of North Carolina Press, 2000), as well as numerous articles and essays on Sino-American relations. He is a co-editor of *The Encyclopedia of the Cold War* (Routledge, 2008).

Index

Abrams, Creighton 79, 83–7, 215
Acheson, Dean 81
Afghanistan and Iraq, comparisons of Vietnam xi, 9, 55, 75, 81, 83–5, 102, 104, 112, 142–4, 148–9, 163–4, 166, 186, 189, 217, 228–9
Allen, George 77
An Loc 84, 87–8
An Nam 22
Anderson, David 151, 153, 171, 175, 208
Ap Bac, Battle of 10, 129, 165, 203, 220–1
Apocalypse Now 7
Asselin, Pierre 63

Ball, George 142
Bao Dai 103, 106–7, 140, 150, 181, 184
Berlin, Isaiah 86, 88
Berman, Larry 153
Betts, Richard 104
Bidwell, Shelford 5
Birtle, Andrew 124, 162–6
Blackadder Goes Forth 1
Bradley, Mark 9, 56, 64, 117–19, 182
Braestrup, Peter 92
Buddhist crisis 10, 43, 57, 133, 151–2; alleged communist ties 81, 161–2, 172, 195–7, 202, 204–5, 213, 216–19, 221–2
Bunker, Ellsworth 79, 84, 87–8
Bush, George H.W. 228
Bush, George W. xi, 55, 112, 148–9, 226, 228
Buttinger, Joseph 31

Cambodia 24–5, 42, 46, 50–1, 53, 64, 87, 102, 104, 165, 192, 209, 219
Carter, James 11, 33
Catton, Phillip 11, 29, 59–62, 93, 114–15, 152, 154, 178, 219
Central Office for South Vietnam (*see* Viet Cong, People's Army Vietnam)
Chapman, Jessica 11, 56, 113, 151–7, 159, 161–2, 211
China 67, 71, 85, 87, 104, 106, 108–10, 149, 153, 173, 178, 183, 209; at Geneva 40–2, 48–51, 68–9, 94, 154; Vietnam relationship pre-20th century 17–25, 59; willingness to respond to U.S. invasion of North Vietnam 42–6, 51–3, 64–6, 69–70, 77–8, 82, 141–2, 172, 187–9, 193–4, 214–16
Clark, Alan 4

239

Colby, William 103–5, 192, 201
Cooper, Sherman 104

Decree 10/59 180, 211
Deer Hunter, The 7
Diem, Ngo Dinh 6, 9, 44, 51, 76–7, 81, 92–3, 95, 106–7, 130, 150–1, 196, 209–10, 216–17; assassination of xi, 31, 57, 63, 103–4, 115, 120, 133–7, 144, 149–50, 164–5, 172, 175, 180, 194–5, 201–2, 227, 229–30; effectiveness and leadership philosophy 10, 29–36, 40, 43, 59–62, 82–3, 92–3, 104, 114–16, 118–20, 124, 126, 131, 133–7, 140–2, 144–5, 154–7, 161–7, 172–3, 176–84, 195, 200–6, 211–14, 218–21, 227, 229–30
Dien Bien Phu 40–2, 48, 63, 68, 76, 79, 94
Dingeman, James 75, 140–1, 165
Dodd, Thomas 174
Doidge, Michael 224
Domino theory 10, 40, 44, 65–6, 92, 94, 149, 171, 173–4, 176, 201, 209, 227
Dommen, Arthur 147
Dong Son 18–19
Doyle, Arthur 3
Duiker, William 49, 173, 178, 210
Duncanson, Dennis 103
Durbrow, Elbridge 126

Eisenhower, Dwight 106–7, 109, 118, 150, 153, 173, 214
Elegant, Douglas 105, 111
Elliot, David 56, 97, 161, 180, 184, 211–13
Enlai, Zhou 41, 50–1, 53, 78

Fall, Bernard 5, 29, 36, 97–8, 103
Fishel, Wesley 103
FitzGerald, Frances 7, 31, 59, 180
France 5, 21, 25–7, 32, 40–3, 48, 50–1, 53, 60, 64, 68–9, 76, 79, 103, 106, 108, 113–14, 117–19, 127–8, 130, 149–50, 154–6, 179–82, 184, 205–6, 210–11, 213–14, 230

Fulbright, William 104
Fuller, J.F.C. 3

Gaddis, John Lewis 105
Gaiduk, Ilya 42, 63, 154
Gelb, Lesley 104
Geng, Chen 53, 70
Giap, Vo Nguyen 41–2, 107, 214
Gilbert, Marc Jason 151
Graham, Dominick 5
Graves, Robert 3, 7
Green Berets, The 7
Guevara, Che 109
Guillemot, Francois 95, 146

Ha Tinh 23–4
Habib, Philip 83
Haig, Douglas 1–4, 11
Halberstam, David 5–6, 31, 33, 43, 58–9, 81, 111, 128, 150–1, 195, 216
Hammer, Ellen 62, 201
Han Empire 18–20
Harkins, Paul 58, 77, 127, 131, 134, 165, 192, 205–6
Harriman, Averell 142
Hart, Liddell 3–4
Herman, Arthur 57
Herr, Michael 7
Herring, George 30, 36, 56, 125, 153
Hess, Gary 57, 183
Higgins, Marguerite 32, 81, 196, 216
Hill, Charles 79, 142–3
Hilsman, Roger 34, 136, 142
Hue 24–6, 148, 208
Hunt, David 56, 96, 147

Immerman, Richard 56

Jacobs, Seth 9, 56, 64, 117–19, 153, 178
Japan 44–5, 64–5, 103, 143, 148, 155, 209
Jian, Chen 41, 43, 154, 178, 188, 193
Johnson, Lyndon 9, 45, 48, 51–2, 65, 76–8, 82–3, 88, 104, 110, 135–7, 142–3, 167, 172–3, 186–8, 191, 193–4, 214–16
Jones, Howard 64, 153

Kaiser, David 56, 153, 175
Kai-shek, Chiang 51, 53, 70
Karnow, Stanley 8, 31, 41, 59
Kendrick, Alexander 97, 147–8
Kennan, George 173
Kennedy, John 65, 76–7, 80–2, 88, 129, 135–6, 153, 173, 187, 201–2, 227
Kerry, John 226
Khanh, Nguyen 142, 196
Khrushchev, Nikita 41, 63, 68, 109,
Kimball, Jeffrey 153
Kissinger, Henry 87–8
Kolko, Gabriel 8, 150
Kovic, Ron 7
Krepinevich, Andrew 9
Kutuzov, Mikhail 87–8

Laderman, Scott 90, 144–9
Lafeber, Walter 56
Laffin, John 2
Lansdale, Edward 115, 125, 172
Laos 25, 42, 44, 46, 50–1, 53, 62, 64, 67, 87, 102, 104, 135–7, 165, 176, 187, 189, 192, 209, 214–15, 219
Latham, Michael 118–19
Lawrence, Mark 56–7, 175, 209–13
Le Van Duyet 25
LeMay, Curtis 104
Lemnitzer, Louis 76
Lewy, Guenter 8, 92, 103, 192–3, 201
Lind, Michael 8, 92, 186, 192, 201, 214–15
Loan, Ngoc Nguyen 6
Lodge, Henry Cabot 82, 103, 144, 150–1, 195, 202,
Logevall, Fredrik 9, 64, 90, 153, 175
Loicano, Martin 11

M*A*S*H 7
Mac Dynasty 23
Marr, David 146, 230
Masur, Matthew 11, 120, 152, 162
McAllister, James 57, 94, 151, 191, 215–18, 222
McGarr, Lionel 126–8
McHale, Shawn 95, 146

McMahan, Robert 31
McMaster, H.R. 9
McNamara, Robert 76, 104, 110, 173, 206
Media in Vietnam 6–7, 81, 91, 110–11, 228
Military Assistance Advisory Group (MAAG) 125–31
Military Assistance Command Vietnam (MACV) 124, 127, 131
Miller, Edward 56, 114–15, 152, 165, 178, 199, 209, 218–22
Minh, Ho Chi 8, 10, 40–2, 48–9, 50, 53, 62, 66–8, 81, 92, 103–5, 106–9, 115, 140–1, 149–50, 153–4, 156–7, 162, 177–9, 181, 183, 195, 209–11
Moïse, Edwin 94, 97–8, 145–7
Mounier, Emmanuel 32, 61
Moyar, Mark allegations of historical misrepresentation 41–4, 48–9, 52–3, 70–1, 91–8, 116, 119, 149, 153, 156, 173–4, 176, 196, 203–6; defense of revisionism 56–8, 60, 144, 148, 150–2, 215, 219; on orthodox school 56–8, 60, 141, 143–4, 148, 151–3, 208, 219; on politicization of academia 54–6, 58, 140, 142, 151, 153, 222
Muong 22–3

Nan Zhao 22–3
Nehru, Jawaharlal 183–4
Newman, John 76–7, 131, 134
Nghe An 22–3
Nguyen Family 24–5
Nguyen Phuc Anh 25
Nhu, Ngo Dinh 33, 35, 60–1, 93, 144, 204, 210
Nixon, Richard 82, 87–8, 171

O'Brien, Tim 7
Oh! What a Lovely War 4
Onion, The 224
orthodox school x-xii 7–8, 10–12, 30–31, 33, 35–6, 39, 43, 54, 56, 59–60, 62, 79–80, 91, 102, 114–15, 141, 143, 148, 151, 171, 175–80, 183, 186, 191–2, 197, 199–200, 202, 206, 219, 224–31

People's Army Vietnam (also referred to as North Vietnamese Army) 63, 84, 105, 111, 125–6, 131–3, 135, 142
Personalism 32–5, 60–1, 204
Pham Van Dong 50–2, 68–9, 105, 194
Pham Xuan An 111, 150, 217
Phillips, Rufus 57, 172
Phoenix and the Birds of Prey 54, 157, 164
Pike, Douglas 105
Podhoretz, Norman 192
Porter, Gareth 56, 94, 145
Prados, John 56–7, 124, 148
Preston, Andrew 153
Pribbenow, Merle 152
Prior, Robin 4–5

Qing Empire 21–2
Quang, Tri 57, 94, 162, 196–7, 202, 204–5, 213, 216–18, 221–2
Quiet American, The 5, 7
Quinn-Judge, Sophie 114, 154, 178

Race, Jeffrey 159–60, 182, 212–13
Radvanyi, Janos 41, 63
Reagan, Ronald 90–1, 98, 102, 173
Reischauer, Edwin 65
Remarque, Erich 3
Republic of Vietnam Armed Forces (also referred to as Army Republic of Vietnam) 82, 84, 86–8, 116, 126–32, 158, 163–6, 201–2
revisionism school xii, 8–12, 30–1, 33, 35–6, 39, 56–7, 62, 79, 80, 84–5, 92, 102–3, 115, 150–1, 171, 175–8, 180, 183, 186, 191–2, 195, 197, 199–201, 206, 215, 224–7, 229–31

Safer, Morley 6, 111
Sassoon, Siegfried 3, 7
Schelling, Thomas 82
Schmitz, David 117, 119
Schulzinger, Robert 153
Scott, Peter Dale 57
Serong, Francis 129
Shaplen, Robert 33

Sheehan, Neil 6, 43, 58, 195, 216
Sheffield, Gary 5
Sherriff, R.C. 3
Simkins, Peter 5
Snow, Edgar 70, 77, 187
Song Dynasty 19–21
Sorley, Lewis 192, 215
Soviet Union 11, 21–2, 41–2, 46, 49–50, 66–9, 78, 87, 94, 104, 107, 109–10, 117–18, 141–2, 154, 173, 178, 183, 188, 209, 215
strategic hamlets 34–5, 60–2, 83, 115, 127, 132–4, 154–5, 165, 172, 195, 204, 213, 219–20
Stueck, William 39, 63–6, 68–70, 94, 114
Summers, Harry 8, 110, 186–9, 192–3

Tang Dynasty 18–20, 22–3
Taylor, A.J.P. 192
Taylor, Keith 17, 58–9
Taxi Driver 7
Terraine, John 4–5, 10, 12
Tet Offensive 11
Thailand 44–5, 53, 64–5, 67, 70, 109, 143, 187, 209
Thanh Hoa 22–3
Thieu, Van Nguyen 87–8, 107, 196
Thim Kim Phuc 6
Thompson, Robert 34
Timmes, Charles 130
Tolstoy, Leo 86–8
Tonkin, Gulf of 43, 51–2, 57, 69, 77, 94, 145–6, 167
Trager, Frank 103
Travers, Tim 5
Trinh Family 23–5
Triumph Forsaken (*see* Moyar, Mark)
Trullinger, James 160–1, 182, 212–13
Truman, Harry 81, 155, 171, 173
Trung Sisters 18
Turley, William 57, 97, 147
Turner, Robert 92, 102, 149–50

Vann, Paul John 129, 192
Viet Cong (also referred to as People's

Liberation Front) 6, 34, 43, 67, 76–7, 82, 84–7, 103, 105, 108–9, 124–8, 131–3, 141, 157–61, 164–6, 181–3, 196, 201–3, 211–12, 214–15, 219–21, 224
Viet Minh 40–2, 60, 63–4, 68, 76, 95, 103, 109, 114, 119, 150, 154–5, 178–9, 183, 205, 210, 213, 216
Vlastos, Stephen 151

Wallace, George 104
Westmoreland, William 7, 11, 51, 84, 86, 124, 127, 136, 186, 192, 215
Westphalia 80
Wheeler, Earle 134
Wiest, Andrew 1, 11, 57

Willbanks, James 11
Williams, Samuel 126, 163, 192
Williams, William Appleman 150, 191–2
Wilson, Trevor 5
Wilson, Woodrow 179, 210
Winters, Francis 62

Young, Marilyn 56

Zedong, Mao 42–4, 49, 51–3, 68, 70, 77, 107, 109, 187–8, 193–4, 209
Zhai, Qiang 41–3, 48, 67–71, 154, 178, 188, 193
Zhang, Xiaming 188, 193
Zhu Di 20
Zinn, Howard 56

eBooks – at www.eBookstore.tandf.co.uk

A library at your fingertips!

eBooks are electronic versions of printed books. You can store them on your PC/laptop or browse them online.

They have advantages for anyone needing rapid access to a wide variety of published, copyright information.

eBooks can help your research by enabling you to bookmark chapters, annotate text and use instant searches to find specific words or phrases. Several eBook files would fit on even a small laptop or PDA.

NEW: Save money by eSubscribing: cheap, online access to any eBook for as long as you need it.

Annual subscription packages

We now offer special low-cost bulk subscriptions to packages of eBooks in certain subject areas. These are available to libraries or to individuals.

For more information please contact webmaster.ebooks@tandf.co.uk

We're continually developing the eBook concept, so keep up to date by visiting the website.

www.eBookstore.tandf.co.uk

Printed in Great Britain
by Amazon